Letters from the Mountains

Between the Years 1773 and 1803

VOLUME 1

ANNE MACVICAR GRANT
EDITED BY J.P. GRANT

CAMBRIDGE UNIVERSITY PRESS

Cambridge, New York, Melbourne, Madrid, Cape Town,
Singapore, São Paolo, Delhi, Tokyo, Mexico City

Published in the United States of America by Cambridge University Press, New York

www.cambridge.org
Information on this title: www.cambridge.org/9781108033480

This edition first published 1845
This digitally printed version 2011

ISBN 978-1-108-03348-0 Paperback

CAMBRIDGE LIBRARY COLLECTION

Books of enduring scholarly value

Women's Writing

The later twentieth century saw a huge wave of academic interest in women's writing, which led to the rediscovery of neglected works from a wide range of genres, periods and languages. Many books that were immensely popular and influential in their own day are now studied again, both for their own sake and for what they reveal about the social, political and cultural conditions of their time. A pioneering resource in this area is Orlando: Women's Writing in the British Isles from the Beginnings to the Present (http://orlando.cambridge.org), which provides entries on authors' lives and writing careers, contextual material, timelines, sets of internal links, and bibliographies. Its editors have made a major contribution to the selection of the works reissued in this series within the Cambridge Library Collection, which focuses on non-fiction publications by women on a wide range of subjects from astronomy to biography, music to political economy, and education to prison reform.

Letters from the Mountains

First published in 1806, and revised and edited by her son for this 1845 sixth edition, this collection of letters by Anne Grant (1755–1838) tells her story of thirty years' residence in the Scottish Highlands. Described by the author as 'sketches of a life spent in the most remote obscurity', it was one of the first works to acquaint the public with the romantic scenery of the Highlands. Her lyrical descriptions of the landscape and characters of the rural parish of Laggan caught the imagination of a generation captivated by the poetry of Scott and Burns. Volume 1 begins with Anne MacVicar's arrival in the Highlands, describes her marriage, and offers frank revelations of personal tragedies. The work is an important example of a woman's literary contribution to the Romantic movement. For more information on this author, see http://orlando.cambridge.org/public/svPeople?formname=r&person_id=granan.

Cambridge University Press has long been a pioneer in the reissuing of out-of-print titles from its own backlist, producing digital reprints of books that are still sought after by scholars and students but could not be reprinted economically using traditional technology. The Cambridge Library Collection extends this activity to a wider range of books which are still of importance to researchers and professionals, either for the source material they contain, or as landmarks in the history of their academic discipline.

Drawing from the world-renowned collections in the Cambridge University Library, and guided by the advice of experts in each subject area, Cambridge University Press is using state-of-the-art scanning machines in its own Printing House to capture the content of each book selected for inclusion. The files are processed to give a consistently clear, crisp image, and the books finished to the high quality standard for which the Press is recognised around the world. The latest print-on-demand technology ensures that the books will remain available indefinitely, and that orders for single or multiple copies can quickly be supplied.

The Cambridge Library Collection will bring back to life books of enduring scholarly value (including out-of-copyright works originally issued by other publishers) across a wide range of disciplines in the humanities and social sciences and in science and technology.

LETTERS

FROM

THE MOUNTAINS;

BEING THE CORRESPONDENCE WITH HER FRIENDS,

BETWEEN THE YEARS 1773 AND 1803,

OF

MRS. GRANT OF LAGGAN.

EDITED, WITH NOTES AND ADDITIONS, BY HER SON,

J. P. GRANT, ESQ.

IN TWO VOLUMES.

VOL. I.

THE SIXTH EDITION.

LONDON:

PRINTED FOR

LONGMAN, BROWN, GREEN, AND LONGMANS,

PATERNOSTER-ROW.

1845.

PREFACE

BY THE EDITOR OF THE SIXTH EDITION (1845.)

The death of MRS. GRANT OF LAGGAN in 1838, and the subsequent publication of her MEMOIRS AND CORRESPONDENCE in 1844, have revived the public interest in her earlier writings; and, in order to meet the numerous inquiries for one of the most popular of these productions, the LETTERS FROM THE MOUNTAINS, which have been for some years out of print, the present Edition has been revised and carefully corrected by her Son. The Editor has also, occasionally, introduced some short explanatory notes respecting the persons and incidents referred to in the Correspondence, and several letters, not included in the former editions have been added.

The "Letters from the Mountains" were published nearly forty years ago, and being one of the very first works which made the public acquainted with the romantic scenery of the Scottish Highlands, and the interesting character and primitive manners of their inhabitants, the work soon attained considerable popularity, and passed through several editions. Circumstances induced the Author to withhold, in the first of these editions, her own name, as well as those of her Correspondents; but it was found that the motives of delicacy which led to this suppression occasioned misconception in some instances, and particularly, a belief that the Letters were a fictitious correspondence. To remove this impression, the second and subsequent editions were printed with the names of the Author and of her Correspondents, to which allusion is made in the short Address to these friends by Mrs. Grant, which follows this Preface.

It may interest the readers of the following Letters, and prepare them, in some degree, for their perusal, to be made acquainted with a few of the more prominent events in the life of the Author, and the different localities in which that life was passed. With this view, the following brief Notice is added:—

Anne Macvicar (the maiden name of Mrs. Grant), although a Highlander by descent by both parents, was born at Glasgow on 21st February 1755. She was the only child of Lieutenant Duncan Macvicar, "a plain, brave, pious man,"—to use her own expression,—descended from a respectable family in the parish of Craignish in Argyllshire, and of Catherine Mackenzie, whose parents were settled in the same county, and who, on the maternal side, was descended from the ancient family of Stewart of Invernahyle, in the northern district of Argyllshire. Mr. Macvicar having obtained a commission in the 77th Regiment of Foot, was ordered, not long after the birth of his daughter, to accompany his regiment to North America, where his wife and child soon followed him, the latter being then (1758) only three years of age. Mr.

Macvicar remained in America for ten years, most of them passed in active service for sometime in the 77th, and afterwards in the 55th Regiments of Foot, in various parts of the British Provinces, during which period his wife and young daughter generally resided in or near the city of Albany, the capital of what was then the British Province of New York. They occasionally accompanied Mr. Macvicar and the military party to which he was attached, to more distant parts of the American continent, particularly to Fort Oswego, on the banks of Lake Ontario, where Miss Macvicar passed a year with her parents.

In 1768 Mr Macvicar, having sometime previously retired from the army, and obtained an extensive grant of land from the British Government in the province of New Vermont, as a reward for military service, resolved to revisit Scotland. He was then undetermined whether to dispose of his American lands and settle at home, or, after spending sometime in Scotland, to return to America and pass the rest of his life on his transatlantic property; but, on the breaking out of the Revolution in America, sometime afterwards, he decided not to return to that country. Upon arriving in Scotland with his family in 1768, he took up his residence for a few years in the city of Glasgow, where his daughter had an opportunity of forming several youthful intimacies, which afterwards ripened into warm friendship.

In 1773, Mr. Macvicar received the appointment of Barrack-Master of Fort-Augustus, situated at the western extremity of Loch Ness, in the county of Inverness, where he resided with his family for several years. Upon leaving Glasgow to take up her residence in this remote part of the Highlands, Miss Macvicar, then in the nineteenth year of her age, commenced the correspondence with her youthful friends, which occupies the earlier pages of the following Volumes. She continued at Fort-Augustus with her parents from 1773 until 1779, when she was united in marriage to the Rev. James Grant, a gentleman who had for sometime discharged the duties of Chaplain to the Fort, and was then the minister of the neighbouring parish of Laggan, a mountainous district upon the river Spey, in the central highlands of Inverness-shire. Here Mrs. Grant early devoted herself to the acquirement of a knowledge of the language and manners of the Highland population among whom her future life was in all probability to be passed; and she soon succeeded not only in being able to converse in the Gaelic language, but in the more rare accomplishment of reading it. She continued, at such intervals as the superintendence of a numerous family, and the varied cares and duties of her Highland home permitted, to correspond with her friends in the south of Scotland, and in England, her letters to whom, as unacquainted with Highland manners and the romantic scenery of the region in which she resided, naturally conveyed frequent descriptions of the people and objects around her.

In December 1801, Mrs. Grant was deprived by death of her husband, and was thus left a widow with a family of eight children,—two sons, and six daughters. Four other children had died during the life of their father. In 1803, she removed from Laggan to a beautiful and retired residence in the neighbourhood of Stirling, called Woodend, where she resolved to continue the education of her family. About the period of this removal, Mrs. Grant first became known as an author, by the publication of a Volume of Poems, which, by the advice of her friends, were published by Subscription, and obtained a very extensive circulation.

The "Letters from the Mountains," commencing in 1773, at the period of Mrs. Grant's removal, in her nineteenth year, from Glasgow to Fort-Augustus, terminate in 1803, when, as already mentioned, she transferred her residence from the Highlands to Stirlingshire. These Letters, accordingly, form an unconscious biography of the thirty years of her residence in the Highlands. The subsequent events of her life, from 1803 to 1838, are in like manner related in the recent publication of her "Memoirs and Correspondence." It may be sufficient here to mention that, in 1806, Mrs. Grant removed from Woodend to the neighbouring town of Stirling, about which time the following Letters were published. These were followed in 1808 by her "Memoirs of an American Lady." This work contains sketches of society and manners as they existed in America previous to the Revolution, and Reminiscences of Mrs. Grant's early years in that country, with notices of Madame Schuyler, a distinguished American Lady of whom Mrs. Grant speaks as "a perfect model of female excellence," from whose society she enjoyed much advantage during the youthful period she spent in the city of Albany, and its neighbourhood.

In 1810, Mrs. Grant removed with her family from Stirling to Edinburgh, where she continued to live for twenty-eight years, until her death on 7th November, 1838, in the eighty-third year of her age. She survived the whole of her numerous family of twelve children, with the exception of her youngest son, the Editor of these volumes.

The only works which proceeded from Mrs. Grant s pen, in addition to those particularized above, were two volumes of "Essays on the Superstitions of the Highlands of Scotland," published in 1811, and "Eighteen Hundred and Thirteen, a Poem," published in 1814.

J. P. G.

EDINBURGH, JUNE 16, 1845.

PREFACE

TO THE FIRST EDITION (1806.)

Lest any of my readers should indulge in the expectation of meeting, in the ensuing pages, either ingenious fiction or amusing narrative, it is but candid to undeceive them.

The simple and careless Letters here offered to the public, carry in themselves the evidences of originality. They are genuine, but broken and interrupted sketches of a life spent in the most remote obscurity. Of the little interest such sketches might possess, much is lost by the necessity of withholding those parts which contained most of narrative and anecdote.

Why Letters should be published at all, comprehending so little to excite interest or gratify curiosity, is a question that naturally suggests itself. It cannot be truly said that the gratification of the reader could form an adequate motive for their publication: and, from the nature of them, it is obvious that the unknown Author* could have no purpose of vanity to answer by it. Yet may not a picture, seldom drawn, peculiar in its shades and scenery, true to nature, and chastely coloured; may not such a picture amuse, for a while, the leisure of the idle and contemplative?—

* The Work was originally published without the Author's name.—ED

and it is hoped, that the images here offered of untutored sentiment, of the tastes, the feelings, and habits of those, who, in the secret shades of privacy, cultivate the simple duties and kindly affections of domestic life, may not be without utility.

The soul that rises above its condition, and feels undefined and painful aspirations after unattainable elegance and refinement, may here find an inducement to remain in safe obscurity, contented with the love of truth, of nature, and the "humanizing muse;" while those distinguished beings, who are at once the favourites of nature and of fortune, may learn to look with complacency on their fellow-minds in the vale of life, and to know that they too have their enjoyments.

The hope of such a result might, in some degree, console the writer of "Letters from the Mountains," for the painful circumstance that has elicited their publication.

MARCH 18, 1806.

TO

MY SURVIVING CORRESPONDENTS.*

[PREFIXED TO THE SECOND EDITION—1807.]

To you, my dear Friends, whose affection has been the cordial of my life, and whose sympathy has been the solace of my afflictions; to you, whom neither absence, distance, nor the revolution of years have estranged from me; you, whom the influx of prosperity never raised above me, and who never withheld the consideration which mind pays to mind, from the darkest hour of my adversity—To you I inscribe these Letters, which you have kindly permitted me to illuminate with names, which accredit the writer, and totally destroy the unjust surmise,—that you are all, "like some gay creatures of the element, the creation of an exuberant fancy." To those who should suppose me capable of such an imposition, I only wish that, by being connected by ties as tender, with minds as estimable, they may be convinced of the possibility of your existence.

ANNE GRANT.

JANUARY 27, 1807.

* This Address, prefixed to the Second Edition of these Letters, refers to a doubt expressed in some Review of the First Edition, whether the Letters were really genuine, the initials alone of the Author's correspondents having been printed in the First Edition, which appeared without the Author's name.

CONTENTS

OF

THE FIRST VOLUME

LETTERS.

1773.

LETTER 1776. PAGE

1777.

1778.

1785.

1786.

1787.

1788.

1789.

LETTERS

FROM

THE MOUNTAINS.

Letter I.

TO MISS ISABELLA EWING, GLASGOW.*

Oban, Argyllshire, May 1, 1773.

My dear Isabella,

I had it not in my power to fulfil my promise at Inverary; however, I have taken the first opportunity of troubling you with the recital of my trifling adventures, if such they may be called. After I parted with you, I was too much engrossed by thinking of the dear friends I had left at Dumbarton, to make many observations. How good it was in your aunt to treat you and Harriet Reid with this excursion, which lingered out the painful parting hour so much longer. Alas! it is a bleak prospect for a poor traveller, scarcely seventeen, to go she knows not where, to do she knows not what,

* Now Mrs. Smith of Jordanhill, Renfrewshire; the early and faithful friend of the Author of these Letters.—1807. This venerable lady still survives (1845), in the ninetieth year of her age.—Ed.

and live with she knows not whom. But, I carry my affections and my hopes with me. We shall meet again, and that as people do in heaven, with increased love and knowledge.

When I began to recover my spirits, and look about me, I was greatly pleased with the romantically variegated banks of Loch Lomond. Luss, with all its evergreens reflected in the purest of mirrors, enchants me; there is a peaceful gloom about it that reminds me of what I used to feel, when musing between the Fir Park and the Bishop's Castle at the Cathedral.* I believe one great reason of my preference of you and our dear Harriet above every body, was, that you seemed to feel and think as I did of that favourite place. I can always get people to laugh with me, and I like to laugh too, at times; but the difficult thing is to get one "soft, modest, melancholy female fair," that will be grave with me, and enter into my serious and solemn reflections, when I have them. I think, if there was such a thing allowable, or, what is the same thing, fashionable, a nunnery (a Protestant one, remember) might be very agreeably situated here. What would you think of such a scheme? Do not mistake me; I would not altogether intend this for a place of penance and mortification, but rather as an asylum from the levity and dissipation of the age; where we might, uninfluenced by fashion, and undisturbed by pride and all the malignant passions that distract the giddy multitude, enjoy the tranquil pleasures of a rural retirement. There, too, we might cultivate friendships, which might rest on the

* Of Glasgow, where the Author had resided for some time previously.

basis of reason, not only through time, but through eternity.

I think I see you smile, and hear you compare me to the fox in the fable, while from this solitude I rail at the lost pleasures of the dear town. I arrived here last night at eleven, after a tedious journey, in a very rainy day, through the *Mona Lia*,* or grey mountain, an endless moor, without any road, except a small footpath, through which our guide conducted the horses with difficulty. The height of the mountain is prodigious; crossing it, we were enveloped in the very region of storms and clouds. A small dreary lake, or abrupt grey crag, was the only variety which interrupted a scene enough to fill any susceptible mind with awe and horror. I am now sitting, in the same rainy weather, in a house on the very edge of a sea sprinkled with numberless islands. But I mean to give you an account rather of myself than of the country, when the fatigue and depression produced by yesterday's awful journey are over. I refer you to Harriet for an account of the delight with which I beheld Inverary. I do not know whether I am most dazzled with the Duke's house, which has all the antique grandeur of a Gothic castle, without its dismal gloom and petty incumbrances, or with the gaiety and frankness of the people. But my fancy was most of all struck with the great beeches on the lawn, and the beautiful crescent which the smooth sandy shore makes round the bay on which the town stands. I am fallen

* The Mona Lia is a long dreary mountain, without any road but the path of cattle, which the traveller crosses to go the direct road from Inverary to Oban.

in love too, deeply, hopelessly, in love, with the old gentleman;* so would you, if you were here; he is so lively, well-bred, and intelligent; your commercial beaux would appear clowns, and your military ones coxcombs, compared to him. Pity he is about seventy, and has been thrice married. Mary looks very pretty, is very busy, and very much a housewife; she sends kind wishes to your sister, whom she likes almost as well as I like you. Farewell, affectionately,

ANNE MACVICAR.

LETTER II.

TO MISS HARRIET REID, GLASGOW.

Lochfyne, near Inverary,
April 28, 1773.

My dearest Harriet,†

I have been seriously thinking all the way to Luss, how little we know ourselves, and what odd beings we are. We left Balclutha ‡ so mournful, "thin darkness covered our beauty, and we looked forth from our hill, like half seen stars, through the rainy clouds of night. The sigh of the manly youths

* Collector Macvicar, of Oban, distantly related to the Author, whose daughter, Mary, had the year before resided for some time with her family.

† Miss Henrietta Reid was a very amiable and deserving young lady, connected by marriage with Miss Ewing; and by the more endeared intimacy both with her and the Author. This triple cord was never slackened by difference or distance of situation, but continued unbroken till the conclusion of that excellent person's life.

‡ Glasgow is called Balclutha in the language of Ossian.

awaited our departure, and we went away very sad indeed." I am sure if St Mungo's spire were capable of gratitude, it owes me some, for the many sad looks I cast back at it. I shall ever love my dear native Balclutha, not only for what I enjoyed, but for what I suffered in it. What I have suffered, was the common lot of humanity; what I have enjoyed was much more, for who ever had such friends as mine? But now to our recollections. Who would have supposed, when we were at Dumbarton, that we should ever have dried our eyes? Yet, when we met in the great room, where the sea-born swains from Greenock joined us, and when "the flame rose from the burning oak," we rose to serene, thence to cheerful, and, had we not been forced to part so soon, we might have got up to *hilarity*. Then, when the great struggle came, and we did really part, I thought my heart would break; and your last words sounded in my ears like a knell; and I thought I should not smile this whole summer. I read the folded paper James Hall gave me to amuse me when I stept into the carriage, about which you were so curious; it related to real events, and was

> "So sad, so tender, and so true."

It was from a young man of merit and parts, who, by a love marriage, had, alas, condemned himself to perpetual poverty. He had gone to scramble among the wealth of England for a subsistence. Why should I tell of his sorrows and disappointments! Finally, my sister, he wrote this letter to a friend (probably James Hall himself) under those impressions which approaching death inspired. That princely knight errant, Francis the First, wrote to his mother from the field of a lost battle, "Madam, all is lost but honour;" good, but this is better still. "The result is, all is lost, but a sure confidence in the Divine mercy." And what else can a poor finite creature hold to, when the world, and all that is dear and lovely in it, fades from his sight? It was a most affecting letter. "I wept abundant, and I wept aloud." Yet, alas! I fear they were not such generous tears as you might suppose. If I had not been so very sorry myself, I should not have been so easily melted. Well, now I was very sure I would not smile this summer, nor yet read any book but the Bible and the Night Thoughts; even the Odyssey* was to be rejected. And thus I travelled on, so serious and so sad. I had got far beyond moralizing; and then came on such small, soft, melancholy rain, and Ben Lomond's great head was wrapt in such a veil of thick clouds, that the nearer we drew, the less we saw of it. And as to my three friends, they showed at first as much sense and feeling as Job's did, whose silence, on an occasion which common minds would have seized to say common things, I always admired. In short, the whole party seemed lost in meditation, till the sight of Loch Lomond roused us. What a happy faculty is an active imagination to combat the evils of sickly sensibility! I passed over all the beautiful groves and corn-fields that adorn the lower side, for I had seen such things before, and they brought images of happiness and tranquillity which my mind could not relish in its depressed state. But the solemn

* The Night Thoughts and the Odyssey, were favourite studies among these friends, to which they were wont to make many serious and playful allusions.

and melancholy grandeur of the lofty dark mountains, and abrupt rocks tufted with heath and juniper, that rose on the other side of the lake, and seemed to close its upper end, arrested my attention at once. I peopled their narrow and gloomy glens with those vindictive clans, that used to make such fatal incursions of old. I thought I saw Bruce and his faithful few ascending them, in his forced flight from Bute. A train of departed heroes seemed to pass on their clouds in long review, and, do but guess who closed the procession? no other than the notorious Rob Roy,* riding up the Loch side with the lady he forced away, and the "twenty men in order," who make such a figure in the ballad. My mother knew the family, and tells the whole history of the transaction. The lady, it would appear, was too delicate a subject for such a rough adventure, for she died of grief very soon after. I saw M. M.'s dwelling, beneath romantic cliffs, and by a roaring stream, but I was not near enough to trace her stately steps. I made a happy transition from Rob Roy, to think of her, and her good books, and her cheerful piety; such an example to us all. Pray tell her I will never forget her.

All this brought us to Luss, which I am too lazy to describe twice; so must refer you to Isabella. But I will tell you how I took a pensive walk to admire Inchmarron,† and the setting sun, while dinner was prepar-

* Rob Roy Macgregor, the leader of a train of banditti; the last person in Scotland who carried off an heiress forcibly.

† Inchmarron is a beautiful island in Loch Lomond, three miles long, narrow and woody. It serves as a park for deer, and is the more interesting from being chosen sometimes as a retreat for harmless maniacs, who roam at large, and lodge with the forester. 1807.

ing. There "I chewed the food of sweet and bitter fancy," and felt some of those painful twitches, or spasms (are they not?) in my breast, that remind one how much the soul is superior to the frame that is thus influenced by it. Dinner brought us together; conversation grew insensibly cheerful; our Greenock friend amused us with amphibious humour, such as all the west coast abounds in; and before tea, your friend, who was not to relax a muscle this year, more than half smiled, and by supper time laughed outright. But truly might I say, that, "in the midst of laughter the heart is sad." Give me credit for my honesty, imitate my sincerity, and tell me when *you* laughed first. In the meantime I will tell you something to laugh at. My three friends being engaged in a long discourse, replete with Argyllshire genealogy, I was for a while quite abstracted; my Ossianic mania returned with double force; while every blast seemed to touch a viewless harp, and every passing cloud, brightened with the beams of the moon, appeared to my mind's eye a vehicle for the shades of the lovely and the brave, that live in the songs of other times. How softly sweet, how sadly plaintive, were the strains that now arrested my attention! From the dark caverns of the kitchen they proceeded, and, through the loose disjointed floor of our apartment, they

"Rose like a stream of rich distill'd perfumes."

This music was both vocal and instrumental; but no such voice, no such instrument, had I ever heard. Could I sit still when curiosity was so powerfully excited? Believe I did not, but, stealing down on tiptoe, beheld a great dark-browed Highlander, sitting double over the fire, and playing "Macgregor na Ruara"* on two trumps† at once, while a nymph, half hidden amongst her heavy locks, was pacing backwards, turning a great wheel, and keeping time with voice and steps to his mournful tones. I retired, not a little disconcerted, and dreamt all night of you and Malvina by turns. Spring appears here but in early infancy. Yet how can I tell you how mildly beautiful the sun arose over the distant hills of Morven; or, with what secret veneration I traced the footsteps of my fathers, along their blue gleaming lakes, or through their narrow vales. I saw, in the course of this morning's ride, in a secret nook at the head of Loch Lomond, Glen Falloch, I think it is called, a name signifying the hidden vale, and hidden it certainly is. One would think it a sad exile to live in one of these recesses; yet, by what I can gather from the conversation of our friends, people somehow contrive to be both gay and busy here.

I have already forgotten the name of the place‡ we breakfasted at; but there our fellow-traveller, or attendant rather, forsook us; and there we picked up an original of quite another kind. The carriage was detained while one of the horses was shod, and I took that opportunity of gathering some of the freshest prim-

* "Macgregor na Ruara," a beautiful plaintive tune, very popular in the Highlands. The mourner, in a pathetic and very peculiar strain of poetry, laments the slaughter of an outlaw, who appears to have been rightful possessor of Glenlyon. A very close translation of this interesting poem is given, by the Author of these Letters, in the 4th vol. of Mr. Thomson's Scottish Music.

† Jews' harps.

‡ Probably Tarbet or Arroquhar.—Ed.

roses I had ever seen, from the roots of a weeping birch, that actually "wept odorous dews" upon me, as I sheltered under its drooping branches. How I do love these artless bowers, and how much I wish to have you with me here, to tell you things that no other mortal would understand or care for! My walk was stopped by a stream, whose descent into the lake was covered by thick shades of alder and hazle, that reminded me of the creek where Ulysses went on shore in Phæacia, and then I wished I had my Odyssey out of the chaise. But, alas! no Odyssey was to be had. Then I was called to breakfast, in an upper room, the floor of which was much worse than that at Luss; and indeed pervious to every sound. We had taken possession of the only tolerable room, and a newly-arrived traveller was heard growling for his breakfast below. He did not swear, but was so fretful and querulous; so displeased with everything that was given or said to him, and his manner of growling, too, was so amusing, he showed so much ingenuity in discovering faults in everything, that I burst out a-laughing, and said we were certainly haunted by the ghost of Smelfungus, of whom Sterne gives such an amusing account. By the by, we had the previous day passed, with "reverence due," the monument of the original Smelfungus, which rises near his native spot, beside his favourite lake, which he delights to describe in Humphrey Clinker. Tea was prepared, but still thunder muttered hoarse below.

My father, inquiring about the stranger, and finding he was a gentleman's son of the country, very good-naturedly sent him an invitation to breakfast; for he concluded the house, a very poor one, could not furnish two breakfasts, with their apparatus, of equal elegance, and that this occasioned the ill humour by which we were incommoded. He was a student, travelling home from college : he left all his irritability below, and came up with an air so manly, well-bred, and accommodating, that, had we not received some previous intelligence of his character through the floor, we should have thought highly of him ; yet, through the strong lines of a marked and sensible countenance, the scowl of discontent was but too obvious. I, who for my part detest every mode of selfish luxury, could not endure to see a native Highlander make his good humour dependant on a good breakfast, and was moreover disgusted by certain learned strictures on new-laid eggs, which, I am sure, made no part of his college acquirements.* Then his appearance was so manly, that this puppyism was doubly provoking ; however, he sweetened by degrees into an agreeable and intelligent fellow-traveller. But, O ! not a single spark of enthusiasm. Ossian himself was never blinder than he is to the soul-moving beauties of that bard.

Why, after tiring you and myself with such a detail, should I tell you of the horrors of Glencroe, through which we travelled in a dismal rainy day ? In one particular, I dare say, I agreed with the stranger, for I really thought dinner the most interesting

* Among the peculiarities of Highland manners, is an avowed contempt for the luxuries of the table. A Highland hunter will eat with a keen appetite and sufficient discrimination; but were he to stop in any pursuit, because it was meal time, to growl over a bad dinner, or visibly exult over a good one, the manly dignity of his character would be considered as fallen for ever.

event of this day's journey, not merely as a repast, but the manner of it was so novel. There was a little inn, thatched, and humbler than any of the former; we came very cold to it; we found a well-swept clay floor, and an enlivening blaze of peats and brushwood, two windows looking out upon the lake* we were to cross, and a primitive old couple, whose fresh complexion made you wonder at their silver hairs. All the apparatus of fishing and hunting were suspended from the roof; I thought myself in Ithaca, though Homer does not speak of peats or trout, and far less of grouse. The people showed an alacrity in welcoming us, and a concern about our being wet and cold, that could not have been assumed. I never took such a sudden liking to people so far out of my own way. I suppose we are charmed with cheerfulness and sensibility in old people, because we do not expect it; and with unservile courtesy in the lower class, for the same reason. "How populous, how vital is the grave!" says your favourite Young; "How populous, how vital are the glens!" I should be tempted to say here: but after the "stupendous solitude," through which we had just passed, the blazing hearth and kindly host had peculiar attractions.

Shall I tell you of our dinner? Never before did I blot paper with such a detail; but it is instructive to know how cheaply we may be pleased. On a clean table of two fir deals we had as clean a cloth; trout new from the lake, eggs fresh as our student's heart could wish; *kippered* salmon, fine new-made butter

* Lochfyne.

and barley-cakes, which we preferred to the loaf we had brought with us. Smelfungus began to mutter about the cookery of our trouts; I pronounced them very well drest, out of pure spite; for by this time I could not endure him, from the pains he took to mortify the good people, and to show us he had been used to lodge and dine better. I feasted, and was quite entranced, thinking how you would enjoy all that I enjoyed. Dear Harriet, how my heart longs for you, when I think how yours is made to share all my wild pleasures!

The boat was crossing with other passengers over the ferry, which is very wide. We were forced to wait its arrival two hours—to me very short ones; one of them I have given to you, for I could never tell you all this when the warm feeling of the minute had worn off. I have kept my promise of being minute, most religiously; there is merit in it. For you I have forsaken Smelfungus, who is yonder walking on the Loch side, in all the surly dignity of displeasure. I am going to tea, and will put him in good humour, with questions about his college.

What a pleasant tea-drinking! The old landlord knew all my father's uncles, and the good woman was so pleased with my interest in her household economy! It produced a venison ham, sacred to favourites, and every other good thing she had; every one was pleased, and Smelfungus himself became,

> "As mild and patient as the female dove,
> When first her golden couplets are disclosed."

And here I conclude this long letter to begin another

at Inverary. Innocent, beloved, and amiable, what more can I wish you, that will not risk a share of your happiness? Adieu, Beloved!

A. M.

Letter III.

TO MISS REID, GLASGOW.

Inverary, April 28, 1773.

If such a snarler as Smelfungus is so undeservedly happy as to have a Harriet to care for everything he does, and think his rambling letters interesting, I fancy he is now pouring out to that favoured fair one a doleful complaint of those "vapours, and clouds, and storms," which only exalted me to "solemn thought." He, indeed, has a better title to call them "kindred glooms," yet he does not seem very fond of these aërial relations. He and I are a complete contrast; he has nothing of a Highlander but by his birth; now that is the precise and only circumstance wanting to make me a complete one. Such a day as we had after crossing the ferry! such torrents! Our carriage stood us in good stead, when we left the boat, in which, indeed, we got completely wet. But, alas! for the unsheltered head of Smelfungus, and for the new hat he was so careful of. Wet and weary, late and dreary, we arrived; and yet I was not depressed. O that I could share with you the musings that absorbed my whole soul this evening. They pertained not to the earth, nor any of its present inhabitants. There are some solemn hours, when the wings of the soul are expanded to pursue the flight of the departed;—when, balanced betwixt hope and fear, we hover over the abyss we are forbidden to explore, and anticipate the hour when the "graves shall give up their dead." Did you not tell me to write my thoughts just as they occurred? How else should we converse in absence; how keep the flame that warms my heart alive? Believe me, I carry the same sentiments and recollections with me here, that used to be my companions at the Fir Park, or the Bogton Linn, to which latter present my respects, when you trace my old haunts. The approach to this city of the mountains was so veiled in mist, that I could only admire, through watery moonbeams, the semicircular sweep which the beach forms round the lake; but I shall be here all to-morrow, and tell you all that pleases me. I leave to Smelfungus to chronicle complaints; if he felt as acutely as I do, he would have no pleasure in recording his painful feelings, which is to suffer them twice.

29th April. Five in the Morning.

What a long sweet oblivion of sorrow and fatigue have I had since nine last night! After discharging superior duties, I am greatly tempted to worship the sun. His first appearance from the sea was so overpowering after his long absence. There he is, "round as the shield of my fathers;" teaching the mountains to rejoice, and the waves to roll in light. "Whence are thy beams, O Sun?" I am not mad, most *gentle* Harriet, though you may think I do not quite speak the words of truth and soberness. But consider that it is the spring of day, of life, and of the year, and indulge me in rejoicing a little, after I have mourned so much and so truly. How could I exist, feeling sorrow so poignantly, if the fair face of nature had not peculiar charms, endless sources of delight for me. Though my sorrows should be multiplied, as very likely they may, I shall have consolations peculiarly my own, that, like Milton's sweet music,

> "Will breathe
> Above, about, and underneath."

How literal this truth is, the dulcet sounds that stole through the floor at Luss may testify. A little dress, a little Odyssey, a little breakfast, and then—I shall behold the faces of my kindred.

I have seen them; and here they come in succession. . . . . Now, I trust, you are tired of characters, and may come willingly down to still life. Last summer you heard half a dozen descriptions of Inverary; this summer, it is very likely, you may have as many more; and that from people not so subject to the digressive infirmity as your friend. Depend upon these matter-of-fact people for an account of this princely edifice,* and its dependencies; I shall merely tell you of particulars that struck me most forcibly, premising that this Castle, as they call it here, is not finished within. First, then, the Gothic grandeur of the hall, open to the very top, and lighted by a cupola, delighted me; it is like a receptacle for the train of a mighty chieftain, and quite in unison with the boldness of the neighbour-

* The Duke of Argyll's Castle at Inverary. It was commenced in 1745, but not finished for some years afterwards.

ing scenery. There is a kind of gallery or corridor carried round this hall, from which you enter the upper rooms; the doors of these you see all in one view, as you stand in the hall. It is not like anything you ever saw before; yet I am sure you would admire it. We were suddenly ushered into a charming summer parlour, which had a sashed door that opened into a beautiful lawn. Will you believe me, when I tell you that I thought, for a moment, I was in the open fields, surrounded by people engaged in rural sports, the scene was so lively, and rushed so suddenly on me. The first thing that awoke me to the knowledge of what I was about was the different style of the countenances from those I was accustomed to see. What should this be but a room hung with Gobelin tapestry, whose magical perfection of resemblance made you think the hay-makers and children lived and moved. And for the trees, I am sure your nephew Francis would have tried to climb them. I said, reluctantly, "Adieu, ye woods!" And yet, after all, I am not sure I should like such a room, unless merely to wonder and gaze at. Can it be the love of truth in the mind, that recoils at a very near deception? Wax figures, and very excellent trees in tapestry, make me something like Young's monkeys, who

> "At a mirror stand amazed,
> They fail to find what they so plainly see."

I did not "peep and chatter," but my wonder felt something like disappointment. I was disappointed, too, in seeing so few pictures. I should like to find portraits in this region of beauty, the Lord and Lady of which, only, could have been parallels to each other.

I am told their children excel even the Hamilton family. So they should, having a double claim; their father having been a model of manly grace in his day. And here I could find in my heart to stop and rail at the world, which, you know, I bear no great good will to. One hears so little about him, he is so quietly passed over to make room for dashers, and boasters, and fighters, and talkers. *He* does not wish to be talked of, it is certain; but then I would not have them quite so complaisant as to give him all his will in this particular. Seek for a great man's true and solid praise at his own door, among his tenants and neighbours; and let it be a material part of his praise, that he has neighbours; that is to say, that he lives at home among them. In this particular the Duke of Argyll is unrivalled and alone. Every mouth here will tell you of some of these "quiet waters, soft and slow," that steal silently on, carrying bounty and beneficence into all the corners of obscurity. Do not be tired, now, for I have a whole volume to write of this good Duke's worth and wisdom, which improves and blesses the whole country; but I can no more

> "Let him still the secret joy partake,
> To follow virtue even for virtue's sake."

Yet, I hope, when this modest and amiable benefactor of mankind sleeps with his fathers,* and when the

* That time is arrived; for last year (1806), Scotland was deprived of this venerable Duke, who, independent of the rank he adorned, and the power he used for the best purposes, was beloved in life and lamented in death, as a worthy private character, and a genuine patriot. [He died in the 87th year of his age, having married, in 1759, the Duchess Dowager of Hamilton, formerly one of the Miss Gunnings, so celebrated for beauty, and was succeeded successively by his sons George last Duke, and John, present and seventh Duke of Argyll. 1845.—Ed.]

tenants have ceased to say, "He is the best of countrymen" (a word equivalent to patriot), some powerful voice shall say with effect,

> "Rise, Muses, rise, add all your tuneful breath,
> Such must not sleep in darkness and in death."

For, as much as I was bent on dying last winter, I may still hear these notes, "sweet to the world, and grateful to the skies." You will say I am quite carried off; but I feel the patriot passion strong myself, and am charmed when I find one actually doing all that I dream of doing.

The offices of this fabric are magnificent for their purposes, and the roads leading to them wonders; but what I greatly wonder at is, that they should place the offices at such a distance as to require such roads. I believe there is no danger of my ever living in a great house, and I am not sorry for it. There is such a stately absence of all comfort; everything that unsophisticated nature delights to cling to, is put so far away; and the owner seems, somehow, alone in the middle of his works, like Nebuchadnezzar, saying, "Behold now this great Babylon which I have made." I should be very sorry to have my poor houyhnhams where I could neither hear them neigh, nor see them shake their necks clothed with thunder. Suppose me above looking at hens and ducks, I should not like to have my stately peacocks and majestic swans swimming and sweeping a mile off. The gardens, too, must keep their distance. What have poor Flora and Pomona done, to deserve banishment? As for the sheltering Dryads of antiquity, they are all marched off, for no reason that I can think of, but their being grown old maids, and the bleak blasts seem invited in their stead. I wonder whether people are to live longer in these temples of Eolus than they did in the sheltered halls of other days, where everything around them was animated and interesting. I wish you could but once see the moon shine on Lochfyne, and the shadow of Duniquaich* falling on the great house. Now, you must observe, the bay forms a perfect crescent; the Castle, surmounted by Duniquaich aforesaid, and skirted at great distance by offices, adorns one end of the crescent; on the very edge of the bay stands Inverary, a mean-looking, yet cheerful and populous place, deriving a peculiar beauty from its situation. It is one street facing the water; and beyond it a fine road, surrounded by a beautiful lawn, sprinkled with prodigious beech trees, sweeps from one horn of the crescent to the other. I hear, and, being no friend to alterations, am sorry to hear, that this ancient town is to be transported and removed to the other horn of the crescent, where the inn and custom-house now stand. This will augment the solitary grandeur of the house, by throwing everything far from it. The Duke, who does everything well that he takes in hand, will, no doubt, raise finer buildings; but they will only look like children's card-houses, as the present set appear like molehills. Nature here is so vast and grand, that the works of art diminish to nothing in her awful presence. I dare say, looking from one of the surrounding mountains, the Castle would appear attached to Duniquaich, like Grildrig's box at the girdle of Glumdalclitch.

* A picturesque hill behind Inverary Castle.

We spent the evening with the same relations we had seen in the forenoon. Our old friend, the Collector's sister, is a most singular evergreen; indeed she resembles himself a good deal; thin, lively, tall, erect, with a keen expressive eye, and a fresh youthful complexion, though much above seventy; awake and alive to everything; always amusing, occasionally facetious, and abounding in anecdote: she has seen many sorrows, and borne them firmly, to say the least. There were assembled at supper . . . . I like the kindness and frankness of these friends vastly.

A sister of Dr. M., whom you may remember with us last winter, is newly married to one of these cousins. She has been growing wise for half a century, without cooling in her benevolence in the region of celibacy. She was always a good creature, and a friend to all the friendless; and has now an occupation well suited to such a disposition. I am sure he married her, beautiless and moneyless as she was, that she might be a kind stepmother; and so she is, and seems so pleased with having a family to rear. She puts me very much in mind of a hen with an alien brood of young ducks. If I were to marry at all, which is very unlikely, thinking on many subjects as I do, I could be easily reconciled to a ready-made family, supposing them docile and grateful. I can easily comprehend how one could adopt them to one's affections. Then think of being quit of their plague while they are mere vegetables, and then become mere animals; and think of the credit one should get for being kind to these ready-made innocents; and, moreover, the strong hold such generosity would give you of your lord's affections. Now if there was any office that would insure one against paying mother Eve's penalty, I think breeding ducks would be no bad speculation. But indeed you may depend upon it we shall never be so happy as we have been; no, never.

The Collector's horses are just arrived; we must leave Inverary to-morrow, and it will rain; and I am so sorry; and I have not half seen it, nor taken leave of poor Smelfungus. I will take leave of you, however; and, if I reach Oban alive, will rise at five every morning to write to you. Good night, beloved!

A. M.

Letter IV.

TO MISS HARRIET REID.

Oban, 1st May 1773.

My dear Harriet,

I arrived here last night, but dreadfully tired;—tired of rain; tired of riding; tired of long moors, but, above all, of long descriptions. See my letter to Isabella,* where you will find how I came through the Mona Lia. Oh! never was moor so long and so solitary.

You will say my active imagination might people the brown desert; so it did, but it was with fleeting spectres, and half-seen visions, melting into grey mist. *Apropos* to our ducklings, you cannot think how my spirit was refreshed by a flock of wild ones, that

* Page 1.

took flight from a small lake in that same dreary moor. I saw, or thought I saw, two or three deer through the mist, and that did me a great deal of good. Still more, I was supported by a benevolent project for the reformation of some of our friends; I mean such of them as do, or say, no great harm, but who so bewilder their brains and waste their time among endless mazes of ribands and lace, and tattle and tales, and "pribbles and prabbles," as honest Parson Evans calls them, that, I am convinced some solitary pilgrimages over the brown desert might wean them from this endless trifling, and teach them first to think, and then "on reason build resolve," which might be found "a column of true dignity," even in woman. But I will no longer bewilder you among my meditations. The general result, however, was, that we should be oftener alone. I am sure I have little merit to claim from superior reflection or culture. Could I have indulged myself in the society of others of my age, I should, most probably, have done as they did. Had I been educated like other people, I should not have felt the necessity of educating myself.

If, therefore, my thinking and reading have been of any advantage, they are merely the result of certain painful and discouraging privations. If others were secluded like me, or exiled, as I am about to be, from all that was wont to please, they would be forced to seek resources within themselves. This, too, might be a cure for vanity. I can easily suppose recluses proud, but it is among frivolous society that people grow vain. We are proud of what we certainly possess; but vanity only seeks credit for seeming, and is just as well satisfied to be admired for rouge as for native bloom. It lives in the breath of others, and dies when it is no longer seen.

Do not think I am so new-fangled as to begin to rail at the town, which I have just quitted, out of fondness for a country which is so new to me, and which, very probably, I may not like; but I am so provoked at the tiresome sameness of treading one insignificant round for ever. Were it a week, a month, a season, that was to be consumed in impertinence and insignificance; but all day long, and every day, and to grow old in it, and die without having lived to any considerable purpose! People in the country may be abundantly silly and selfish, but the passion for despicable and corrupting novelties is not so constantly fed. When the heart is chastened by adversity, or softened by sorrow, the salutary impression is not too soon effaced. The mind is in a manner forced on the contemplation of nature; and I do not know how any one can see one's Maker in his greatest works, without being the better and the wiser for it. Yet to those who are truly desirous of improvement, the town affords greater choice of society. That, and that alone, I regret in leaving it. I forgot to say, that, as we drew near Loch Awe, we caught a distant glimpse of Barabreack,* familiar to me as the often-described abode of my paternal ancestors. Here we had a long detail of their simple manner of life, their humble virtues, and the affectionate confidence that subsisted between them and their co-partners in the same pos-

* Barabreack or Barbreck, in the parish of Craignish, Argyllshire.

session. My father delighted to show us the stream where he first caught a trout, and the little island which had been the object of his first excursion in search of nuts and raspberries; and I listened with delight to tales of other times, told with so much animation. I felt as proud of the genuine worth and unstained probity of my ancestors, as if they had been all that the world admires and envies, and only wished that I might not prove unworthy of them.

I will not be so cruel as to carry you back to the moor, but I will tell you how it terminated. We descended into low grounds, in view of the sea, about twilight, and there was my spirit exhilarated with the sight of Glenfeochan. The sweet stream that winds by it, the green pastoral vale, sheltered by an overhanging mountain, in which it lies; the birch grove, in which the house is embosomed; and, above all, the air of "animated peace," which it derived from the return of the cattle and the servants, at the evening hour; and, moreover, the idea of the warm welcome I should receive from that agreeable romp, Mary Campbell, whom you have seen with me last winter; all this pressed so forcibly on my mind, that I would have given anything to stop here. But this indulgence was not permitted, so, with a heavy heart, I went on, and did not reach Oban till eleven.

Are the cares of a household productive of the same alteration in manner that we have often observed to be the result of matrimony? Mary Macvicar and I were too unlike to be congenial; but kindred, and those who live together in a perpetual interchange of kindness, may love without assimilating, and even though their views and pursuits should be very different. That was precisely the case with Mary and me, when she lived with us. Though she has little taste, no refinement, and not the smallest thirst for knowledge, she is not heartless, has a good understanding, and a quick apprehension of the ludicrous. I am sure, too, she loves me as well as she does any one else, and so she ought; indeed, she seems to love me still, and is all kindness and attention, yet there is a visible constraint about her. She is often absent, and does not enter into the spirit of raillery, or what she used to call fun. Who could ever think of Mary's being abstracted, and yet abstracted she certainly is. I wonder much how people should be so fond of marrying, when the cares of a household make such an alteration on a girl not sixteen. She manages surprisingly, and pays an attention to everything, which, I am sure, I could not do, though I am older,* and accounted more sedate. It is very encouraging to her to see how much her father is pleased with everything she does. And I am so pleased with her father; he is a delightful old man.† If his are the manners of the old court, I wish I had lived a little earlier. He is not the least formal. Indeed, he has lived so much among military people, and has so much of their general knowledge, and general politeness, that his are rather the manners of an old officer. He delights to talk of his "last friend," who, I believe, was an amiable woman, and lived happily with him, for the short time their union lasted;

* The Author was then in the nineteenth year of her age.—Ed.

† Collector Macvicar was a polished, intelligent, and public-spirited character, and was a great favourite of the late Duke of Argyll.

though the difference of age amounted to little less than fifty years. I must surely have told you the singular history of that marriage. The only fruit of it, a little girl not three years old, is a creature you could not see without loving. He dotes upon her, and I do not wonder at it; every look and motion of the dear little orphan charms one. She is pretty, too, though not remarkably so; but she shows sense and feeling that is incredible. The sweet creature follows me already; I never saw a child half so interesting. Good-night; I will tell you to-morrow what kind of place this is;—this day I have devoted to the people. Besides, it snows so hard as to remind me of your favourite poem,

> "Oft for the prospects sprightly May should yield,
> Rain-pouring clouds have darken'd all the air,
> And snows untimely whiten'd o'er the field."

Letter V.

TO MISS HARRIET REID.

Oban, May 2, 1773.

My dear Harriet,

The morning is clear and mild, and something like what May ought to be.

The Collector's dwelling-house forms part of the custom-house; it stands on the verge of this fine bay. The tide flows up to the door, but retires half a mile back, and discovers a scene very new and amusing to me, who have never been at the sea-side, except in embarking and debarking. Vast stones, where the footing is difficult, mixed with gravel, shells, and sea-weed, compose the extensive beach, which the ebbing sea leaves naked. I propose indulging my delight in overcoming difficulties, and exploring odd places and odd things, by many a walk in pursuit of the retreating sea nymphs. For you must know, it is settled I am to stay till June, when the Collector and Mary are to conduct me to Fort-William, where my father will meet me. I am glad of it, I shall not be kept so busy, and will have more society and amusement. Here is an excellent library, left to the Collector by that ill-fated brother* who was the patron of my father's orphan childhood. His fine talents, and finer feelings, served only to embitter misfortunes such as could not have happened to a common man. His morals were spotless; and he was not the victim of rashness and imprudence, as is often the case, with these "fine souls too feelingly alive;" nor was poverty among the number of those misfortunes which pursued, and at length overwhelmed him. His fate was very singular indeed; he might have been said to die a martyr to wounded honour. Had he died when the wound was inflicted, his fate would have been comparatively mild; but a man whose form, whose manners, whose mind, were distinguished, above all others, by peculiar elegance, to languish in painful obscurity, branded by a set of miscreants with the disgrace of treachery, which his soul abhorred! All his patriotic plans for the improvement

* Captain Macvicar, of the 42d Regiment of Highlanders, who retired from the army about 1749, in consequence of being most unjustly suspected of being privy to some projects then in agitation by the Jacobite party.

of the country, all his plans of life, and hopes of happiness, blasted by a malignity too base and secret to be exposed, and too barbarous to be resisted! When forced, by the machinations of his arch-enemy, Lord J.,* to sell his company in the 42d, he tried to amuse himself by rural occupations in his native country; for his mind was too deeply wounded to find solace in those literary pursuits, to which he had been formerly so much attached, and in which, if we may judge by his letters, he was so qualified to excel. A hypochondriac affection, which made life burdensome to him, and often tempted him to throw off the load, made him frequently change his abode, though well aware that "change of place was only change of pain." Melancholy, solitude, and the corroding remembrance of an irremediable misfortune, soured the most gentle and benignant of mortals into absolute misanthropy. I am interrupted, and cannot detail the painful story of his death. It was a sad termination indeed, but not self-urged: such a man could not be so utterly forsaken. He has haunted me ever since I came here. I shall never open a book of his without a pang.

What a transition, from the person I have been describing, to those I have just left! You must remember a good natured, giddy, but very genteel looking youth, who was in town last winter, a relation of ours; he is the heir of a very long ancestry, a very small patrimony, with abundance of *original sin* attached to it, and of two of the best old people in the world.

* Lord John Murray, who was himself misled by a designing sycophant, and afterwards prejudiced the Duke of Cumberland against this hard-fated gentleman.

Though these good people cared for nothing earthly but each other, and their children, and lived in as primitive and frugal a manner as Baucis and Philemon, they long struggled vainly with their incumbrances. At length they began to get above water, and actually built the shell of a house, to be finished by young hopeful; for a Highland mansion is generally the work of two generations. This consummation, so devoutly to be wished, was to take place when the said heir began to thrive in some lucrative profession; or by some wealthy match, to which, it was supposed, his fine figure and family pretensions might entitle him. He has, in the meantime, a younger but cleverer brother in the army.

But, mark the sequel. A very little, very pretty, and very thoughtless girl, the daughter of a neighbouring gentleman, came home from the boarding-school, as usual very full of dress, vanity, and music: she was scarcely sixteen, quite childish looking, and in frocks. However, cousin and she met, and, in two or three days' acquaintance, sung, and played, and romped, and trifled themselves into matrimony. No fortune to compensate this rash act, what should the good old people do?—Just brought them home with all the patience imaginable; and here they are, and often, I am told, they come; it is quite a second home: their own is half a mile off. How I shall be teased! yet conscience says I should like my kindred, and they are most obliging; but I feel something revolting, when people love me dearly at first sight. I cannot love others so: my mind shrinks from strangers. Then, how should they like me at once? I am sure our old friend must tire of the incursions of these nothing-doing people.

I am vexed to see that Mary is fondly intimate with them. Say they are quite harmless, as I dare say they may be, they favour her own bent too much. Good night. I am very tired; but you know my day, from five in the morning till midnight, admits of doing much to make me so.

A. M.

Letter VI.

TO MISS HARRIET REID, GLASGOW.

Oban, May 3, 1773.

My dear Harriet,

I wrote letters of duty in the morning, walked out all the forenoon, except a short time I spent with the sweetest of children and her father; and now I shall account to you for the remaining hours. After dinner we left our two old gentlemen together, and set out for Soroba: the walk Soroba-ward is charming. It is a sweet place, sheltered by a small hill; a brook, fringed with willows and alder, runs by it; beautiful meadows lie below, and towering mountains rise opposite. I never saw a place of a more pastoral aspect. I love the good old people; there is something so artless, primitive, and benevolent about them. I think I could guess them, by their looks, to be what every one describes them. Do you know, the Highlanders resemble the French, in being poor, with a better grace than other people. If they want certain luxuries or conveniences, they do not look embarrassed, or disconcerted, nor make you feel awkward by paltry apologies, which you do not know how to answer; they rather dismiss any sentiment of that kind by a sort of playful raillery, for which they seem to have a talent. Our visit, if not a pleasant, was at least a merry one. The moment tea was done, dancing began; excellent dancers they are, and in music of various kinds they certainly excel. The floor is not yet laid, but that was no impediment. People, hereabouts, when they have good ancestry, education, and manners, are so supported by the consciousness of those advantages, and the credit allowed for them, that they seem not the least disconcerted at the deficiency of the goods of fortune; and I give them great credit for their spirit and contentment, though it should provoke the appellation of poor and proud, which vulgar minds are so ready to apply to them. Is it not a blessed thing that there yet exists a place where poverty is respectable, and deprived of its sting?

O this incurable disease of wandering! I will return to my description of the Collector's house, which I broke off yesterday, on the ebb shore. Behind the house, then, is an excellent, though, as yet, infant garden, for this is quite a new establishment; a range of offices stretch along the shore on each side; the King's wherry and other boats, and such vessels as may chance to arrive, lie a little westward, and animate the spot where the joint wisdom of the Duke and the Collector have projected a future village, the rudiments of which already begin to appear.* From this chosen spot,

* The village, or rather town, of Oban is now become a very flourishing one, much resorted to by tourists on their way to the Island of Staffa, and other parts of the Western Highlands.—(1845.)

where a large brook discharges itself into the sea, a peaceful, long, green valley* opens from the shore, of which the Duke has given an advantageous lease to the Collector, who is a great favourite. The cottages lie in clusters on the sides of the sloping hills, or in sequestered nooks, below rocks interspersed with patches of earth, tufted with yellow broom, or mountain ash, which nods so wildly! And the people have so much the air of loving and helping each other, and their goats are such familiar, fanciful looking creatures! I am so fond of the kids, that dance and frisk with so much humour and meaning, and cry so like children; I would fain have one of them follow me tame, and am sadly distressed when I must needs eat them. I think if ever I run wild on the rocks, which at times I feel much inclined to, I will not be a shepherdess, but a goat-herdess. These creatures have more sense and spirit than heavy-headed sheep; they differ just as Highlanders do from plodding Lowlanders.—To return once more. On the other side of the house, and within a small distance of it, rises a hill quite detached from all others, and as like a sugar-loaf as if the resemblance had been designed by art. It is small, compared to the lofty heights that overlook it. The fine prospect seen from the house, is commanded to great advantage from this little eminence. I climbed to the very summit, which *we* should call high, but it is nothing here. There I found a white scallop shell, a diminutive of those used at Fingal's feasts. I was quite glad, thinking it a most orthodox shell, left by the deluge; but

* Glenshealeach, or the Vale of Willows, is the name of this verdant and pastoral glen.

was so laughed at—and very justly, when I think of it; for it would, in that case, have mouldered to lime a thousand years ago. Well, I hope this will be a lesson against being positive and conceited.

Good night. I go to church to-morrow. Now I think of it, I will not go to sleep without finishing what I have so often begun. Of the fine views from this spot, I cannot enumerate the islands I see, nor the groupes of fantastic dark blue mountains, rising before others too distant for distinction. Just such a prospect, I dare say, Ulysses had from the heights of his dear, rocky Ithaca; he looked on Zante and Cephalonia, as I do on Mull and Lismore. Some of these isles are inhabited by one gentleman, his family, and a few tenants. What an undisturbed little kingdom, and how happy one could make every subject of it! What an exile, what a prison, would such a sea-girt domain prove to some crowd-dependant people we know!

Mary is, and will be down stairs, getting flattery and comical sea stories, of which she has a great many, that are too much in the style of these inferior regions. Good night again.

Letter VII.

TO MISS HARRIET REID.

Oban, May 5, 1773.

Kilmore, where we heard sermon, is four miles off, at least, being three of Highland computation. It is by no means a Jewish sabbath that is kept here; it would be bold even to call it strictly a Christian one; be that as it may, it is a very cheerful one. We set out on horseback in a shower of snow, which people here mind no more than hair-powder; it hinders nothing. We picked up the young couple at Soroba, whose unmeaning mirth made me grave, and set me on pondering. Yet, when I observed the perpetual flow of spirits that buoys up the emptiness of ——, I revered the goodness of Providence in making people happy at so small an expense of intellect. I am not sure but their lot would be preeminent, were they all as innocent as my good-natured cousin. But their imbecility makes them tools to the wicked and designing; so that I believe it is as well to have some reflection, after all. This was an odd, old church, almost ruinous. But when the preacher came in,* he roused all my attention. I never beheld a countenance so keenly expressive, nor such dark piercing eyes: he is very like his sister, Flora Macdonald, and resembles her in a superior musical genius, being a distinguished composer, as well as performer, on the violin. When I began to look about, the dresses and countenances of the people presented new matter of speculation. This is certainly a fine country to grow old in; I could not spare a look to the young people, so much was I engrossed in contemplating their grandmothers. They preserve the form of dress worn some hundred years ago. Stately, erect, and self-satisfied, without a trace of the languor or coldness of age, they march up the area, with gaudy coloured plaids, fastened about their breasts with a silver brooch like the full moon in

* The Rev. Peter Macdonald, Minister of Kilmore, distinguished for musical talents. 1807.

size and shape. They have a peculiar, lively, blue eye, and a fair fresh complexion. Round their heads is tied the very plain kerchief Mrs. Page alludes to, when Falstaff tells her how well she would become a "Venetian tire;" and on each cheek depends a silver lock, which is always cherished and considered, not improperly, as a kind of decoration. These, you must observe, were the common people; the old *ladies* were habited in the costume of the year one.

I was trying to account for the expression in the countenances of these cheerful ancients (many above four-score), while the pastor, with vehement animation, was holding forth in the native tongue. Now here is the result: people who are for ever consecrating the memory of the departed, and hold the virtues, nay, the faults of their ancestors, in such blind veneration, see much to love and revere in their parents, that others never think of. They accumulate on these patriarchs all the virtues of their progenitors, and think the united splendour reflects a lustre on themselves. The old people, treated with unvaried tenderness and veneration, feel no diminution of their consequence, no chill in their affections. Strangers to neglect, they are also strangers to suspicion. The young readily give to old age that cordial, by which they hope to be supported when their own almond trees begin to blossom. But fine people do not seem ever to think they shall be old. Now, in their way, I should love my father not merely as such, but because he was the son of the wise and pious Donald, whose memory the whole parish of Craignish* venerates; and the grandson of the gallant

* The Author's father, Mr Macvicar, was a native of the parish of Craignish, in Argyllshire.—Ed.

Archibald, who was the tallest man in the district; who could throw the *putting* stone farther than any Campbell living, and never held a Christmas without a deer of his own killing, four Fingalian greyhounds at his fireside, and sixteen kinsmen sharing his feast. Shall I not be proud of a father, the son of such fathers, of whose fame he is the living record? Now, what is my case is every other Highlander's; for we all contrive to be wonderfully happy in our ancestry; and by this means, the sages here get a great deal of reverence and attention, not usually paid to the "Struldbruggs" of other countries. Observe, moreover, that they serve for song books, and circulating libraries; so faithfully do they preserve, and so accurately detail, "the tales of the times of old," and the songs of the bards, that now strike the viewless harp on wandering clouds. All this, with their constant cheerfulness, make them the delight of the *very young*, in the happy period of wonder and simplicity; and their finding themselves so, prevents their being peevish, or querulous. Ossian was never more mistaken than when he said, "Age is dark and unlovely;" here it appears "like the setting moon on the western wave," and we bless the brightness of its departure.

I was waked out of the pleasing reverie which the sight of so many fine ancients inspired, by the beadle's coming to the seat to ask if I understood Gaelic, because if I did not there was to be an English discourse. Judge of my self-importance, in having a sermon preached for my very self. Poor souls! will you ever compare yourselves to me again? Meg

Morison,* when she was composing her meditation upon "Worm Jacob, threshing the Mountains," had not a higher idea of the consequence of her single, sinful, soul. A new, and very amusing scene opened, when service was over: we were ushered into a kind of public house, where it seems all the genteel part of the congregation (and very genteel some of them were) usually meet, converse, and take refreshment, while their horses are preparing, &c. Mary Campbell and I met joyfully. I recognised her new blush-coloured lustring, as soon as I went into church; but at such exhibitions I no longer wonder. The *Kirk* here, is literally accounted a public place, and frequented from very different motives. People *not singularly pious*, cross ferries, and ride great distances in bad weather, not solely, I fear, to hear the glad tidings in church, but to meet friends in this good-humoured, kindly way, after sermon, who can tell them all about their eighteenth cousins in India and America. All this is very animated, and I contrive to be much interested. There is little scandal; for scandal is the dregs and sediment of conversation, after better things have been discussed; and we talk so much of the dead, that the living escape. Your belles and beaux would not relish this, for there is no chance of being admired by the dead. I am resolved, for my part, to die in the Highlands, that I may avoid the sudden oblivion which swallows up the departed among polished people, who disguise selfishness under the pretence of not being able to endure to have their

* A conceited bigot in low life, who used to compose and sell what she called her Meditations, one of which had the above title.

fine feelings disturbed with the mention of the dead. Honest Donald feels no such repugnance, but calls up the joy of grief in tender meditation, cherishes the memory of his fathers, "and walks in the light of their renown."

> "Why should I speak of General Chumley,
> And Mr. Muster-master Gumley?"

Why should I introduce you to the Cynosure of the assembly, the old Major, with his tartan coat, his large silver buttons, worn in Montrose's wars by his grandfather, and his redundant silver locks adorning a countenance the picture of health and benignity? Nor will you care a farthing for his three thin upright sisters, though they are, amidst their oddity, very like mountain gentlewomen; nor for his nine cousins, tasteless thing that you are! Among this singular group, were some very well-bred, fashionable-looking people, who had been abroad in the world, without being spoiled by it, and treated their antiquated rustic relations with a respect and kindness which was both amiable and exemplary. If I were to stay and frequent this church a twelvemonth, hearing and retaining as I generally do, I doubt not that I might be qualified to compile the heraldry of Lorne,* so skilled should I become in its antiquities.

The sun shone on our social repast, but when we set out, Eolus did not perform the task Thomson assigns him in the opening of Spring; instead of "calling off his ruffian blasts," he let them loose in great fury, and the demolition of my new hat awakened my remorse for making so merry with poor Smelfungus's misfor-

* The name of one of the Northern districts of Argyllshire.

tune of the same kind. Blinded with snow, and in instant danger of "mounting the whirlwind's wing," we were accosted by a most respectable-looking gentleman, who brought us into his house, which seemed the chosen residence of comfort;—so they told me, for I could look at nothing but the mistress of the mansion, she had been so very handsome, and was still so very engaging: her countenance had so much soul in it, her person and demeanour were so graceful, and her manner so graciously kind. The Collector says, she is all her appearance premises; I felt sorry when I thought I might never see her again. After all, "What's Hecuba to me, or I to Hecuba?" My friends laughed and talked louder than the storm, all the way home; I was lost in lofty meditation, and, to own the truth, was writing this letter in idea; and then I was so glad to find myself at this fireside, with the Collector's sweet little girl in my arms.

I am going to bid good night to the moon; the storm is over, the undulating waters are like living light, while the same beams repose so sweetly on the shadowy sides of far-seen mountains, that arise in distant isles.

> "—— In such a night,
> Stood Dido with a willow in her hand
> Upon the wild sea bank, and wav'd her love
> To come again to Carthage."

Ungrateful cur that he was! Adieu; may you never wave a willow, or spend a good day as idly as I have done this. It is past midnight, and remorse is preying on me. Adieu, again, my dearest.

A. M.

LETTER VIII.

TO MISS HARRIET REID.

Oban, May, 1773.

Now, my dear Harriet, I have commenced a bad custom both to you and myself. I write so minutely, that when I settle and have something else to do, I must needs be concise, and then you will think me careless; but you must not, for my manner of writing to you is so like our old wandering chit-chat, that I fly to it as Lizzy does to her snuff-box; and this so often, that I neglect those I ought to like and attend to, and would attend to, if I did not feel as if I had you always, in a corner, to run to. I will not write these two days, unless a little matter-of-fact before breakfast, and a gossiping whisper at bed-time. My taste for solitary amusement, and indifference to the volatile chit-chat of some people, begin to excite much observation. Shake off the imputation as we please, every one has their own mode of selfishness, and I feel mine to be that of running away to my solitary pleasures. I repent, will mortify myself, and "do penance in gay young company."

Evening.

I am reformed, and amended, but cannot fatigue myself or you with the description of this day; you will find it in Thomson: "deceitful, vain, and void, passes the day." Why should I speak with peevishness of good-humoured, harmless people, who show a wish to please me? Why am I not pleased with trifles, when the best of us are doomed to pass great part of our lives in a manner which our own reflections must call trifling? But then I should like to trifle in my own way. I could play half a day with sweet little Anne, or even with a sportive kitten, or puppy; I could gather shells and sea-weed on the shore, or venture my neck for nests, which I would not plunder after finding them; nay, I could talk nonsense, as we used to do, and laugh heartily at vagaries of our own contriving. But the nonsense of these good people I cannot for my life relish: they think it wit, and I cannot accredit it as such. Then they think cunning wisdom, and mistake simplicity for folly.

Very rural all this; here is gossiping for you with a witness! Do not think that I indulge myself in the conceit of not caring for any body, unless they have the taste for reading, which great leisure and solitude, in a manner, forced upon me. But I would have people love truth and nature; I would have them look a little into the great book which their Maker has left open to every body. I would have the rising and setting sun, the blossoming trees and opening flowers, give them the same pleasure, which many taste without knowing their alphabet. O! when, or where shall I see another Harriet, uncultured and untaught, yet awake to all that is grand or beautiful in nature, all that is excellent or desirable in knowledge—whose intuitive sense of what is delicate and proper, is worth volumes of instruction! The more I know of others, the more I regret you; and the best use I ever could make of the knowledge which I have accidentally acquired, would be to impress it on the fair tablet of your spotless mind. Good night, my dear; I am neither very well nor very easy. I have got cold in these meadowy traverses. My father and mother go away to-morrow. Were it not for the dear old man, and his little girl, and his library, I would go too. Write to me here, and never mind incorrectness; you will daily improve; or, though you should not,

> "Thou hast no faults, or I no faults can spy,
> Thou art all beauty, or all blindness I."

Letter IX.

TO MISS HARRIET REID.

Fort-William, May 12, 1773.

Be astonished, O Harriet, for here I am. Ask why I am here, and I can only tell you it was owing to the strangest caprice. Yet, so it is, and you know I do not use to be fickle. The day after I wrote to you, it was settled that my father and mother were to proceed from Oban to Fort-William in the King's wherry. "Mark that, Mary Jones." Two o'clock was the hour fixed. Mary Macvicar proposed a forenoon walk,—I went reluctantly, on condition of not passing the boundary rivulet on the way to Soroba. There she lingered with teasing perseverance; hoping, no doubt, that some of our friends would appear. At length I would go, fearing my parents might go without seeing me. The first object that met my eyes, crossing the hill, was His Majesty's wherry, going full sail up the bay. I grew cold as lead; I felt the oddest sensation; surprise and remorse for being away, and a strange forlorn feeling I cannot express, stupified me for a few moments, and then my eyes filled, and I was relieved. Yet I felt as if I were alone in the world, and cared for nothing. After dinner there came a sudden violent blast, with drift and squalls. The Collector retired to write, and I to the library.

Just as we all met at tea, lamenting the sad evening, there came an outcry from below, that the wherry was seen returning. I was so agitated. In short, the storm had driven them back, and I was seized with the strongest desire to go with them; I knew I should miss many pleasures I had promised myself; that, for instance, of seeing Kitty Macalman, whom I like better than any one ever I knew from this quarter. But it was odds if I should get away till the end of summer; I had lost all influence over Mary's mind, and I saw clearly she was in hands I could not take her out of: so far from profiting by advice, I knew she would dislike me for advising her: she might sink into vulgarity or folly, but why should I grieve myself with seeing what I could not mend? I knew the Collector would be sorry to part with me. I hope it was not cunning, but delicacy, that made me beg my mother to say that she had changed her mind, and would not leave me. How my heart pined for the sweet little girl! I should have delighted to take her with me, and make a little sister of her.

We left Oban at five next morning, for then the tide made. Poor Mary was not so indifferent as I thought. After we had parted, while the boat was putting off, she sprung, as from a sudden impulse, on a great stone, and from thence to the boat again; she silently embraced me, with a tear on her cheek. If we never meet again I shall remember this as ominous, for Mary is unused to the melting mood. I thought she never looked so pretty: what a fine face her's would be, with suitable expression!

The morning was clear, though cold; I enjoyed very much the views on each side, betwixt Mull and the coast, and saw the old castles of Dunolly and Dunstaffnage on rocks projecting into the sea, and many other places of old renown. Do you know, that the Collector, who knows but everything, says, Robert Bruce held a parliament in Dunstaffnage, where all the barons spoke Gaelic. We passed the pleasant and fertile island of Lismore, a name signifying a large garden, and on the other side saw the coast of Appin, rich in early verdure, and sheltered with groves of oak. The scenery is various and beautiful. This estate is at present possessed by a gentleman of taste and liberality,* who has improved it exceedingly, and, though not a native, seems very much attached to the place. He has built a stately mansion on it, and, being an enthusiast in regard to antiquities, and a lover of nature, is regarded by the people with as fond an attachment as any of their native chiefs. He is indeed, they say, very good and kind to them. I never saw a place that had more attractions for me; it is wild,

* Henry Seton, Esq. of Touch. The beautiful estate of Appin has since belonged, successively, to the Marquis of Tweeddale and the late Robert Downie, Esq. (1845.)

without being savage; woody, but not gloomy; and fertile, but not flat. I wish I were to go no further. I should like to tend a flock of goats among those picturesque crags that form the back-ground of that fine picture. A contrary wind gave me leisure to survey these beauties, but cold rain and driving blasts coming on, his Majesty's own wherry was in danger of being overset, like a common boat; and his Majesty's own officer began to be afraid, like any other man. I feared nothing but cold and wet, yet was very glad when I heard a proposal of hauling in to shore, which we did opposite to Appin, at the foot of a steep green hill, on the side of which was a dwelling newly erected; not sumptuous, but, by its neat outside and sashed windows, distinguished from those of the common people. We climbed the hill, and were received with a kind of stately civility by a tall, thin, erect person, a widow,—pale, wan, and woe-begone. She never asked who we were, till a good fire and most comfortable tea-drinking, with many other good things, put us in humour to make replies. She then asked my mother if we were connected with the country. Now we had just left my father's country, and entered my mother's. She told the good lady her whole genealogy, by no means omitting the Invernahyle family, on which the old lady rose with great solemnity, crying, "All the water in the sea cannot wash your blood from mine." This tender embrace was succeeded by a long dissertation on the Invernahyle family,* &c. There is an

* Stewarts of Invernahyle, an ancient family, in Appin, Argyllshire, from whom the Author's mother was descended. The late Alexander Stewart, Esq. of Invernahyle, fought at the battles of

adventure for you, which will form a suitable conclusion to this important epistle! Adieu, for the present.

Letter X.

TO MISS REID, GLASGOW.

Fort-William, May 14, 1773.

The hospitable matron who received us so kindly, is, alas, a childless widow, yet not poor, as poverty is understood here; and I really think the standard is better fixed than with you. Is it not due to Providence, to say one is easy, having every necessary and some comforts? I should like elegance dearly, if she were not so nearly allied to luxury—and luxury too I could tolerate, if she were not so abominably selfish. I can never believe that a being, whose wants are endless and numberless, can spare even a thought to the wants

Prestonpans and Culloden, and was afterwards concealed in a cave, in his native district, for several weeks, while soldiers were searching for him. The dangers he was exposed to on this occasion form the foundation of similar incidents in the account of the Baron of Bradwardine, in the novel of Waverley. In the Introduction to that work, Sir Walter Scott, speaking of Invernahyle, says, "I knew him well. He was a noble specimen of the old Highlander, far descended, gallant, courteous, and brave even to chivalry. He had been out, I believe, in 1715 and 1745, was an active partaker of all the stirring scenes which passed in the Highlands betwixt these memorable eras; and, I have heard, was remarked among other exploits, for having fought a duel with the celebrated Rob Roy Macgregor, at the Clachan of Balquidder." The Laird of Invernahyle, here referred to, was granduncle to Mrs. Grant, the Author of these Letters, being the brother of her maternal grandmother. He died towards the end of last century; and his only son died, unmarried, about 1823. See farther as to this family, in a letter printed afterwards in this volume, dated 18th April 1779.—Ed.

of others. Very luxurious people do some charitable things, but they are induced to do them by vanity, example, or solicitation. You always hear of heroism and great exertions of all kinds in poor countries. Patience and fortitude, the virtues our helpless state most needs, are the growth of barren soils. I always delighted in Gray's Ode to Adversity; read it once again, and compare its ennobling tenor with my ideas. It is happy I think so: if wealth was everything to me, as it is to many you know, it would make me miserable to see so many deserving creatures, what you would call, very poor; but they do not think themselves so, and therefore they are not so.—I know nothing so silly as the disgust and wonder your cockney misses show at any custom or dress they are not used to. I now think plaids and faltans (fillets) just as becoming as I once did the furs and wampum of the Mohawks, whom I always remember with kindness.*

As this long digression cannot much please, I hope it will greatly improve you. We landed on the west side of a promontory, and to save sailing round a long point, resolved to walk to Ballachulish† by the light of the moon. It was a bleak evening, and the wind whistled dolefully while we were passing, in utter darkness, through a small wood; the moon broke through a cloud, and the owl began to hoot most opportunely. I started, and was shown the cairn (or rude monument of loose stones)

* Alluding to the years of the Author's childhood spent in North America, where her father was stationed with his regiment on the banks of the Hudson, and of Lake Ontario.—Ed.

† An estate on the northern border of Argyllshire; then possessed by Mr Stuart, a relation of the Author; and now by his grandson, Charles Stuart, Esq. (1845.)

where Campbell of Glenure had been murdered, and where every passenger throws a stone. I cannot convey to you the impression, which this assemblage of gloomy images made at once on my mind, aided by the recollection that a worthy and innocent gentleman, related to my mother, suffered death in consequence: though it appeared afterwards the murder was committed by a soldier in the French service, who lurked in the country since the year 1745, for that purpose.* The eulogium and history of this victim of prejudice, kept our attention engaged till we reached Ballachulish. The lady was not at home; I was sorry for it. She is a person of more than common understanding and virtue, whom I greatly esteem. She has built a fruit wall, a thing before unheard of here, and does much good among the common people, with the productions

* Reference is here made to a memorable occurrence in that part of Scotland. In 1752, Mr Campbell of Glenure, who was the manager for the Crown of the forfeited estates in that district, was shot from behind a rock, when riding on the highroad. Suspicion fell upon a man of the name of Allan Breck Stewart, who had been a sergeant in the French service, had come over in 1745, and lived afterwards as an outlaw. He was never seen after the murder, and was supposed to have gone to France. A gentleman of the name of Stewart, of the family of Ardsheil, in Appin, was taken up, indicted, and tried at Inverary, on suspicion of being privy to the murder. The Duke of Argyll, the head of the Campbells, then Justice-General, a nominal office, which did not require him to act at all, presided at the trial, and selected the jury, eleven of whom bore the same surname as that of the murdered gentleman, between whose clan and that of the prisoner a feud had long existed. The result, as might be expected, was, that Mr Stewart was found guilty. He was soon afterwards executed, near the spot where the murder was committed, and hung in chains. Traces may still (1845) be seen on an eminence behind the inn, on the south side of Ballachulish Ferry, of the place of this memorable exhibition. The whole transaction caused a great sensation, and the justice of the verdict and execution has always been much doubted. See an article on the subject of this trial in the *Edinburgh Review* for October 1821.—Ed.

of her garden, where she has medicinal herbs, which she shows much skill and humanity in applying to their proper uses. I have changed my mind about herding goats, and now the result of my moonlight meditation in the wood, and my reflections on this good lady's well-earned praise, have determined me to seek forthwith,

> " A hairy gown, and narrow cell,
> Where I may sit and nightly spell,
> Of every star that heaven doth shew,
> And every herb that sips the dew."

What fine transitions one might make, from the bright eye of the celestial bull, to the soft eye of the terrestrial daisy, by thus studying stars and herbs together. A pair of hermits, were that possible, would be a double felicity; but, perhaps I may see something to-morrow at my grandfather's, which may suggest a new mode of life to me. But, whether nun, goat-herd, herbalist, or star-gazer, depend on my being unalterably yours.

Letter XI.

TO MISS HARRIET REID.

Fort-William, May 17, 1773.

I dare say I am the more prejudiced against this place, because I was brought here so soon against my inclination. The young ladies of Glencoe, with whom I have a remote connection, and who were at the dancing-school with me the first winter I was in Scotland*

* The Author returned to Scotland, with her parents, from America in 1768, in the fourteenth year of her age.—Ed.

(and great companions for the time we were), sent urgent invitations, and were within two hours' ride. I should have liked very much to see them; the youngest is a fine creature,—all heart and soul, without a thought to hide. Glencoe she has often described to me as very singular in its appearance and situation;—a glen so narrow, so warm, so fertile, so overhung by mountains, which seem to meet above you,—with sides so shrubby and woody!—the haunt of roes, and numberless small birds. They told me it was unequalled for the chorus of "wood notes wild," that resounded from every side. The sea is so near that its roar is heard, and its productions abound; it was always accounted (for its narrow bounds) a place of great plenty and security.* In this romantic retreat, where a blue stream bends its course, with a half circular sweep, through the most peaceful and secluded of narrow vales, the matchless melody of the sweet voice of Cona first awaked the joy of grief. On that account you may well believe the glen is peopled with images, that are "pleasant, yet mournful to the soul." Why did I not go there to meet the fair spirit of Malvina in the haunt of roes? Happy daughter of Toscar, to have thy spotless faith, thy virtuous sorrows, and thy soul-inspired beauties, immortalized in the sublime and tender strains of thy heroic friend! Thrice happy to have the heavenly employment of pouring the balm of sympathy into wounds of the heart, that could not be closed; of supporting the feeble steps of age and blind-

* The latter part of this description applies rather to Invercoe, the family residence, which is situated at the lower end of Glencoe, on the banks of an inlet of the sea, called Loch-Leven.—Ed.

ness; of soothing, with the melting music of thy voice and the soft sound of thy plaintive harp, the sorrows of the venerable bard, and of hearing him awake those divine strains, that consecrate to future ages, the fame of thy generous hero, and all thy mild graces and gentle virtues!

Daughter of Toscar, dear and frequent to my nightly visions, come, like a moonbeam, to the chamber of my repose! I wish, with all my heart, that I could design and paint like Angelica. Then would I give "a çombination and form indeed," to the beautiful image that exists in my mind, of the fair mourner of Lutha. The sweet sadness of her eyes you should only imagine; I would not have them profaned by vulgar gaze; she should sit on the ground beside the prince of bards, her white arm thrown carelessly over her silent harp; she should look pensively down, as fixed in tender recollection. Her thick locks, blown aside from her fair forehead, as by the autumnal gale, should by chance, as it were, display the pensive grace, marking those fine formed brows, from which she took her name; her beauty should appear fast fading, like the many-coloured foliage on the back-ground, and mild composure should denote a soul that feels a sad enjoyment in its sufferings, and would not purchase ease at the price of oblivion. Humbler pursuits and duties are wisely assigned to me. In conformity to that designation, which was certainly meant for my happiness, I shall come down to the safer walks of common life, and tell you the sad story that has made this glen frequent in the songs of modern bards, and has even found its way to the page of history, to blot it with crimes unequalled in our age and country.

But, first, that you may estimate duly the renown of this little glen, I must tell you what a tuneful and warlike tribe inhabited it. The tribe of Macdonalds, called MacIans, or sons of John, who dwelt in this sequestered spot, were all, as the country people say, born poets; and this belief was so well established, that, if a MacIan could not rhyme, his legitimacy was called in question: whatever his other merits might be, he was no genuine MacIan. This is not only very strange, but very true; but I think we may credit it, on the principle of the old by-word, "Bode a gown of gowd, and ye'll aye get the sleeve of it."* The first possessors of this peaceful retreat were led to take a powerful interest in the songs of Selma, by the proud consciousness of dwelling on the spot made sacred by the birth of the tuneful hero.† The profound seclusion in which they lived, encouraged meditation; the noble objects which surrounded them, and shut out the world, sublimed it. The plenty their retreat afforded to their hunting and fishing pursuits, afforded leisure for the Muse. Poetry was universally familiar, where every eminent character rejoiced and mourned in measured strains. All the most obvious images, phrases, and rhymes grew so common, that nothing could be easier than stringing rhymes together like those you have seen me get from —— and ——, who, I doubt not, thought it incumbent on them to be poetical as well as the MacIans. Rosalind says, in As You Like it, "I could rhyme you so for a year together—dinners, and sup-

* A proverb, indicating, that a strong confidence of success, will, at least, procure a degree of the object aspired to.

† Ossian is said to have been born on the banks of the Cona, or Coe, which issues from Glencoe.

pers, and sleeping-times excepted." Whether it was by those mechanical means, or by superior powers of imagination, it appears this tuneful tribe claimed all the respect due to superior talents; to which was added, that paid to distinguished courage. When they were induced by the fatal feuds, so common in old times, to attack any other tribe, it was not easy to pursue them into their retreats; and then they sallied forth again with the hardiness produced by impunity. Thus, they became fearless themselves, and feared by others. To be concise, they were always with the Steuarts of Appin, their neighbour clan, and against their opponents, which, in the end, provoked no common vengeance.

In the end of the year 1691, it was required that all heads of tribes in that district should take the oaths to Government at Inverary. Now, this was a hard pill; for the Highlanders could never forgive King William for dethroning his uncle. It was quite out of their style of doing injuries; and the reasons for so doing were beyond their comprehension. Probably MacIan was not in the least sorry that a violent storm made the mountains impassable about the last days of grace; so he made a declaration before some magistrate at Fort-William that he would have gone to take the oaths if he could. This informality was seized on as a pretext by some enemy whom he had in the army, whose ancestors had probably suffered from the fury of a Glencoe irruption. A company marched out from the fort, under pretence of quartering in the glen till the oaths were taken. They were received with the most hospitable kindness; the officers were lodged in Glencoe's house; the soldiers with his tenants. This happened in the joyous days of Christmas, when it is, if ever, that these people have plenty and good cheer. Glencoe was not well, but sat up and played at cards the last night, out of courtesy to the officers. At midnight the soldiers got the word of command; every man went in and shot his host, and then bayonetted the boys and old people. It was a clear frosty night. The discharges of shot through the echoing glen alarmed those who had given up their beds to their guests, and slept in bye places. Of these I cannot exactly recollect how many escaped to the mountain, to suffer every extremity of cold, hunger, grief, and fear. I have not nerves for the whole detail; suffice it, that Glencoe's last breath was spent in a devout aspiration; that his superannuated father was murdered in his bed by an Ensign, whose name should never be pronounced or written; and that his eldest son, in his eighth year, was stabbed by the same ruffian, when on his knees imploring mercy.

The present laird, grandfather to my young friends, was an infant two years old, and was carried off to the hills by his nurse unobserved. The only other male in the chief's house who escaped was the bard; I am sure he did not, like Phemius, cry out, "O spare the poet's ever gentle mind;" nor, by any means, owe his safety to his tuneful powers; but as every shift had been made to accommodate the strangers, he slept in some odd corner. Next day there was neither smoke seen, nor voice heard, in this close-peopled glen, which before contained about three hundred inhabitants. The bard sat alone upon a rock, and, looking down, composed a long dismal song, which I would give all my ear-rings to understand. They say it has not much poetical merit. No wonder—" Small heart had he to sing."

Now you are waiting to hear, with savage delight, of the punishments inflicted on those midnight assassins, and the exemplary vengeance that pursued their cruel chief. No such matter; the cry of blood resounded over all Europe, and the hero of Nassau heard it as if he heard it not. This was a great blot in his character; but, no doubt, he had been made to believe that Glencoe was some sanguinary monster, who lived by rapine. Princes adjust their accounts of this kind very easily; it is but calling people savages, and then their blood is of no value, and their lives of no consequence. Why should a musical, poetical, and patriarchal Highland chief fare better than the Incas of Peru, " where dwelt the gentlest children of the sun." William was a hero after all. But authority, pure at the source, is often poisoned in the channels. Yet, though he could not remedy the evil, he ought to have avenged it. Now, you would know how the chief agent in this villany ended. He died at a ripe age, abundantly prosperous. But who saw his nightly visions, or felt his secret pangs? The Judge of all the earth never fails to do right, though we cannot always see how.

Satiate with blood, I bid you good night. It is very possible I am going to occupy the same room the Ensign slept in when he returned from the depopulated glen; he will, may be, come and smile on me like the blood-smeared Banquo.

> " From fairies, and the tempters of the night,
> Guard me, good angels!"

Morning.

I am awake, and have not seen the Ensign. Let his memory perish, as well as that of all the wretches who perverted mercy, and abused authority in this place. Of the many shocking details I have been pained with, I shall only recite one. There was an English major, who, in the absence of the governor, commanded the garrison of Fort-William in the dismal year 1746. There was, at that time, after much previous severity, a free pardon offered to all the lower class, who would deliver up their arms: those found with weapons in their possession had no mercy to expect. After supper, when the commandant and his officers were enjoying their bowl in this house, the sergeant of the guard came in, and said, there were three men brought in with their arms,—what should be done with them? "What but hang them!" said the Major, impatient of disturbance. Now, this was owing to the sergeant's inaccuracy of expression. The poor men, in fact, were coming in with their arms, to deliver them up, and, meeting one of the out-parties by the way, accompanied them to the garrison. "When the giant awoke from his wine," it was the first thing he did to look out of the window; and the first object he saw, was the bodies of these unhappy men, hung over a mill opposite! He was filled with horror, not recollecting his last night's order. When it was explained to him that the poor creatures came to receive the proffered mercy, the intelligence threw him into a deep and lasting melancholy. My father, though of all Whigs the bluest, speaks with horror of this transaction, and says he saw a very pretty young widow come to that mill the following winter, whose father, brother, and husband, had been the sufferers.

Oh ! when shall I have spirits to relish the kindness I receive from very worthy people here, and give you some idea of Inverlochy ? Dismal, dismal it appeared to me; drenched with cold rains, and covered with clouds of unusual darkness. The shore so flat and unmeaning ! A long low moor spreading behind; very little verdure in sight; no peaceful vales or sweet streams; the very river Nevis to me looks gloomy and stupid; 'tis a little Acheron. Ben Nevis is a great clumsy mountain, without any fanciful breaks, or fine marked outline, like those of Morven. It is great, without sublimity, and seems to nod above this ugly town, and shake a perpetual drizzle from its misty locks. As far as a mountain can resemble a man, it resembles the person Smollet has marked out by the name of Captain Gawky. I wonder much how any one lives here, who could live anywhere else.

Yet, I am told, Glennevis has rural beauties, and is very sweet and placid, when once you get into it, which I have no desire to do. The village, which stretches from the Fort, along the banks of Loch Linnhe, is a very tolerable one, could I but think so; but this Fort, " with many a foul and mid-day murder fed," looks just like a place to kill people in, it is so gloomy and uncouth: it is triangular; the soldiers' barracks are of wood, grown black with the constant rains. We are in the best of the officers' apartments, occupied by a very worthy family, the master of which holds the same half-military employment here, which my father is to exercise at Fort-Augustus. I was not in the humour for liking these people if I could help it, but I find I must; they grow upon me every moment. Mr. Gray* is a native of the Border, quite an original: harsh-looking at first, yet, when the smile of benevolence lights up his countenance, and his humour, anecdote, and observation begin to unfold, you would not think him the same person. Mrs. Gray is just recovering from illness; mild and beautiful I am sure she has been; and they have a little boy, more lovely than the Cupids in Glasgow college; if he could but speak, he would almost rival Anne the well-beloved. I say so much of people so new to me, because they are the only objects here that I can regard with any complacency. If Fort-Augustus be such a place, I will certainly become a votary of the

"Pensive nun, devout and pure,
Sober, stedfast, and demure,"

whom we used to admire so much. Expect to see me when we meet,

"With sable stole of cypress lawn,
O'er my decent shoulders drawn."

I have no spite against this place, but I am provoked at its superabundant negatives. It is a seaport, without being animated; it is a village, without the air of peace and simplicity; it is military, without being either gay, or bold looking; it is country, without being rural; it is highland, without being picturesque or romantic; it has plains without verdure, hills without woods, mountains without majesty, and a sky without a sun. At least his beams appear so

* Mr. Gray was Barrack-master and Post-master at Fort-William; had large farms, trading vessels, &c., and was in easy circumstances and much respected.

seldom, that I wonder the Lochabrians are not dazzled into idolatry, when he walks in his brightness.—O, this is a bad country for a butterfly, a bee, or an enthusiast, to expatiate in; but it is the best place in the world to remember an absent friend in! "Thought strays a wretched rover o'er the pleasing past;" I feel the spark of fancy kindling at the torch of memory; but, as Gray says of Jove's eagle, "the thunder of whose beak, and lightning of whose eye" were to be quenched, I too will quench my mental light in "dark clouds of slumber." Meet me in my dreams, daughter of winding Clutha! Adieu!

Letter XII.

TO MISS HARRIET REID.

Fort-William, May 20, 1773.

My dear Harriet,

I dare say you are ready to cry out, "Lochaber no more!" and I am sure I am ready to echo the same note. Yet who ever left a happy family without regret? and I am about to leave a very happy one. Our host improves upon us every hour. He has good sense, and a good heart; and is a perfect cabinet of that sort of old-fashioned knowledge that I like. He is from near the Law of Berwick, and knows all the traditionary history of the Border; of the Humes and the Elliots. He is, in fact, a true-blood old Scotsman; shrewd, cautious, and sarcastic, yet kind and affectionate where he loves.

Do you know, if ever I break a resolution you wot

of, it shall be in favour of an ugly man. Ugly is a harsh word, I only mean plain looking, rather harsh, like Mr. Gray; he should be much older than myself too. Those are the people likely to be most grateful for attention, from a person whose youth, &c. &c., might make it presumed that she had made some sacrifices. I do not suppose myself capable of having any thing to do with folly or knavery; but, put those out of the question, and if I had a choice of fifty, it would not be the wisest, the wittiest, the wealthiest, nor, by any means, the handsomest that I should choose. No; it would be the person capable of most affection, if one had scales that could weigh such a thing: but, wanting these, him who, having the least opinion of his dear self, is likeliest to value another; him who, having outlived early vanity and romance, can best value "the sober certainty of waking bliss," such as this good couple most deservedly enjoy. Mrs. Gray is amiable, gentle, and well-bred; a person of family too. He looks with such calm complacency at her, and is so charmed with everything she says. The respect she shows him, is so softened by affection! She has a sister here (Miss Graham); not the least like her, but an excellent creature; good-hearted, frank-spirited, and active. They all form such a harmonious group, and the little boy is so lovely. There is one in the cradle too; but I only mind those that can "softly speak, and sweetly smile;" for the boy of boys has some pretty half-formed words. My father went on, a week ago, to Fort-Augustus, to regulate matters for our removal; but his predecessor's family are ill of fevers. We have been urged to stay here till matters are in a train, but have resolved to proceed; I am sure I shall feel much concern when I go away. There is a Major Cochrane here, a man of taste and ingenuity, who pleases me much by the delight he takes in talking of his wife, who is certainly very pretty. He has her picture, drawn by himself, with a most angelic expression. Happy artist, who can thus give a visible and lovely form to the predominant image in his mind. If I could but sing and draw true likenesses of my friends, I think I should not be an unhappy exile, after all.—I will not write another word from hence. I am busy with a piece of work, which I mean as a memorial for sweet Mrs. Gray; and will not bestow a minute on you, till I see myself in Loch Ness. Good night, my dearest. Write, or not write, my spirit is with you; and I feel a pleasure in thinking I can contribute to your amusement.

Once more adieu: when I meet with another that possesses your native delicacy, your disinterestedness, your purity of heart, I will forget you,—forget all our past happiness, and those that shared it. Peace be with you, my own Harriet.

Letter XIII.

TO MISS HARRIET REID.

Fort-Augustus, May 23, 1773.

My dearest Harriet,

I am very much disordered by my journey; but, while I am able, I shall endeavour to describe it for

Isabella Ewing, as well as for you, and it is needless to tell you both the same thing.

On Monday we set out on horseback, good Mr. Gray conducting us to Highbridge; and a most instructive and interesting companion he was. Why did I leave Lochaber without introducing you to the Castle of Inverlochy? You never saw such a castle in your life. I mused the whole night after I saw it, on the strange manner in which the inhabitants must have lived. It is large and square, and has the remains of four round towers; and is built of round stones, that never were touched by the hammer. You may guess its venerable antiquity, from the circumstance of Achaius, "our gude Scots king," having signed a league with Charlemagne here, in the eighth century.* Only think how kings could choose such a residence; but they were great hunters, and the dark moors in view were all a forest then. The sea running up so far into the bosom of the mountains, was also a favourable circumstance; besides, it stands in the mouth of the singular and important Glen More, which I shall hereafter describe to you. It is somewhat singular that sixteen thanes, or chiefs, of the name of Cumming, witnessed this league.

The progress and declension of power is worth tracing; it makes no unimportant part of the history

* Inverlochy Castle is situated on Loch Eil, and near the town of Fort-William. The building, which forms a court, has round towers at the angles, of the most massive proportions, the whole fabric covering a space of 1600 yards. It had once wet ditches around it, and must have been one of the strongest castles of the kind in Scotland. Inverlochy gives its name to the brilliant victory of the Marquis of Montrose over the Campbells, which took place in front of the Castle in February 1645.—Ed.

of human nature. In those days the Cummings were unrivalled in the north, and potent everywhere. The wisdom and valour of some distinguished individuals, no doubt, procured this influence at first. When they acquired it, they abused their power, and, by their joint influence, bore down every other name, till, in the end, they became the objects of universal fear and jealousy. There were doubtless, among so great a number, unworthy individuals, whom the spirit of clanship led the more deserving to protect and support in some instances of violence or fraud. This created a kind of combination against them; and the treachery of the Red Cumming, which provoked Robert the Bruce to stab him in the cloister of the Grayfriars at Dumfries, was a mortal stroke to their declining power.

What an astonishing instance it was of our great Robert's royalty of mind, that, when hunted from place to place, pursuing a precarious title to a despoiled crown, he could, in the glow of virtuous indignation, perform such a deed in such a place, without losing all popularity! It was the blindness of zeal. The cruelty of the times, attended with bitter exasperations, prevent its being a stain on our liberal-minded hero. Do not think I am diverted from my favourite star in the galaxy of fame; I always see the spirit of Wallace superior and alone, like Hercules reposing after his labours. Do not tell me of his being bloody; no doubt he thought it was the "sword of the Lord, and of Gideon, that he drew:" "Nothing he did in hate, but all in honour." I reverence his hallowed shade as much at this present moment, as when we were trying to lift his two-handed sword in Dumbarton Castle.*

Now I was as full of the idea of the Castle of Inverlochy as possible, when these heroes carried me away. The strength of this venerable pile is wonderful. Mr Gray has told us how they built these strange walls. There was a frame of boards made of their height and breadth, into which dissolved lime and stones of all sizes and sorts were poured: when these consolidated, the frame was taken away, and the wall was everlasting. Pray thank me for your first lesson in architecture, which, at any rate, will do you no harm.

Now I am going to commit to your prudent secrecy a flight among the clouds, which I ventured on a very stormy day, and a very melancholy hour.

Rave on, ye demons of the storm!
The skies disturb, the seas deform,
And urge the whirling blast!
Commix the waves in wild uproar,
And howl along the desert shore,
While nature shrinks aghast!

From the dark chambers of the sky,
I see the lurid lightnings fly
With quick illusive glance;
While thunders murmuring from afar,
Proclaim the elemental war,
And nearer still advance.

Methinks, with horrid joy elate,
Avenging ministers of fate
Now mount the whirlwind's wing;
And, while they trace their destin'd path,
Tremendous pour the vial'd wrath
Of nature's awful King!

Rage on, ye blasts! unmoved by fear,
Your fierce conflicting strife I hear;
For what have I to dread?
Not storms, whose fury rends the sky,
Nor thunder, pealing from on high,
Awake the unconscious dead.

* We had visited this relic the day we parted.

Since dead to hope, and love, and joy,
Why should your pow'r my peace destroy,
Or break my mournful calm?
Your deepest bass, your loftiest tone,
Grateful to me, and me alone,
I feel, like sorrow's balm.

Thus, pleas'd, the sea-fowl cry aloud,
While toss'd aloft from cloud to cloud,
With heedless course they roam;
With stern delight, unmix'd with care,
They wander through the troubled air,
Like me, without a home!

This, you say, is an exaggeration, for both the sea-fowl and I shall find our home in due time. True; but this is the language of deep despondency, which aggravates everything, and looks to no future comfort. The poetry of sorrow, however real the sorrow may be, sees images through mist, and enlarges them. In those cases, where there is imagination and an ear for harmony that predispose one to it, solitude and sadness very naturally lead the mind "to feed on thoughts that voluntary move harmonious numbers." This amusement may tend to soothe and to refine the mind, but whether one is the happier for refinement, is a doubtful case. Though I were wise enough, I am too drowsy to decide this point. The account of my journey must also be deferred till to-morrow, when, I trust, my head will be clearer, and my heart lighter. I will tell you of the diabolical quotation from Milton, which occurred to me on entering the chamber which is to be mine:—

"Receive thy new possessor, one who brings
A mind not to be chang'd by time or place."

24th May.

I left my narrative yesterday to mount the clouds and chase phantoms. I am now very sick, and very sober, and resolved to be methodical. If I grow worse, our correspondence will terminate in the only way it ever shall; if not, I must attend my wonted duties, and lay down my pen. But this day is mine, and shall, therefore, be yours. Know then, beloved, that the Glen More, or Great Valley, is an opening from sea to sea, across Scotland, through some of the wildest parts of the Highlands. On the east, the spacious Firth of Moray, at the head of which lies Inverness, runs up between Ross-shire and Moray, a great way inward, till it reaches the Highlands; then, on the west, you sail in between Appin, Lesmore, and Mull, till you come to Loch Linnhe, an inlet of the sea, on which Fort-William stands. A little further, as you go towards Fort-Augustus, you meet with the Lochy, a river which, coming in a westward course from Loch Lochy, discharges itself into Loch Linnhe, at the old castle of Inverlochy, properly signifying the discharge of the Lochy. Over brown and unvaried moors we travelled, after leaving Fort-William, still in sight of this short river, till we arrived at its parent lake,* long, narrow, and remarkable for nothing but its occupying some miles of Glen More, and having had the last battle between adverse clans fought on its banks, which are a dull flat. What gives it interest is, that when you arrive at the east end of it, you see and feel yourself in the centre betwixt the two seas, and see at once the Lochy and the Oich on each side of you, running in

* Loch Lochy.

opposite directions, one making its way through Loch Linnhe to the west sea, and the other through Loch Ness into the Moray Firth, on the east. It is those fast-following lakes, linked by filial streams, that form the opening which the three forts were meant to guard, and which, they say, invites art to the aid of nature in forming a canal, that should, in a manner, divide Scotland; but that will be the business of a wiser and a richer century.* I should have told you in the right place of my passing Highbridge, eight or nine miles, I think, from Fort-William. It crosses the Spean, a small river, which, rushing down from the central mountains, has worn a channel of astonishing depth. Over this two shrubby crags project; the bridge is thrown across from the one to the other, and the arches, founded in the river, are ninety feet high. You know how little I understand or care for buildings; but fine bridges, cast over deep chasms, have that kind of grandeur that seizes on my gothic imagination. The effect of this one must be forcible, I should think, on every mind. After so much dreary moor, the shrubbery and verdure about it refresh the eye; and the simple majesty of those lofty arches forms a fine contrast to the noble, though irregular piles of rock-work, which they connect. The boiling and wheeling of the waters below animate the view; and even its dizzy horror pleases, after the long pause of dreary stillness you have just quitted. Another far-seen object gives sad variety to

* This prediction has since been fulfilled by the formation of the Caledonian Canal, commenced in the beginning of this century, and completed in 1822, at an expense exceeding one million sterling.—(1845.)

the prospect before you leave the languid sameness towards Loch Lochy; it is Locheil and the ruins of Achnacarry, once the mansion of the gentle chieftain of the Camerons.* I call him gentle, because he really was so. His disposition was milder, his manners softer, and his mind more cultivated, than those of his companions in misfortune, to use a soft word. He was like Brutus among the conspirators, whom you used to admire in the play:—

> "The rest did what they did in envy of great Cæsar,
> He only, in a general honest thought," &c.

No man sacrificed more domestic comfort to mistaken principle than Locheil; no man had clearer views of the fatal result. In vain he endeavoured to dissuade the Adventurer, who landed near his house, from carrying on his ill-supported project. When he saw his doubts were misconstrued into fear, he took a tender leave of his family, and plunged into the gulf where he foresaw destruction. Can I possibly quit Achnacarry, without proudly reciting an instance of the generous attachment of the tenants to their exiled Chief? His estate was forfeited after the rebellion of 1745, and they paid the usual rent to the Crown; besides this, they voluntarily paid a rent to support Locheil's family abroad. When the demesne was taken by some friends for their behoof, the tenants stocked it with cattle of all kinds. This, too, was a pure benevolence; and to this my grandfather, one of that faithful band, amply contributed.

* The estate of this respectable exile, forfeited in the year 1745, has been by his present Majesty restored to his descendant, the present Locheil.—(1806.) A handsome modern residence has lately been erected at Achnacarry by Locheil.—(1845.)

Mr. Gray is provoked at my stupidity, in not being lost in admiration and astonishment at the military roads. Highbridge, which makes a part of them, I do admire, but have no clear apprehension of their general beauty, or wonderful usefulness. I do not quite take it for granted, that they are to civilize the country so speedily and effectually ; the people were very *civil* when they were well treated; they were so agile and familiar with their own bye-paths, and so accustomed to go

> " Over moor, over mire,
> Thro' bush, and thro' briar,"

that I am not clear they will always forsake their old short cut, for the pleasure of going ten miles round on hard gravel. These roads will afford access to strangers, who dislike and despise the natives, because they do not understand them ; and to luxuries they cannot afford to pay for, and would be happier without. Early accustomed to savage life, I have not the horror at it that wiser people have. As far as merely regards this world, I am not sure how much my old Mohawk friends have to gain by being civilized; nor are my expectations very sanguine of the felicity which more knowledge of good and evil will produce here. They know the plain, the narrow path which revelation has traced out to a happy immortality; and what more can they know, that will not be vanity and vexation of spirit, to a country which nature meant to be poor. I am sure savages have more useful and pleasing knowledge than people imagine, were it only that of birds and plants. This, perhaps, is saying too much ; but I am so provoked at seeing shallow, artificial people, who have no ideas but what they borrow, treating the inventive children of the wild with scorn. Those who pace all their lives on in an even-paved road, doing every day just what they did yesterday, are unable to estimate the powers of those, who must bend their mind every hour to some new and unpremeditated exertion.

After we passed the centre of Glen More, where the waters divide, I was much pleased to find woody hills, and green plains, narrow, but beautiful, opening before me. Laggan-a-chadrom charmed me ; it seemed so rural, so peaceful, and so social. Thinking what innocent sylvan beings dwelt in those huts, I contemplated them with secret pleasure; and so would you, knowing no more than I did. I am sure there were forty distinct buildings spread out on a smooth little plain, of the softest, freshest verdure. The broad end of Loch Oich, the prettiest of all possible lakes, forms the base of this triangular plain: the steep green hill of Letterfinlay, on the slope of which the light foliage of the drooping birch waved in the evening gale, formed one side, and the variegated slopes and broken copses on the Glengarry side, the other. Mr. Gray had left us to return to Fort-William. We had a boy, very smart and intelligent, who took care of our horses. Lost in contemplation, we were enjoying this pastoral scenery, when we were interrupted with—"Ladies, the greatest thieves in all the country live in these houses." We were shocked, but found, upon inquiry, that this sweet hamlet was really inhabited by the only remaining horde of those plunderers who used to consider making a *spreath* as a gallant exploit; now, a spreath was carrying away forcibly a herd of cattle, and fighting their way through all opposition. I felt a kind of horror on finding that the cluster of innocent peasants' cottages I had been admiring, was merely a den of thieves. I now began to hold the military road, and civilizing the natives, in all due reverence. Nay, such a complete convert was I become, that I felt inclined to admire a happy thought of a worthy good-natured Irishman, Governor Caulfield, at Fort-George, who most poetically exclaimed,

> " Had you seen these roads before they were made,
> You would hold up your hands, and bless Marshal Wade."

I wish I could share with you the pleasure I felt, in admiring, in a sweet still May evening, the scenery round Loch Oich and Invergarry; the declining sun was shining, immediately after one of those soft warm showers that steal silently down, refreshing all nature, and awakening the whole woodland melody. A blackbird, on one side of Loch Oich, poured out the fullest strain of wild music I ever heard; while a wood-lark, from the streaming birch-trees on the other side, seemed emulous of his notes, and was more sweetly liquid, though not so loud. Do the birds really sing sweeter here, or does the wild scenery of these narrow vales reverberate the sound, and produce a tone of feeling more accordant to the music of nature? I never before felt the magic spell of sweet-according sounds so powerful. O, how I wished for some one to share a luxury that wealth cannot purchase, and that thousands are not born to taste.

> " O blind to truth, to virtue blind,
> Who slight the sweetly pensive mind,

On whôse birth the Graces mild,
And every Muse prophetic smil'd."

"These are the spirits born to know and prove
All nature's charms immense, and heaven's unbounded love."

From this trance I was waked by a bright gleam of the parting sun, which threw its yellow radiance on the opposite windows of Invergarry House. This has all the characteristic features of the seat of a Highland chieftain—the lake, with little wooded islands, that seemed to float on the calm surface before it; the rapid river rushing down from the mountains, pouring its full stream into the lake beside it; the remaining tower of the ancient castle frowning proudly on the modern house; the long habitable glen opening back from the mansion of the chief, embosomed in woods and rocks, and animated by clusters of warm peaceful hamlets. From these every peasant rushes to arms, when his master's honour or safety is endangered: here every man is a hunter, a fisher, and an architect, in his own way; and there is a musician in every house, and a poet in every hamlet. Alas, for me, that am "of language strange," and have returned to the land of my forefathers, with only this *Chaldean* English. "Dark sayings on the harp" are dark indeed to me.

I greatly wish you saw Glengarry,* it is so picturesque; the glen that ascends from it, instead of narrowing, as usual, grows broader, as it retires back,

* Macdonell of Glengarry is head of a considerable branch of that powerful clan, who spell their names in that manner to distinguish them from the Macdonalds of the Isles, attached to Lord Macdonald.

till you arrive at Loch-Garry, from whence the river of that name descends. The Castle, surrounded by a very respectable garden, of old renown, is half a mile west of the house. Rich corn fields, a great relief to the eye after the brown desert, fill up the interval; and westward from the Castle, Killeanan, gently sloping, verdant and diversified, closes the prospect with due solemnity: for there the family burial place, a pretty large inclosure, shaded with lofty old trees, arrests the attention. I think the mind broods with more calm and steady attention over the last refuge of mortality, when appropriated in this manner to a particular set of people, whom the imagination can grasp and follow, than over the resting-places of unknown multitudes, where thought wanders, in forlorn confusion, " along the waste dominions of the dead." You must muse alone, as much as I have done, before you can be capable of penetrating the gloom of a paragraph so sublimely obscure as my last. Tombs, like heroes, have a peculiar attraction for me; I cannot get quietly past them.

After having thus transgressed and digressed, I shall keep you at Invergarry, to view the back-ground towards the north, where the prospect rises into the most blue, aërial, and fantastic group of broken rocks and mountains I ever beheld. Through these you can neither ride nor properly walk, but the natives contrive to swim and creep, and wade and leap, much in the way Satan did when he visited the " Anarch old," and then they arrive at another estate belonging to Glengarry, on the sea-side, a wondrous region, called Knoydart, where there are no first floors at all, but all is garret or cellar; inaccessible precipices, overhanging mountains, and glens, narrow, abrupt, and cut through with deep ravines, combining with rapid streams, dark pools, and woods so intricate, that the deer can scarce find their way through them. Yet the natives are looked upon as happier than others. Redundant grass and luxuriant heath afford abundance to their cattle, who are never housed in winter. Deer, wild fowl, and fish are in great plenty; salmon, in particular, crowd their rivers, and shell-fish of all kinds abound on their rugged coasts. All this they enjoy without a rival or competitor, for who could go for it, or carry it away? Bread, indeed, is a foreign luxury with them, as they raise little or no corn; a ship, however, comes once or twice a year, and brings them a supply of meal in exchange for butter and cheese. This is the asylum of the Catholics; all who live in the country are of that faith, and, wonderful to tell, a gentleman of family, great learning, genteel manners, and most spotless life, a Bishop of their communion, spends his life in this truly savage abode; he has no other motive but the desire of doing good to those who can make him no adequate recompense. There, too, in the most secluded recess of these wilds, in a corner so obscure that the sun can scarcely shine on it, is a seminary, where boys are educated for the priesthood (that is, prepared for foreign seminaries), amidst very great poverty and hardship. Surely these people imagine they suffer for conscience' sake; and, absurd as their tenets are, to say the best of them, we must not think they can dissemble for a whole lifetime, nor have we room to think, that any one can lead a self-denying and upright life without the Divine aid. I fear we poor creatures are merciless to each other; I do not like to think of their opinions, yet am happy when I hear of the gold of good intention glittering through the dross of error.

How I have wandered! but the thing nearest my heart, now that I care so little for most worldly matters, is to show to you every object in the clearest light in which it appears to myself. I would carry you with me wherever I go; I would teach you to think, that you might supply the defect of timely tuition, by giving, yourself, some culture to that excellent understanding. Your mind is too good a soil to run to waste. When I think of your native taste, your delicacy of feeling, and that rectitude of judgment, which is your peculiar excellence, I grieve that you know so few who comprehend what you possess, or know what you are capable of acquiring. How pleasing to see the beauties of such a mind expanding! (Will that pleasure ever again be mine?) Let me suppose it, in the meantime, a mirror, in which the images that pass through mine will be reflected. I cannot think how any one who has ever tasted the rich banquet of intellectual pleasure, mingled with the sweets of friendship, can exist deprived of it. Surely the Lotos that Ulysses' friends found, was something like it; no wonder they would not come away. If I did not think of you, and could not write to you, how forlorn I should be, and how little would "the charm of earliest birds," or the wild scenes of enchantment, that rise here and there amidst the brown desert, avail to comfort me. Adieu, my dear. It is time to leave off "chewing the food of sweet and bitter fancy." Good night.

Letter XIV.

TO MISS HARRIET REID.

Fort-Augustus, May 25, 1773.

My dear Harriet,

Small heart have I to write, and can as yet tell you little of Fort-Augustus. It was dark before we descended to the house which is to be ours; of which I can only say, that it stands in something like a grove, and that this grove rises on a point at the confluence of the Oich with Loch Ness. We drank tea with our predecessor's family; they are still convalescents. The clergyman of the place* was the only stranger; of whom I was previously told that he was handsomer than any body; he appeared more modest than most handsome men, who are less tolerable, I think, than mere handsome women. . . . . . . The Barrack-master's family cannot remove for ten days, and here am I very much indisposed, "in the worst inn's worst room;" and, to mend the matter, just above the best bad room, where all strangers are received; and, worse still, this room has a vocal floor, like the one at Luss. Oh for a carpet! the only luxury, not intellectual, that I have longed for since I left you.—Worse and worse—if I do not get better, remember the last word I write is, my benediction to you!

* The Rev. James Grant, afterwards Minister of Laggan.

Letter XV.

TO COLLECTOR MACVICAR, OBAN; ON THE CLANDESTINE MARRIAGE OF HIS DAUGHTER.

Fort-Augustus, May 25, 1773.

My dear Sir,

I know not how to console you, nor, indeed, how to mention the event that has grieved us all so much; yet, after all, this new connexion is a gentleman by birth and education.

Very great blame there certainly is, but a small part comparatively remains with those who are, in a great measure, sufferers from their own imprudence. The contrivers and abettors of this rash union are more deserving of your anger than the parties themselves. Marriages thus hasty and clandestine, have sometimes proved fortunate beyond all expectation. It was, perhaps, too great a charge for a creature so young and lovely, without a protector of her own sex, to manage a family, and be obliged to entertain all kinds of company. I know, I am certain, your heart must relent towards her, when you consider fully of it. The Regiment, I am told, is ordered abroad; they may be years without meeting; she will return home penitent and thoughtful, to take charge of your affairs; and, her fate being now fixed, will have no object to draw off her attention.

I am confined here; and reading some of the books I had from you is my only consolation. When I am well enough to write more at large, I shall endeavour to amuse you with my crude opinions, for which I shall make no apology, as it is in compliance with your own desire. I am, very sincerely, yours, with much esteem.

LETTER XVI.

TO COLLECTOR MACVICAR.

Fort-Augustus, May 28, 1773.

My dear Sir,

Since I wrote to you last, I have been most intent on biography, and quite engrossed by heroes and legislators. I am afraid and ashamed, after all my promises of frankness, to tell you who is my favourite. When I look up to the great legislator of the North,* like Shenstone's little boys,

> " I do in passing wonderment abound,
> And think *he* been the greatest wight on ground."

I am astonished and borne down with the force of that mighty mind, which burst all the golden chains of imperial pomp and prejudice,—which came streaming like the aurora borealis, to pour its splendours on the regions of darkness; and which stooped, like the fabled Antæus, to gain strength from the earth, and rise with fresh vigour. Self-abasement, matchless patience, and stubborn perseverance, virtues dealt sparingly to the hero kind, were his pre-eminently. I survey his new creation with astonishment; I see him presiding at the birth of intellect with reverence; and yet, I respect and admire, without loving or esteeming this extraordinary character. He was a heartless barbarian after all; his

* Peter the Great.

views were often just and always great, but he did not care whom or what he trampled on, to attain to the completion of them. Only think of him, like another Herod, sacrificing so many hundred innocents to his preposterous salt-water experiment. It was an insolent and impious attempt to conquer nature. Then how many thousands fell victims to his ambition of building that shocking town Petersburg! He might have made the principal street of dead men's bones (as children say of London Bridge in the old ballad), provided he applied the remains of the poor peasants to that purpose. Five hundred thousand people to be sacrificed with such cool deliberation, to create a seaport! I am sure, though he did conquer nature there, it was a dear-bought victory. Which of Shakspeare's heroes is it that says with such bitter regret,

> "If I am forced
> To draw this sword to be a widow-maker,
> Bear witness Heaven," &c.

That was generous, open war; fatal and depopulating at best, no doubt, yet a field for noble exertions, and for the display of some shining qualities. But, to go calmly and coolly with a hatchet and trowel to be a widow-maker to such an extent,—I have no patience with the cold-hearted tyrant.

If you *will* know what I think of the great Czar, you must not call it prudery when I express insuperable disgust at his marriage, and at the blind admiration which that circumstance of his life has excited. To divorce his wife without a pretext, to give the example to a great empire—which he professed to enlighten and reform—of a father's bringing not merely his own mistress, but the mistress of other men, to rule over his family, and to be the mother-in-law of his son, the heir of that vast empire! What father could place confidence in his son, or give him lessons of virtue, when conscious that he had forfeited all claim to his reverence? What husband, what father, can find felicity exclusive of his family? What laurels, what eulogies can extract the sting of domestic misery? The wretched, withered heart pines unrefreshed, like Gideon's fleece, that lay dry while all nature shared the genial influence of the dews of Heaven. On the evil consequences resulting to society, from breaking down the partition-wall which separates the undeviating from contagion, volumes might be written, replete with instruction corroborated by facts. But a single fact selected from the life of this mighty legislator, contains the essence of volumes; it is that of beheading a gentleman of his bed-chamber, a handsome favourite of the Empress, on the mere surmise that this favour extended beyond due limits. You will recollect, too, that the Czar had his head exposed on a pole in the pathway, and he drove out his happy Empress in a sledge past the pole. She did not ask what head it was, nor did he make the least allusion to it. What easy intercourse, what perfect confidence!

Now, there could be only two ways of viewing this circumstance: Catherine was guilty, or she was not. If she was guilty, how peculiarly aggravated was that guilt,—how depraved was that mind,—how vicious those habits,—how hardened that ingratitude,—which, in spite of the light of her own excellent understanding, in spite of the dangers and spies that surrounded her, could add a deeper blot to all former stains, and could look with cool dissimulation on the dreadful result of her crime! Now, had Peter, as he ought to have done, if convinced of her guilt, hurled her down to contempt and infamy, the world would have approved the justice of his vengeance, and her memory would perish with the opprobrium of that very world, which now applauds her because she was prudent and fortunate. Add the reflection, of what life a man of a great mind and strong passions must afterwards lead with a person whose infidelity and ingratitude he was convinced of; how the mere shame of having debased himself by such an alliance must have made him swallow his injuries. Consider, too, how totally that delicacy, which inhabits every pure and noble mind, must be extinguished, before a man could live on with a person whom he inwardly despised. Say then, that, in a rash fit of jealousy, he, a legislator, a self-conqueror, neither young nor romantic, had taken the life of a man whom he afterwards found reason to believe innocent? Can there be a stronger testimony of the disquiet, distrust, and restless perturbation, which must result from such an alliance? Othello talks of

> "The minutes he tells o'er
> Who dotes, yet doubts; suspects, yet strongly loves."

What, then, must be his fate who begins his married life by laying a broad and just foundation for jealousy? What woman who hopes for protection, would marry a known coward? Is life, or anything pertaining to it, so dear as that honour, that very existence of his family, which a man intrusts to his wife? Though surrounded with glory, and admired by all the world, is it to be wondered at, that the great Peter so often drowned in wine the bitterness of reflection? Had he built fewer ships and towns, and begun his great work with reforming the morals of his subjects by his own example, his work might have been slower, perhaps, but it would have been surer. Elegance and refinement are easily added to wisdom and virtue; they are indeed produced by them. When a man is brought to think rightly and act justly, his taste improves apace; and we see all over the world, that where virtue languishes, the arts decay.

I must now return to justify my limited admiration of your favourite hero, who, I suspect, stands the higher with you for being an artist, like your own Duke Archibald.* How a man should be great without generosity, seems wonderful; and yet great the Czar was, and generous he was not: no, not in a single recorded instance. His promoting foreigners, who would not stay among his bears without promotion, I should only call sound policy. I shall not detail what every page evinces; I will not grate my feelings with the recollection of the accumulated cruelty and injustice which sent the brave Swedes—prisoners of war, gentlemen, and servants of a generous and heroic master—to expiate the crime of obedience in the deserts of Siberia; which sent generals, who had struck terror into the heart of Moscow, and dazzled all Europe with the splendour of their actions, to build huts in Siberia with their own hands, and teach his half-rational slaves to plant turnips on the banks of the Oby. To sum up

* Archibald, Duke of Argyll.

all, I consider Peter as a man wise and brave without virtue. Perhaps his hard unbending character was as well calculated to make political reforms in Russia, as the sanguine and ferocious temper of John Knox, for making religious ones in Scotland.

I will not apologize for this long letter. You bid me read biography, to teach me to think; I have thought, and here is the result. If I have not made you very angry, I will next give my thoughts of his rival hero. Will you, dear sir, continue to think that I respect your opinions, reverence your judgment, and shall always be your obliged friend and obedient servant.

Letter XVII.

TO COLLECTOR MACVICAR.

Fort-Augustus, May 30, 1773.

I rejoice, dear sir, that you are pleased with my sincerity, and not displeased with my enthusiasm. I hope it will not, as you seem to think, evaporate with *you*. I trust I shall be an enthusiast in friendship, and in the love of virtue and of nature, all the days of my life. How could spirits, aspiring after something better than this world affords, exist in this gloomy uncongenial clime without it? When torpor threatens to chill the soul, enthusiasm warms and animates it; when the mind tends to be languid and enervated, it invigorates and braces it. It is the fan of a warm climate, and the fur of a cold one. Who ever did much good to others, without a degree of enthusiasm to loosen the faculties from their cohesion with self-love? I will no longer bewilder myself among figures, for I see you ready to compare me to Hudibras,

> "Who could not ope
> His mouth, but out there flew a trope."

Yet is not enthusiasm pardonable, when about to enter on the discussion of a life of wonders, where all is true yet nothing probable, even the right marvellous life of Charles the Twelfth?—The unfortunate have few friends. This remark is neither so trite nor so invidious in my application of it as it may at first appear; we are not always malignant, but we are very often lazy; people's misfortunes are so often owing to their own misconduct, that, without examining into particulars, we are ready to take it for granted in most cases, and become unjust, to save ourselves the trouble of candid investigation. Never was there a human being whose character was more modelled by peculiarities in his situation and education; by irresistible impulses from without and from within, all driving him on to that ardent extreme, to which his natural temper too forcibly inclined. Reared under a father cold and stern; defectively educated; taught from childhood to value nothing but military glory; left so very young to act for himself, and surrounded by people little skilled in the elegant arts, who had not learned to estimate truly the softer graces and milder virtues of civilized life; young and inexperienced, yet full of valour, generosity, and integrity, a storm broke around him, which involved all his future life in tempests. The perfidious Confederacy of the three Royal robbers, who, under the mask of friendship, had agreed to take advantage of the minority of a brother sovereign, to despoil him of his crown, and divide his territories, while it called forth the military talents of the young Prince to prompt and astonishing exertion, gave, at the sametime, an inflexible bias to his mind. The more upright and pure he felt his own sentiments, the more indignation this conduct must have excited. There is no motive that could stimulate the human mind to persevering hostility, but what mingled in this case; revenge, which the provocation had almost exalted into virtue; the patriot passion burning for his injured country; emulation, excited by rivals, brave, powerful, and invidious; the ardour of youthful enthusiasm animating a frame of iron and a soul of fire; and, finally, the

> "Fatal love of fame, that glorious heat,
> Only destructive to the brave and great."

Stern, obstinate, and uncultured, highly exasperated and signally victorious; what was the conduct of this Prince, when the proud city of Copenhagen lay at the feet of a victor, scarcely seventeen? Piety, moderation, clemency, and magnanimity, marked every step of his progress. Had he not outlived that year, it would have been very unjust to characterize him as a mere warrior. Even then he was something more, and something better.

After granting terms dictated by lenity and probity to this faithless enemy, let us view his conduct to the more faithless Czar, after the victory at Narva; that victory whose rapidity distanced belief, while its splendour dazzled imagination. Still we find him acting with the generosity of a true hero, and the courtesy of a *preux chevalier* without fear or reproach; ascribing all glory to the God of battles, and treating the vanquished with unequalled humanity. Could it be expected, that, in the midst of this brilliant and rapid career, he should readily listen to terms of accommodation, dictated by those very fears that insured his future victories; from an enemy, too, who had planned the destruction of his country?—Would the great Gustavus, wise and pious as he was, have done it in the same circumstances? Besides, he was actuated by the spirit of chivalry, and considered his courage as the gift of Providence, bestowed upon him to redress the injured and protect the weak. How different would be the judgment of the world, regarding his conduct in Poland, had success attended him to the end of his career! Was not Augustus a perjured prince, without honour or morality; who governed by intrigue, broke every compact, and violated every duty both to his Saxon and Polish subjects? What did Charles do, but remove him from a throne which he had degraded to venality, and stained by his vices? He sent him back to Saxony, which he should never have left. Finding that the Poles, corrupted by the example of a king, at whose disposition they rejoiced, had neither virtue nor concord remaining, sufficient for the purposes of a free election, he pointed out to them a young man, noble, brave, virtuous, and candid, to whom he seemed attracted by congenial rectitude of mind, and who represented one of their most illustrious families.

Why does not the scene close here? Why not stop,

while we have the pleasure of contemplating this extraordinary man, with hands unstained by cruelty and injustice, and a heart pure from every sinister motive, "acknowledged lord of pleasure and of pain," neither to be attracted by the one, nor repelled by the other; dispensing crowns and dignities with the most disinterested liberality; receiving the homage of the north and the splendid embassies of the east, with unvarying modesty; and uniting in his habits of life the activity and ardour of a soldier, with the simplicity and abstemiousness of an anchorite? He, indeed, was a hero to his valet-de-chambre, for he had nothing to conceal, nothing to be ashamed of. But who could drink so deep of the cup of prosperity, without being in some degree intoxicated? Who can pass through life without committing some fault, the consequences of which cloud and embitter it? His treatment of Patkul was indeed very barbarous; I never think of it without horror, and feel little inclined to be the advocate of cruelty; but, from the undeviating rectitude of his general conduct, —this being the sole instance in which he was charged with injustice—it is but candid to suppose that he considered himself as inflicting death on a traitor. The manner of it is not to be palliated; it is a great but a single stain. His subsequent schemes of ambition were doubtless extravagant and injudicious; and the rashness of endeavouring to combat the elements and subdue nature, in his march to Pultowa, was still more so. Yet he led his men to no hardships that he did not share with them; he was certainly deceived by flatterers, who attacked him on his only vulnerable side, by persuading him he could overcome difficulties from their nature insurmountable. Can you withhold your pity and your admiration from him in that sad crisis of his fate, when the sun of his prosperity set, to rise no more; or when he bore the utmost bodily pain, and the most wringing anguish that a great mind can suffer, without a change in his countenance or temper? Can anything equal his fortitude and patience in Turkey, or his wild heroism at Bender, where his liberality and simple manners, his unstained morals and undaunted mind, won reverence and affection from the very Janizaries; or his unshaken perseverance in Demetica, where he lay eleven months in bed, in perfect health, to escape the risk of degradation, to him the greatest of evils? I own his reign was a misfortune to his people: I confess it was happy for him and them that it terminated so soon; when exasperation, injuries, and disappointments, had driven him to a kind of obstinate desperation. Yet still I admire and regret him, and look upon him as a man, brave and virtuous, without wisdom; whose great qualities may be safely admired, without the least danger of their being imitated. He is unique, and will continue so. You wonder at my preference, but I cannot give much of my admiration without some of my esteem.

Again, this self-subdued hero serves to establish my favourite maxim: without self-denial and self-conquest, I have no idea of any consistent virtue. Who can depend for a moment, on a character open to all the attacks of passion, all the allurements of pleasure? A case like his, where so many causes concurred to urge him on to pursuits so fatal and pernicious, can occur but very seldom. But what soldier, emulous of his well-won fame, would not benefit by imitating his temperance, his probity, his contempt of pleasure, and his abhorrence of meanness? Peace to his shade, which has doubtless, ere now, claimed kindred with a far more amiable hero, but his only equal in unwearied perseverance, romantic and extravagant courage, unconquerable strength of mind and body, and unblemished purity of morals. You have found out, ere now, that I mean our own unequalled Wallace. They both early began the race of glory; both stemmed the torrent of adversity with unshaken fortitude; both refused honours and dignities with steady magnanimity; and both, at a very early period, fell victims to misfortune. Our Scottish hero had a manifest superiority in the uprightness of his motives. Unbiassed by ambition or vanity, he lived and died a generous patriot. Conqueror to the last, he subdued the rigour of his fate by the calm cheerfulness with which he met it. The noble sentiments he displayed in the last scene of suffering, overcame the resentment of a hostile nation, so that

> "His fair fame, with clear and radiant blaze,
> Spreads and grows brighter with the lapse of days."

So far the Scot has the advantage of the Swede; a proof that the world is not always unjust.

I have been tedious on this favourite theme. I wish to hear your criticism. Though I am sanguine, like Wallace, I am not obstinate like Charles, and shall yield up my errors to your correction, with all due submission. I am, dear sir, your grateful and obliged friend,

A. M.

Letter XVIII.

TO MISS HARRIET REID, GLASGOW.

Fort-Augustus, June 5, 1773.

My dear, I have been so sick and so studious, and so willing to please and amuse the Collector, under his late severe affliction, that I have given you, and our trusty and well-beloved Isabella Ewing, room to suppose I have already forgotten you. My right hand was at one time very near forgetting her cunning; but my heart, like poor Maria's, is still warm, and while it beats I shall tenderly remember you both. Your letter is, like yourself, all truth, nature, and candour. Do not be discouraged; there lies no fair comparison between us. Forced to read and think from childhood, for want of brother, sister, or companion of my own age; tossed from place to place, and early accustomed to the society of my superiors in age and knowledge; what should my mind do but unfold? You had every disadvantage; I shall never be other than I am, but you will every day improve.

I had no pleasure in writing to you of that marriage which I knew you would hear of but too soon. I certainly should make a very bad Duenna. She is a strange creature, and could not be improved; her pride was in high company, but her pleasure in low; for her equals she never cared, and reading I never could get her to relish. How very vigilant my good angel was the day before I left Oban, when I took that strange sudden desire to come away, which has been so much for my peace and credit! The very night I left them, this marriage took place; it was celebrated in the garden during an ominous shower of snow, with no other witnesses than that happy pair who had acted the same part themselves so lately. Unhappy creature! what a fond parent has she plunged into grief and disappointment. He had great hopes of her; her beauty and plausibility warranted them. . . . . . . Love to our Isabella. I can tell you nothing of this place. My cough has been drowned in decoctions of mountain herbs, given me by the best woman in the world, who keeps this house; I should have died but for her. I have not gone down stairs yet, and am at a loss with this pervious floor, whether to wish myself deaf, or all the guests dumb. If uncle Francis, with his irritable nerves, were here, it would either kill or cure him. Do you know I have not been in Eumæus's pig-house this month, which you used to say was my favourite haunt. The poor dear Odyssey is quite neglected; I have forsaken it for biography; I can speak of nobody less than a king or a general, and shall take the first opportunity of introducing you to Prince Mazeppa. Tweed and Clyde are not worth a farthing now; I can think of nothing but the Dnieper and the Boristhenes. I have some toleration, too, for the Wolga. "O voman, voman!" as Win Jenkins says, "If you knew but the pleshur we scullers have when we conster the crabbit words." You see spirits will return with health, but you must expect no more bulky letters from your unchangeable,

A. M.

LETTER XIX.

TO MISS HARRIET REID.

Fort-Augustus, June 15, 1773.

My dear Harriet,

I will describe this place to you, if I can. It is a miniature of New York as to situation, and upon that you have often heard me descant; only this is on a very small scale. The village, and remains of the old fort, stand on a little rising ground above the Oich, a sweet wild-murmuring stream, that comes down on the west side from Loch Oich and Glengarry. On the south side, the Tarffe steals through deep-wooded glens from the mountain of Corryarrack, and wanders, at length, through a meadowy low valley, bounded by very steep, woody braes on the garrison side, and by a mountain, gentle in its ascent, verdant and cultivated half way up, on the other, surrounded by rugged rocks, that seem to frown sullenly on the sweet scenes below.

The Fort stands on the brink of the western extremity of Loch Ness, and the Oich and Tarffe discharge their pure streams into it on each side. Next the lake, the Governor has created a most picturesque shrubbery and garden in the dry ditch that surrounds the fort, and has covered the wall with fruit-trees, and hid the masked battery with laurels. That beautiful spot, the glacis, is almost an island; the village looks down on it from the west; on the north and south it is inclosed by the Tarffe and Oich, a bridge crossing each, parallel with the fort; on the east, Loch Ness forms a noble boundary, with its pier, and solitary vessel, which the vastness of the surrounding objects diminishes to a toy. The Fort, too, appears the prettiest little thing you can imagine. You would suppose some old veteran had built himself a house, with a ditch and drawbridge, to remind him of his past exploits. I have not been in it yet, but the barracks form the walls, and they are so white and clean-looking, and the bastions so green and rural, and it is so fancifully planted round with the mountain-ash, you would think Vertumnus commanded here, and had garrisoned the fort with Dryads. The lake, which opens in a long vista below, reflects this fairy fortress; and (a still more rural scene), a little to the north, on a long fantastic-looking point, at the junction of the Oich with the lake, stands my father's house, surrounded with tall ash-trees and gardens.* Very near it is that of the Commander of this solitary vessel. The serene grandeur of this lake in a calm is not to be described. Bold, steep mountains rise on the south side; little retiring bays and sloping woods give variety to the north; and the reflection is so fine; nothing interrupts it for twenty-four miles, at the end of which the lake discharges, through the short, rapid river Ness, into the Moray Firth. The immediate scene, in short, is tranquil and beautiful, while the surrounding objects are all rude and majestic.

About half a mile up the smiling meads that border the Tarffe, is the village burying-ground, a place of

* The house of the Barrack-master, here referred to, and in which the Author resided, is still extant (1845), with the ash-trees described in this passage. It stands detached, outside of the Fort, and between it and Loch Ness.—Ed.

old renown, where many a soldier sleeps to wake no more. As I stood at the door in the afternoon, contemplating the scene I have tried to describe, a cannon, fired from the fort, and answered by the vessel, announced an approaching funeral. There was a soft shower, or rather heavy mist, which made everything look fresh, but sad. Wreaths of thin clouds came down on the mountains, as if they, too, wore the veil of sorrow. The procession came out with muffled drums and fifes playing a dead march. A fine youth, intimate with the deceased, and much about his age, walked as chief mourner, and seemed greatly affected; so was every creature. You cannot think how touching it was to see a funeral, where every individual seemed sunk in the deepest sorrow. The mournful music, echoed by the rocks, followed the winding of the Tarffe till they reached the grave. I was chilled when the solemn pause ensued; and, when the discharge of muskets announced the close of the ceremony, I felt as if I were suddenly left alone,—such is the effect of scenery and music. Not that entirely, either; for my feelings were also excited from having heard every one in the place agitated by hopes and fears about the deceased* ever since we came here. He was the only son of a person in some employment about the royal household. A strong passion for a military life induced him to enter the regiment quartered here last winter, as ensign. The superior officer, to whose charge he was entrusted, leaving the place the day before we came, his *protegé* went to see him over Corryarrack. The captain, on

* Ensign Taafe of the 43d regiment.

parting with his young friend, discharged his musket, forgetting it had small shot in it: the young man's knee was shattered; he was carried back, and the amputation found necessary seemed, at first, successful. Sunday night, however, when all was thought secure, the bandages loosened, and he bled to death. He was so much beloved and pitied, that the operation and progress of the cure was every one's theme. I heard nothing through my vocal floor at the inn, but how Taafe was, and what Taafe said, and eulogiums, and regrets. Nobody is so lamented in town, because there people do not think long on any one thing.—Adieu. Night will seem long and dismal; but I can write no more.

Letter XX.

TO COLLECTOR MACVICAR, OBAN.

Fort-Augustus, June 20, 1773.

I am sure, my dear sir, you will incline to think me as mad as my hero, though you do not exactly say so. I suspect he was no favourite with Duke Archibald;* whose opinions, I suppose, you respected many years ago, as I do yours now. I think when you and he joined counsels about removing poor old Inverary, it was a very *Czarish* plan; and I fear it will soon be put in execution. If I had great ancestors, my domains would have a very grotesque appearance; for so much would

* Archibald, third Duke of Argyll, who died in 1761.

my reverence for antiquity combat my love of elegance, that I would not willingly remove a stone from the buildings they had reared.

I expect a kind and favourable answer to the intercessions in my last. I touch, with a trembling hand, on a subject so delicate; and would not touch it at all, if I were not pretty confident of assistance from an advocate in your own breast. In the meantime I will hope the best, and endeavour to pursue Oliver Cromwell through all his crooked paths. I have gone but a short way, my attention having been completely engrossed by a book that has bewitched me for the time; it is the Vicar of Wakefield, which you must certainly read. Goldsmith puts one in mind of Shakspeare; his narrative is improbable and absurd in many instances, yet all his characters do and say so exactly what might be supposed of them, if so circumstanced, that you willingly resign your mind to the sway of this pleasing enchanter, laugh heartily at improbable incidents, and weep bitterly for impossible distresses. But his personages have all so much nature about them. Keep your gravity if you can, when Moses is going to market with the colt, in his waistcoat of gosling-green; when the Vicar's family make the notable procession on Blackberry and his companion; or, when the fine ladies dazzle the Flamboroughs with taste, Shakspeare, and the musical glasses; not to mention the polemical triumphs of that redoubted monogamist the Vicar. It is a thousand pities Goldsmith had not patience, or art, to conclude suitably a story so happily conducted; but the closing events rush on so precipitately, are managed with so little skill, and wound up in such a hurried and really bungling manner, that you seem hastily awaked from an affecting dream. Then miseries are heaped on the poor Vicar with such barbarous profusion, that the imagination, weary of such cruel tyranny, ends it, by breaking the illusion. I have too much, indeed, anticipated your own observations; but my intention was to awake your curiosity, that you might share the pleasure this artless tale has afforded me.

To quit the flowery paths of ingenious fiction for the thorny maze in which I am slowly advancing, is no pleasing transition to female fancy. I make it the more reluctantly, as I have not yet duly considered the character I am pursuing. While Cromwell mounts the dizzy crags of ambition, by ways untried before, which he does not seem to have premeditated, I gaze with wonder, heightened by perplexity; trying, but vainly trying, to discover at what exact time he ceased to have at heart the public good, and that which he thought to be the interests of religion. You see I take it for granted he was sincere at first; and am the more convinced of this, as nothing could be more natural than the first steps of his progress. His early transition from a libertine to an enthusiast, is by no means wonderful. If a rash, impetuous libertine becomes at all devout, the same headlong fervour that hurried him down the precipice of vice, will animate him on his return to virtue. He will feel a more eager aspiration after superior attainments in spiritual improvement, than those who have not been misled, and a revolting horror at the allurements of vice, and all the delusions from whose power he has escaped. Hurrying as fast as possible to the opposite extreme, his speed will naturally kindle enthusiasm. This appears to have been precisely Cromwell's case at his outset. The rigour of Laud soured him into a bigot. The vehement and declamatory style of preaching which prevailed among his sect, heated him into a fanatic. When temporal views, mingling with spiritual, awaked the spark of ambition which lay hid under the specious pretence of zeal for reformation, hypocrisy began to take its turn to reign.

It would be tedious and difficult to trace his progress; yet, marking these changes and gradations in his case, and that of others, would be no useless task. It would help us to a solution of many historical doubts, which, probably, became such by an impatience in writers to decide on the motives of actions, without developing the process of opinion; to cut, in short, the knot they would not take time to untie. It is certainly invidious, as well as injudicious, to brand all those with the stigma of hypocrisy, who were, by the opposition and clashing of parties, the stream of popular prejudices, and the tumult of popular commotions, hurried far beyond their intentions, and involved in a mass, from which there was no possible means of separating.

When we find him, who was not unjustly stigmatized as the Arch-hypocrite of his day, sincerely pious at one period; we must learn that, when it is so necessary at different stages of life, and under different circumstances, to distinguish the same man from his former self, it becomes still more necessary, for the purpose of tracing back the causes and weighing the consequences of actions, that we should attend to the distinction of character among those who, though very different in their views, are, by slight observers, considered as one class. For instance, those who, having little piety themselves, are not aware of its different effects on the minds of others, are very apt to confound all enthusiasts with bigots. Now, an enthusiast sees the bright side of all objects. Except in one of those occasional fits of despondency, which are the common portion of morbid sensibility, his ardent mind gives a bright colouring to all things connected with the object of his desires and contemplations. He is highly benevolent, because the common state of depravity, and the common refuge of hope in an only Redeemer, form a strong tie betwixt him and those who have already, or may hereafter, become penitent like him :

"These share the joy that faith and hope supply."

Enthusiasm in devotion is thus perfectly compatible with cheerfulness of temper, and with the utmost liberality and good-will to all who worship the same God, more particularly those who hold their salvation by the same charter. We may perceive, by a little observation of characters which we are well acquainted with, that bigotry, so often confounded with enthusiasm, is very unlike, indeed, often opposite to it: it is a species of self-deception in those who substitute a strong attachment to certain peculiar opinions, with regard to the ordinances of the Divinity, for a love of his essence; and they mistake a certain vanity in exercising their faculties upon polemical subjects, for a delight in contemplating the Divine perfections. A bigot may be, indeed often is, as sincere as an enthusiast; but his views do not tend to meliorate his temper, or enlarge his heart; they have rather the direct contrary effect. The transition from a bigot to a hypocrite is not necessary nor common, in ordinary circumstances. Yet a person who idolizes his opinions cannot abound in charity; and he who does not love God well enough to love even his defaced and degraded image for his sake, is certainly in greater danger of being misled by self-interest, into a dereliction of his principles, than those whose hearts are warmed and expanded by their devotion. He may insensibly be led to cherish a degree of spiritual pride, teaching him to impose on others—and even on himself, if that were possible—austerity of manners and outward observances, for that religion "which is first pure, then peaceable, gentle, and easy to be entreated." In many instances, it would be the greatest presumption in any human being to say where bigotry ended, and hypocrisy began.

You may observe instances of Cromwell's leaders, especially those who commanded in Ireland, and executed what they called divine vengeance against the Catholic garrisons, perpetrating such deeds of cruelty as human nature shudders at. Yet, so thoroughly satisfied were those men that they were acting according to conscience, that they not only lived a self-denied and pious life ever after, but closed the scene on the scaffold (upon the change of government) with serenity: professing their dependence on the Divine mercy, full of concern for "having fallen short of the glory of God," as they expressed it, and "being unprofitable servants;" yet not feeling the least apparent compunction for cruelties acted and ordered by them.

All this is not mere digression, though it may seem so; for, if one did not read the history of that age of wonders with some attention to the shades and degrees of guilt, that were forced upon some by the rushing cataract of furious party zeal in their associates, and which others slid into when once they departed, in a slight degree, from the unvarying path of rectitude, to do evil that good might come of it; if one did not attend to the gradations by which certain characters sunk in value and efficacy, and thus gave room to unprincipled individuals of the same party to take the lead; we would shrink back with horror from human nature itself, wearing such a deformed and disastrous aspect. The opposite parties, too, were too much exasperated to speak with truth and candour of each other. Yet even those barbarous factions, while they broke down restraints, so as to show the human heart in its utmost deformity and depravity, produced many virtues, elicited much bravery, fidelity, and true patriotism, that would otherwise never have been roused into action.

I have tired your patience, and my own, with this long letter; I shall therefore defer my opinion of Cromwell to another, which you must encourage me to write to you. I must only say at present, that I am not over-dazzled by his abilities: his was a life of contingencies, made or patched up out of the fragments of other people's broken systems: he lay on the watch for casual advantages, snatched them from friends and foes, and pursued them to the utmost.

This a man of plan or system could not have done. When he had converted his warmest friends into his bitterest enemies, his only hope of impunity was, by climbing up out of their reach. In his elevation he found his only safety; but the wretchedness of that elevation, the misery of ruling by cruel and incessant expedients, and living in perpetual dread, and dying at last of ceaseless and secret perturbations, afford a still stronger lesson against

"Vaulting ambition, which o'erleaps itself,"

than even that awful one which history and poetry have blended their powers to impress in the instructive scenes of Macbeth. I have, as usual, wandered, but my hope and intention, dear sir, is to amuse you; and that, perhaps, I may do as much by the starts and excursions of an unformed mind, as by methodically and consequentially detailing opinions not worthy your attention. I hope this will find your domestic peace established, and your mind reconciled to those evils which wisdom cannot prevent; though virtue, and above all, that rarest virtue, patience, may convert them into blessings. Not a word more about Cromwell till you tell me how I acquit myself in the untried region of criticism.—I am always, with great esteem and deference, your obliged and obedient servant,

Anne Macvicar.

LETTER XXI.

TO COLLECTOR MACVICAR, OBAN.

Fort-Augustus, June 28, 1773.

I really cannot determine whether you, my dear sir, are amusing yourself with harmless raillery at the expense of your too presumptuous correspondent, or whether you mix serious opinions with a little grave irony. As I feel myself very unequal to meet you upon the ground of raillery, I shall willingly take it for granted that you are "quite serious," and as seriously comply with your requisition. In short, I will endeavour to point out the sources whence this "premature information and reflection has been derived." Spirit of Biography! (Muse of Biography, methinks I should rather say) on what calm elevation dost thou reside, surrounded by the powers of just discrimination, candid discussion, and true delineation? Could I trace thy abode far, far beyond the clouds of passion, and mists of prejudice, I would invoke thy assistance to portray a faint sketch of the useful and happy life, the estimable and singular character of the friend of my childhood, the instructress of my youth, and the existing model, in my mind, of the highest practical virtue.

Madame, or "Aunt" Schuyler, then (for so, by universal consent, she was affectionately called in the province of Yew York), was daughter to one of the first and most respectable characters existing in that province when it fell under the dominion of the English. His name was Cuyler, and his descendants are still numerous and prosperous in that country, to which prosperity my friend's wisdom and goodness contributed not a little. This Cuyler was the person who brought over the four Mohawk chiefs, who were mentioned by the Spectator as exciting so much wonder in England. He was introduced to Queen Anne, and had several conversations with her; she offered to knight him, but he refused, not choosing an elevation unusual in that country, which would make an invidious distinction betwixt him and his friends. Some years after his return to America, his daughter, Catalina, then about eighteen, was married to Colonel Schuyler, who possessed an estate above Albany, in the direction which led to the vicinity of the French and hostile Indians. He was a person whose calm, temperate wisdom, singular probity, and thorough knowledge of the affairs and interests of the bordering nations, had given him a very great influence, not only in his own province, but among the Indians and French Canadians, whose respective languages he spoke fluently. He was wealthy, and very generous, and so public-spirited, that though he did all in his power to prevent war, being, in fact, a

"Lover of peace, and friend of human kind;"

yet, when he saw it inevitable, he raised a regiment at his own expense, and was the first who gave character or energy to the provincial troops. To detail instances of public virtue in this truly great and good man, would, in fact, be giving the history of the Province during his lifetime. From the place where he lived, he stood, as it were, a barrier between the hostile Indians and the colonists. Of high and distinguished utility was this mild, philosophic, and Christian character; yet, unless he had met a congenial mind, he could neither have done so much good, nor prevented so much evil. Luckily for the public they had no family; therefore, greatly resembling each other, both in taste, and inclination, and intellectual powers, their efforts were all directed one way.

At that time (about 1730), there were not many settlers in the province who were acquainted with the English language;* and these generally entertained a rooted prejudice, nay, aversion, to the very army which came to protect them. In the hospitality, intelligence, and pleasing conversation of this very worthy pair, these officers always found a refuge; from them they met with cordial kindness, sound advice, and useful information. Petty and crooked policy was unknown in this patriarchal family, where a succession of adopted children, judiciously educated, and a number of domestic slaves, very kindly and tenderly treated, formed a happy community, who were directed with such prudence, that they left leisure to their rulers for beneficence still more widely diffused, and for studies of the most useful nature. Their acquaintance with elegant literature was, perhaps, not very extensive; the Spectator, the tragedy of Cato, and the works of Milton and Young, being the only books I remember to have met with, exclusive of history, biography, and memoirs; of these, indeed, there

* The Dutch language was the general one of the province of New York, before its acquisition by the English.

was a very ample collection, which had been carefully read and thoroughly digested, by the owners; and which not only furnished very frequently matter of conversation, but materials for reflection, and for that system of policy by which their plans were regulated. They had three objects in view, besides the great primary one of making their large family as good, and wise, and happy as possible. The first was, to prevent injustice being done to the Indians, to conciliate their affections, and to meliorate their condition; the second, to alleviate the hardships and difficulties to which the British troops were exposed, from marching into unknown wildernesses, by receiving them into their family, making them acquainted with the nature of the country, and the manner of managing the stubborn tempers of the boorish inhabitants, avoiding ambushes, and reconciling Indian nations to our government. On these occasions they would accommodate in the house those officers, whose morals and manners recommended them most, and allow the parties of soldiers, as they passed, a lodging in their offices, and an abundant supply of milk and vegetables. The third object to which their wisdom and humanity were directed, was the protection and comfort of new settlers on their neighbouring boundary, to whom they were ever ready to extend a helping hand, both in the way of advice and assistance. Indeed, so well did they understand the interests and defence of that growing colony, and the important frontier on which they lived, that every new Governor always came up to consult them, and no public measure was thought safe till Colonel Schuyler approved of it.

In the meantime, their house was an academy for morals, for manners, and for solid knowledge. There the best company was always to be met; there the most important topics were discussed, dispassionately and fully; there conversation, properly so called, was cultivated, and tasted. The little embellishments and elegances of life, perhaps, had no great share in these discussions; but she,

" Whose mind was moral as the preacher's tongue,
And strong, to wield all science worth the name,"

was well skilled in the Holy Scriptures, and intimately acquainted with the writings of the best divines and historians. I say she, for the Colonel died in 1757, before I knew Madame Schuyler, after they had lived forty years together, in unexampled happiness; and reared (from the time of their being weaned, till they married, or launched out into active life) fifteen nieces, nephews, or other relatives, several of whom have since been distinguished both for their merit and their uncommon success in various pursuits.

Soon after the death of her lamented partner, Madame Schuyler removed to the town of Albany, that she might more freely enjoy her choice of society, —people, whom experience in the world, or superior attainments, made suitable associates for a mind so sound and so enlightened. Her husband had left her all his possessions. The use she made of her wealth was to keep a kind of open table for strangers who were in any respect worthy of admittance; and to educate, in succession, the children of different relations of her beloved consort.* Many particulars, rela-

* Madame or Aunt Schuyler was a descendant of those Dutch

tive to this excellent person's life and manners, would be well worth preserving; and, if I outlive her (for I hope she still does live), I think I shall, some time or other, endeavour to please myself at least, by preserving a memoir of a life so valuable and exemplary.* . . . . But to the point: In the eighth year of my age (1762), we removed from the Fort to the town of Albany, to make room for some other regiment. Lodging next this good lady in town, I took a great fancy to a beautiful child, a relation whom she was bringing up in the house; and my father attracted Madame Schuyler's notice by his piety, not very frequently a distinguishing feature in the military character. I will not tire you with the detail of all the little circumstances that gradually acquired me the place in her favour which I ever continued to possess. She saw me reading Paradise Lost with delighted atten-

settlers, by whom the province was occupied when the English got it in exchange for Surinam. She was well known over all North America, and to all the British officers of any note who served there in the Canadian war, in the reign of George II. Lord Howe, killed in 1758 at the lines of Ticonderoga; Lord Loudoun, General, afterwards Lord Amherst, General Sir Thomas Gage, Sir William Johnson, and every other person who, during that period, acted any distinguished part in the war, were intimate in her family. Among the children brought up on Aunt Schuyler's knees, was her husband's nephew, General Philip Cuyler, to whom the British troops, under Burgoyne, surrendered at Saratoga; and Brigadier-General Cuyler, her own nephew, who was, and I believe is still (1807), in the British service. Several others of them were distinguished in their own country, though unknown here.

* This intention was carried into effect by the Author, who published, in 1808, "Memoirs of an American Lady," which contain full particulars of Madame Schuyler's family history, and a description of the primitive society and manners of the colony of New York, as they existed before the American Revolution. They also furnish details of the Author's own early years while she resided in America. The work appeared in two volumes, and has been republished in America.—Ed.

tion; she was astonished to see a child take pleasure in such a book, and no less so to observe, that I loved to sit thoughtful by her, and hear the conversations of elderly and grave people. My father, on leaving the army, took a small farm of Aunt Schuyler's, upon the river Hudson, some miles above Albany. She still grew more attached to me, and I lived with her for two winters; she professed a desire to keep me entirely, if my parents would part with me. I was admitted to the honour of being her constant companion, slept in her room, and was entertained with many interesting details, which to hear did I, like Desdemona, "seriously incline," and she was gratified with my attention. Whatever culture my mind has received I owe to her. Beyond the knowledge of my first duties I should scarcely have proceeded; or rather, I should have become almost savage, in a retreat which precluded me from the advantages of society, as well as those of education. It is now three years since I have heard of her. When we left her, in 1768, the discontents against the mother-country were daily on the increase. Her influence, which was very considerable, was all thrown into the opposite scale. I fear her latter days will be darkened by that disaffection to the parent state, which she always dreaded would become the consequence of peace and security.*

Now, dear sir, you have traced all this premature

* "Aunt Schuyler died in 1778, full of years, and honoured by all who could, or could not, appreciate her worth; for not to esteem Aunt Schuyler, was to forfeit all pretensions to estimation."—*Memoirs of an American Lady*, p. 329.

reflection to its true and veritable source; and you will possibly call it parrotism; nay, what is more, and worse, you will possibly not be far mistaken. Adieu! dear sir. Thank me for making known to you a mind worthy of your own; whose place you have in some degree supplied to your attached and grateful, &c., &c.

Letter XXII.

TO MISS REID.

Fort-Augustus, June 30, 1773.

My dear Harriet,

I hope you are now satisfied with my diligent and unwearied endeavours to amuse you, and make you present here as much as possible. I do not know as to the worth of the people. They certainly take a great deal too much pleasure in turning each other into ridicule; one is greatly amused; but I do not know that we ought to indulge such amusement.

I wish you saw how gay and pleasing summer looks here now; but no one will admire it with me, and delight, as I do, in seeing nature unmasked and unfettered. I feel my mind rise to a kind of melancholy greatness, when I contemplate these scenes, particularly by moonlight; but I think I should rejoice *once more* if I met with one that tasted all this as I do. I am seized with longings for you all that are very painful; nobody will care for me here, because nobody will understand me. I cannot blame them. I am too rustic, too simple at least, for people of the world, with whom manner is everything; and though myself uneducated, I painfully feel I have too much refinement, too much delicacy for uninformed people, with whom I feel no point of union but simplicity. It is a pity there are no hermitesses; I should just now like to be one. All the spirit that diverted you in my description of our garrisonians, is evaporated. They are diverting originals, but their restlessness and discontent provoke me. Military people always speak with pleasure of the place where they have been, or where they are going, but never are satisfied where they are. One sees them too near here. They are generally well-bred, and entertaining, but often hard, and heartless at bottom; and always arbitrary in their families, when they have them. They rail constantly at this place, yet, perhaps, they will never be so happy when they leave it. I would rather be a beetle under a stone, than a dragon-fly, blown with every blast. Good night; I am peevish, but not at you, spirit of truth and gentleness!

"Meek nature's child, again adieu!"

LETTER XXIII.

TO MISS ANNE OURRY, AT KINSALE, IRELAND.*

Fort-Augustus, May 24, 1774.

My dearest Nancy,

You see I have lost no time in complying with your

* Miss Anne Ourry (afterwards Mrs. Furzer), to whom many of the Letters in the following series are addressed, was the daughter of Major Ourry of the 15th Regiment, and niece of Admiral Ourry of

most agreeable proposal. Yes, my beloved sister, let us, solitary beings as we are in our respective families, supply that endearing relation to each other. You have only anticipated me, for the thought was my own. Of course you had a right to it. Kindred and united minds like ours should surely maintain a closer intercourse than we have hitherto had it in our power to do. Our separation has made us experience the mournful solitude of the heart, "the craving void left aching in the breast," occasioned by the want of that luxury of affection, imagination, and intelligence, which we have so long shared together. The beautiful caves at Inchnacardach, the wild hanging gardens of Glendoe, and the echoing glen by the waterfall at Culachy, restore your image to my solitary musings; only to make me feel your loss the more.* Never will any one enjoy

Maridge, Devonshire. She was also connected with the family of Sir A. Molesworth, Bart., of Pencarrow, in Cornwall. Miss O. was married in 1794 to Captain Furzer of the Royal Marines, who predeceased her a few years afterwards. Major Ourry's regiment was stationed at Fort-Augustus for nearly a year after the Author arrived there in 1773, and a warm friendship was soon formed between the two young ladies, then in their nineteenth year, which was kept up by correspondence for many years afterwards, as well as by an interchange of visits; Miss O. having spent a summer with the Author and her family at Laggan in 1793, and Mrs. Grant having visited her friend, then Mrs. Furzer, at Plympton, in Devonshire, in 1803, and at Rich mond, near London, in 1805 and 1807. The correspondence commences soon after Miss Ourry's departure from Fort-Augustus, whence she accompanied her father with his regiment to Ireland.—Ed.

* Mrs. Grant appears to have retained throughout her prolonged life a warm recollection of the beauties of the scenery around Fort-Augustus, described in this letter. More than fifty years afterwards, we find her, in her seventieth year, thus directing an American stranger, travelling in the Highlands, to explore those recesses. When arrived at Fort-Augustus, she bids him, in a letter dated in 1824, go to "the house of Culachy, at the foot of Corryarick, and call to give my regards to a poor afflicted widow, a kinswoman of mine, who lives there. Tell her I asked her to direct you to a little

those scenes with me as you have done. Never was the true, the genuine love of nature so strong, in a person bred in the very midst of that society that was, most of all, estranged from it. Can you ever forget the sweet summer evening, behind the great white rose bush, when we first found each other out? Sacred for ever be the hour to virtue and to friendship! The smile of nature brightening every object round that enchanting garden; the full sonorous murmur of the Oich over its fantastic gravelly shores; and the thrush's vesper hymn from Thicket Island, so near, so inaccessible, and so attractive, all opened and soothed our minds, and half an hour did as much, as half an age would have done in any other place—opened our hearts, and made us know we were worthy to mingle them. Surely, if we have guardian angels, they must have smiled together on an union productive of such innocent felicity; may I not add, useful improvement? How sadly I look at eight on the glacis, where we used to spend the full hour from that to nine, in convoying and reconvoying each other. These tender recollections are indeed "pleasant yet mournful to the soul."

I cannot complain much of solitude, in the strict sense of the word; we are now become acquainted with our neighbours all around, and see them often. You know what a wide word neighbourhood is in this

fall of water about half a mile above the house, which dashes down the face of the rock into a little round basin, so dear to many of my tenderest recollections, that I shall like you the better for having washed your hands in it; and, if you should walk a little farther up that glen, depend upon it my spirit will walk with you, and you will meet my wraith."—*Memoirs and Correspondence of Mrs. Grant of Laggan*, vol. iii., p. 64.—Ed.

thin-peopled country. Besides, we are all now tamed and softened, and live on such a good footing with each other, that we are "like young lambkins sporting in a green meadow," as your antiquated friend expressed it. Never being used to see much company, particularly fine company, I have nothing to complain of on that score; but, O, my Nancy, ask your own heart what pleasure mine finds in the society of common acquaintances, selfish, superficial, and possibly deceitful. Christina Macpherson stands a worthy exception to this general character, which you will easily perceive to be the drawing of chagrin. Yet her sound understanding and steady attachment, though valuable in themselves, cannot supply the place of the numberless, nameless links by which our minds were connected; those conversations where perfect freedom, without the least tincture of rude familiarity, unveiled the inmost thoughts of our hearts, which must be depraved and degenerated, before our mutual affection can be abated, far less extinguished. I know not where I am wandering, but I meant to tell you, that there are a thousand things which occur in the course of my reading and observation, to delight and interest me, of which she has no idea; for this she is not to blame, but I am to be pitied. Were it not for the correspondence I keep up with you and my dear Harriet Reid, I should find this exile gloomy indeed. Yet, though I feel unwilling to submit to its wholesome bitterness, my reason informs me that even this exile has its advantages, considered in one point of view. Your penetration enabled you to discover in my mind a strange mixture of wild enthusiasm of imagination, with indolent tranquillity of temper. The retired manner in which I have been brought up, equally remote from the refined artifice of higher life, and the necessary activity and confined notions of the mob, have nourished my peculiarities. So has the little company I have kept; these were mostly of the same primitive cast, and lay under the same disadvantages of being equally unfit for vulgar, and, what the world calls, elegant society. The mournful event* to which you are no stranger, blasting the flattering picture of felicity which my heart had too fondly indulged, fixed in my mind a cast of pensive thought, which has been alternately sustained by the tenderness of friendship, and the reveries of solitude; so that I am now neither fit for any other situation, nor desirous of a change, lest it should prove

"A bitter change—severer for severe."

If Heaven should favour our ardent wishes, of once more meeting, I hope the change will not be a disadvantageous one. I should value your society more than ever, now that I know what it is to be deprived of that or any other suitable to my taste. Whatever change a necessary habit of prudence and reserve may have made on my manners, you will find my heart the same, and we shall meet as if we parted yesterday: my soul foretells that this meeting, and all we have seen since we parted, will only make us value each other the more. I wish we were once more together, with the privilege of teasing poor Captain D'Arippe, by affecting learning, and mispronouncing hard words.

* The death of a young friend.

What a dilemma his desire of appearing gallant and well-bred, combining with his real hatred for the sex, used to reduce him to! He might have furnished a new character for a comedy. Shall we never more hold him in chace, through the windings of the zig-zag road, where he used to pant before us like another Falstaff, little knowing that we only wished to frighten him. I have often smiled by myself at the recollection of our industry in tormenting him, and never hear a hard word murdered, but what *a crowned cat in a nation of ideas** brings him into my head.

I was so much entertained by your lively and humorous description of your place of residence and its inhabitants, that I could not resist reading a part of it to my father, who was quite charmed with it, and, having taken his tour of duty through many parts of Ireland, is the better qualified to judge of the verisimilitude of your description. Vanity has her votaries everywhere; but on the Hibernian shore, she is more devoutly worshipped than any saint of the country. She holds the place there which pride does here; I do not know how to strike the balance. Vanity is in better humour, but pride tells fewer lies; the first is more pleasing, the latter safer. May the dominion of either be far from our peaceful bosoms. I conclude this letter of declamation, by telling you it shall be directly followed by one of faithful narration, giving you a brief history of this little epitome of the great world you are ranging through. Short may your

* "Concatenation of ideas:" a term invented to tease Captain D'Arippe, of the 15th Regiment, who of all things dreaded female pedants.

eccentric course prove. If I were a star, I should like to be a fixed one. Be you in the meantime my guiding planet, and shed sweet influence on your unaltered friend,

A. M.

Letter XXIV.

TO MISS ISABELLA EWING, GLASGOW.

Fort-Augustus, June 10, 1774.

My dear Isabella,

I will make no excuses for leaving your two entertaining letters so long unanswered; but rather show my gratitude, by giving you, as well as I can, some account of my late excursion, which has helped a little to divert the chagrin I felt at my ever dear Miss Ourry's departure. But I must thank you for your sincere sympathy with a grief, that to many would appear romantic or exaggerated, or might at best be considered as the result of a retired life, little acquaintance with the world, and the necessity which a weak mind feels of having something, or somebody, to lean upon. She made my sorrow more excusable by seeming to feel, nay, really feeling, as much herself. Mine might be accounted childish, because I am, as you well know, womanly in appearance, while a mere girl in years and judgment. But this was by no means the case with her. Had you but known her, you would be convinced that it is not merely the pleasure of agreeable society that I mourn over; but that her mind was firm, rational, and enlightened, and her friendship a real benefit as well as honour to me. I know I tire you, but you must have patience, for you will hear a great deal more on this subject, if you indulge me in saying, as usual, what is nearest my heart, and uppermost in my fancy.

This is the best place in the world for cultivating friendship; and therefore, in spite of all the privations to which it condemns me, I will love it, because there is little to scatter the recollection of the days I wish to live over again, or to divert me from self-culture, the only object that now remains to me. Do you remember my mentioning an agreeable neighbour in one of my former letters, who lives a mile off, in a situation equally singular and beautiful? I mean Miss Christina Macpherson. She is an acquisition in her way, sensible, and sincere, though uncultivated. She possesses a fund of genuine humour; and I believe has a regard for me. With this agreeable companion I went down to Inverness in May, making a very pleasant and picturesque voyage down our fine lake in the galley.*

I got your kind letter just as I was setting out, but delayed answering it till I could tell you something of my travels. We meant to stay but a few days, but, betwixt kindness and contrary winds, were detained three weeks. Your extreme delicacy with regard to your Dunbar jaunt, might be an example to me; but I resolve to do good for evil, and carry you north, though you would not give me an ideal jaunt to the

* A small Government vessel attached to Fort-Augustus, and used for conveying supplies for the garrison. It was commanded by Captain Gwynn, some of whose family still reside at Fort-Augustus.—(1845.)

east. Come with me, then, to the capital of the Highlands. Inverness is most agreeably situated at the very threshold of this rugged territory; the mountains of which rise, with abrupt grandeur, to bound the prospect on one hand, the plain being four or five miles in extent, while a large bay of the sea limits it on the other. From the odd looking hill of Tommin-a-heurich, which rises in the middle of this plain, the fertile shires of Ross and Moray indulge the eye with a boundless view of gentlemen's seats, placed generally under the shelter of eminences, and surrounded with plantations (for the gentry here are great improvers), whence we overlook extensive fertile plains, and

> "Softly swelling hills,
> On which the power of cultivation lies,
> And joys to see the wonders of His hand."

Yet, over and above the partiality which we are apt to contract for our place of abode, we found a sameness in that extent of lowland that did not compensate for the variety afforded by our wild hills and winding glens at Fort-Augustus. Besides, its north-eastern situation exposes Inverness to such chilling blasts, as made us reflect with pleasure on the shelter we receive from our mountains; which are like some lofty and revolting characters, who appear stern and awful to strangers, but are all warmth and kindness to their own family. Yet I should like none of these climates, where

> "Winter lingering chills the lap of May,"

if I could help myself.

But to return to the said capital. It is somehow a cheerful looking place, because the people look cheerful; yet not flourishing, though no situation can be better adapted for the purposes of commerce. It has, however, a genteel society; and one meets with many well-bred agreeable people. They have assemblies every fortnight, gayer than your Glasgow ones; which may be accounted for by their being attended by the neighbouring gentry, who are numerous and polite. These gentry, too, have, many of them, been abroad in the army or otherwise, and thus add liberal notions and polished manners to the acute and sprightly genius of the country. Their great distance from the capital often makes their provincial town the scene of their winter amusements. Nothing took my fancy so much there, as the ladies. They are really, in general, showy, handsome women, excellent dancers, and have the best complexions I ever saw. Indeed you can scarcely meet a young lady who does not remind you of the beauties in old romances. They have a great deal of flaxen hair, a skin transparently fair, and cheeks like the opening rose. Yet their features are seldom regular or delicate, and their beauty is of that kind which vanishes with the bloom of youth. Their persons are large, and they are fat as heart could wish; yet, on the whole, they look cheerful and innocent. They certainly speak better English than most Scots do, but with a sharp imperative tone; and they are very frank, and full of professions of kindness. But I tease you with what perhaps loses all interest in my dull description.

We had our share of adventures in coming home, some of them abundantly ludicrous; but the minutiæ would be more tiresome than Clarissa's, without being compensated by the same interest and fancy. We moralized, and wandered by ourselves in a most beautiful wood for two or three days, lodging at night in a great old chateau, where the servants were ordered to give us all we wanted. All this time we waited for a fair wind, to take us up Loch Ness to Fort-Augustus. We had no book or work;—Christina sung like a syren to me, and I caught young wild ducks, which she tried to tame, while I gathered wild flowers. We began at last to suffer "the pains and penalties of idleness." I held out better than she, having more rural taste, and taking more interest in trifles. We came up here at last, by moonlight, in a boat. In the morning we landed at the sweetest place imaginable, the Laird of Glenmoriston's* seat; which delighted me so much with quietness and wildness, and romantic environs, and hospitable, easy people, and beautiful children, that I would describe it to you, if I thought Inverness were not more than enough at once. I should need to have the Princess Schehersade's talents, before I could give you half our adventures. They ended, however, in the laird and lady kindly coming up with us, and spending a most agreeable day at my father's.

I have only time to tell you, that I have heard four times from Miss Ourry; that I thought many times of you every day in the wood, and that I am proud of being two letters in your debt. I am most affectionately yours, &c.

* Grant, of Glenmoriston; a family respectable for its antiquity, and estimable for genuine worth and simple manners; in whose hospitable mansion the spirit of true Highland cordiality loved to linger, surrounded by its attendant graces, ease, courtesy, and cheerfulness. Glenmoriston is situated on the northern shore of Loch Ness, within six miles of Fort-Augustus.

Letter XXV.

TO MISS OURRY.

Fort-Augustus, October 10, 1775.

My dearest Nancy,

Your letter came just in time to relieve my anxiety, and prevent me from absolutely despairing of ever hearing more from you. Need I tell you my uneasiness, or how I rejoiced on receiving another proof of your continued love? My pleasure changed too soon to melancholy, when I understood the dreadful dilemma you are all in about this American voyage, which impends too surely over you : I had indeed heard that the 15th Regiment were under orders for America, but did not dream of Captain Ourry's accompanying them ; and I examined every newspaper, in hopes of finding his name changed, or sold out. How grieved and surprised was I to hear that he is in danger of being once more torn from the embraces of a family so dear to him, who have already spent so many tedious years in lamenting his absence, and this to plunge into the most cruel and horrid of wars ; whose most desirable event can be only that of successfully devastating with bloodshed and destruction a country, lately the most peaceful and happy on earth, but never, never to be happy more, end this as it may. The cup was too full to hold, yet I did not think it would be spilt thus rudely. How dear must victory be bought with the lives of our fellow-subjects and former friends! But I will no longer torment myself or you, with giving vent to all the sad reflections arising from this most painful subject. Yet why were you not more distinct and particular? Alas, I fear all our prayers and hopes for the desired reconciliation will prove fruitless. The Divine justice seems about to display itself in taking signal vengeance on the iniquities of the times. The corruption of the parent state, which leads her to an inordinate enjoyment of those advantages that she possesses in pre-eminence over all others, and her ungrateful neglect of the source of all those blessings, seems arrived at its height; and will be requited by the ingratitude of those colonies which owe their existence to her.

There was a time when such a half-moral, half-political harangue from your friend would have made you laugh; but now fatal necessity urges us to take more than a common share in the public calamity—calamity, how heavy, and how general, when we, who, in the sequestered vale of life, might be supposed exempt from any other share than the tribute which humanity pays to the woes of human kind, are forced for those dearest to us to have our hearts wrung with anguish hitherto unknown! I deeply sympathize with your sufferings, on account of the worthy Captain's illness, and that of your good mother. Alas, my dear girl, we were sisters by sentiment and inclination before, but now I may hail you as a sister-sufferer. You have met, or are likely to meet, with the train of sorrows that have obscured the morning of my youth. These I account salutary drops of bitterness thrown into my cup, lest the tranquil easiness of my temper, and that range of imagination which furnishes me with a boundless store of ideal pleasures, should raise my enjoyment of life beyond what is destined for this imperfect state. You will too feelingly trace the resemblance which I allude to; the daily sufferings and broken spirits of a beloved parent bursting asunder the tenderest ties of affection, and hurrying me away, far, very far, from those whose presence was life and joy to me! I hope you will not finish the resemblance, by being forced to cross the Atlantic with the same desponding reluctance which hung upon the spirits of your friend on a similar occasion. Never shall I forget the emotion with which I saw the Cape of Neversink melt into air, when I bade the last farewell to the dear-loved coast of America, which I am now certain I shall never more behold. My dear friends were beginning to be persecuted for their loyalty before we came away, for even then the storm began to lower.

Poor Letch!* his kingdom is not of this world, that is evident. What a crush to the spirit of a young soldier, to be forced to forsake a profession he was so attached to, at the very time that military merit had the fairest chance for distinction and reward! I wish you had given more particulars of his parting behaviour. I am glad he spoke so plainly, because it no doubt relieved his mind, and the assurance of your compassion and esteem, which was all he could rea-

* Henry Letch was the son of a physician of the same name in London. He was sent very early into the army, full of romantic prejudices, which led him into boundless profusion and endless errors. With great purity of heart, and uprightness of intention, he very early dissipated his patrimony, and soon after was so much in debt as to be obliged to sell his commission, about the period when this letter was written.

sonably hope, would be so consoling to him. You will think my expectations romantic, as usual, but still I will hope our friend Henry has embraced the only profession he is fitted for. The zealous fervour of his attachments, his glowing admiration of superior excellence, and the ardour of his conceptions, will find adequate objects, where the affections of his heart, and services of his future life will, I trust, be dedicated. How happy those whom the storms of life drive so early to their best, their final harbour! That abhorrence of vice which would be a continual source of vexation, in struggling through the scenes of active life, will be very well suited to the duties of a pastor; besides, the emphatic eloquence which makes every word of our poor friend so interesting, will be peculiarly suited to the pulpit.

How many new things have I to tell you of! A new cousin, whom I am much pleased with; he has learning, taste, and understanding; I find him in many respects very congenial with my disposition. Then we have got a new church built by subscription, mind, that it would do your heart good to see, and your soul good to hear sermon in. We have been quite animated all summer, with flocks of wild geese from your country. Lament with me, for we have had another ship load of emigrants, marching off to their Chaldea, for such I know it will appear to them. I have a good mind to pray for a heart of stone. Your old friend, the Honourable Captain Murray,* commands the invalids here, and passed the

* Captain William Murray, brother to the Earl of Dunmore, who had formerly resided near Captain Ourry, and was intimately known to that family.

summer amongst us. He is more helpless than you saw him, but has still equal spirits, and amiable manners. We often conversed about you, and he begs you may not forget him. Mr. G. left us last week to be settled in Badenoch. Our parting was—almost affecting. . . . . He was proud of your notice and remembrance, and begs me to assure you of his cordial good wishes.

I beg you will write immediately on receipt of this. Stay at home one night from your Hibernian Ranelagh, and renounce noise and headache to gratify your friend. Pray explain yourself about being sick of elegance. I do not remember teasing you about the word; but my out-of-the-world education, and primitive notions, and almost savage simplicity of taste, made yours seem to me to border on false refinement. I triumph in your confession, having always assured myself that your native sensibility and ripened judgment would lead you back to the paths of nature and of truth. Then you will fully relish that chaste and sublime simplicity in style, in manners, and in sentiment, which delights the untutored mind. Your change of taste will show you many things which you once thought eccentric, in a very different light. Tell the Captain and his lady I rejoice in their kind remembrance of me, and shall never forget them. Friend Henry, too, shall be remembered with all his imperfections on his head. Adieu! I shall always be very tenderly your sister and friend.

Letter XXVI.

TO MISS OURRY.

Fort-Augustus, November 26, 1775.

My dearest Nancy,

I expected to have your opinion of the general character of the people you have been among in Ireland these two years almost, and should think the comparison which your understanding and observation might enable you to draw between their manners and those of the countries where you sojourned of yore, might be a very amusing one. But my own experience leads me to make the proper apology in this case; for we really both give way so much to the overflowing fullness of our hearts, that neither of us leaves room for the news, description, or usual tittle-tattle which female correspondence is, for the most part, filled up with.

I can the better comprehend your *pair of ducks*, as we have now in the garrison a couple (not a pair) who are newly arrived from Ireland, and always talk with fond regret of Dublin, as the centre of all their joys. They have so much external and superficial elegance, and so little of that refinement of sentiment and manners which emanates from the heart, that I never see them without thinking of your newly-acquired friends. They are natives of this country, and have a singular history. . . . . . . They are fond of company without real hospitality, or the least regard for their guests, whom they look upon as merely implements to kill time with. They behave to each other with a kind of civility which seems rather a substitute for tenderness, than a proof of it. There is a negative merit which must be allowed to those well-bred people, who never offend or oblige you, but are satisfied with amusing and being amused. They are, perhaps, safer than people of mere virtue, who have quicker feelings and more earnestness; they have neither acrimony enough to feel quick disgust at vice and folly, nor benevolence to be delighted with the excellencies of God's creatures. They neither love nor hate cordially, but just consider people as cards to play with. Now, I cannot endure to be a card, since I cannot aspire at being queen of hearts. Yet if you knew how eagerly I set about gardening, and how stoutly I laboured at transplanting, you would be apt to call me queen of spades.

I have dwelt thus minutely on these characters, as I think them a sample or counterparts of those you daily meet with in Ireland. I am sorry the general rage for dissipation, and your indignant feelings at it, should lead you to think your mind contracted;—

> " I do not think my sister so to seek,
> And so unprincipled in Virtue's book,
> And that calm peace which goodness bosoms ever,"

as to suffer the depravity which prevails around her to produce any lasting sentiment but pity, which must indeed on some occasions be mingled with contempt. Whatever you may say in a momentary heat, I am sure your good sense and kindly affections will preserve you from a gloomy disgust at human nature, on account of the vice and absurdity of individuals, to whose nature it belongs to rush into full display, while the pious, the modest, and the good, serve God and their fellow-creatures in quiet obscurity. When we forsake the paths of nature and simplicity, in a restless pursuit of amusement, vanity and ostentation generally take the lead of all the passions. That principle which leads the human mind so eagerly to desire the approbation of its fellow-mortals, was certainly placed within us as a spur, not only to the desire, but to the attainment of applause; and if people applauded only what was right, it might answer noble purposes. But, alas! when conscious we no longer deserve esteem, we grasp at admiration, and endeavour to conceal our want of real happiness and self-enjoyment, under the veil of external gaiety and artificial mirth. The glossy varnish of politeness, which, like the skin of a snake, though bright and pleasing to the view, is cold and slippery to the touch, we are taught to substitute for the lively glow and artless tenderness of true benevolence. Be merciful even to the perversion of Irish hospitality. Excess of good nature first makes them wretched, and then necessity makes them cunning. To be truly and austerely good among such a "perverse and crooked generation," requires the resolution of a confessor at least; but you must at all events preserve your charity, were it but to guard the purity of your own heart.

Occasional solitude is a blessing which every well regulated mind would long for, if deprived of that privilege. Remember what our favourite Young says of

"Our reason, guardian angel and our God."

I have a particular pleasure in reading the pencil-marked lines that we compared together. I wish we could read some more chosen books in that way, whenever we meet, as meet we shall, I trust:—we may then have the satisfaction of tracing the similarity of our respective tastes.

You desire a history of the garrison; but so bad a newsmonger and narrator am I, that unless I go through it *à la militaire*, somewhat in the order of the muster-roll, I shall lose myself. The prime personage,* then, remains much as you left him; if anything he mends; stays more at home, and is content to pry less. But whether this be reformation or decline, this deponent saith not. Gwynn's† good nature and salt-water wit continue to grow and prosper; he will never want a butt while we have a ruler. I have a notion I, too, furnish one occasionally; but it is wit without valour, for his is always an absent butt. I have one way of keeping these gentry in order; I can see they dread my contempt. Now, next to being loved, the best thing is to be feared; and when people know you incapable of meanness and deceit, depend upon it they will fear you. Mrs. Newmarch is still‡ the alternate prey of doubts and despondency: you would pity her if you knew half what she suffers. Yet who can imagine it better than you, by what you saw your own mother suffer in the like situation. To be sure, Mrs. N.'s feelings are on no occasion very lively; yet, though we children of fancy suffer more than

* Probably Mr. Trapaud, the Governor.

† Captain Gwynn, the Commander of the Government Yacht attached to the Fort.

‡ The daughter of the Governor, who remained at Fort-Augustus while her husband was absent with his regiment in America.—Ed.

others, both have many consolations. Besides the sympathy of friendship, and the ardour of hope, we build the prettiest castles imaginable, tenant them with courteous knights and virtuous dames, and then sit, rent free, in these airy dwellings. Mrs. N. seldom hears of her husband; he is prisoner somewhere on the frontier of Pennsylvania. Our new surgeon, Mr. Curtis, is an original, whom I would wish you to know, but I have not colours wherewith to paint him. He was very stiff and pedantic, but that begins to wear off. He is, I dare say, well principled; but, though he has solid learning, I believe, and very sound sense I am sure, he has neither fancy nor feeling, and has the presumption to laugh at sentiment; you may believe I grow very angry, and attempt to be severe, and then he rallies me about morbid sensibility, as he calls it. He is very provoking, and quite incorrigible. I always tell him he will meet an Iphigenia somewhere.*

Remember me respectfully to your father and mother, and kindly to every one you think has any kindness for me. Adieu, dearest Nancy! only sister —beloved friend. Farewell.

Tom cat is well, and lives in clover,
But Perry's harmless life is over:
To tell you that he died quite mad,
Will melt your heart and make you sad:
But when you know he sleeps in peace,
Methinks your grief, like mine, should cease.

* He is now happily married, and settled in Edinburgh; is a particular friend of the Author's, and a valuable member of society. —(1807.)

Letter XXVII.

TO MISS OURRY.

Fort-Augustus, Feb. 15, 1776.
(The month of our nativity.)

My dearest Girl!

I most sincerely forgive your perplexing and mortifying silence, and most willingly attribute the chasm in our correspondence to any other motive than indifference, altogether inconsistent as it is with the sincerity and affection which form so great and distinguishing a part of your character. But now that my forgiveness may be as sincere as I know your penitence to be, let me, with my accustomed freedom, warn you of the consequences of indulging that unfriendly indolence, less pardonable in your active, lively disposition, than in my easy and indolent one. I have admired this vivacity without envy, and am therefore entitled to reap the fruits of it. I was vain of your attainments, and always thought myself deficient in nothing which you possessed; it was enough for me that we had them between us. This is digression—but I resume. In the present unsettled habits of your life, there is nothing you ought to be so careful of as cherishing those friendships which have given you so much pleasure, and done you so much good in your earlier years; for, indeed, as poor Pope said when he was dying, and saw things as they are, "There is nothing worth living for but virtue and friendship;" and friendship is a part of virtue; when the one withers, the other will droop. Friendship is the misletoe growing on the oak of virtue. I fancy when the Druids cut the misletoe with golden sickles, they had a kind of prescience of the dear and close ties that gold was destined in after ages to divide. Seriously, if the friendships that have formed the delight and comfort of the earlier stage of life were once extinguished in your breast, no later formed attachment would ever supply their loss. You will meet with many agreeable acquaintances in your peregrinations; nay, in the country where you are,* you run a chance of being overwhelmed with civility by the one sex, and compliment by the other; but where will you find the playful innocence of a Miss De la Garde, the solid sense and rational attachment of a Sophy Gerard, or the sincere and constant affection of her whom you have thus long neglected? Yes, my dear sister in the best sense of the word, sister of my heart, and of my vowed affection, if you allow trivial motives to estrange you from your friends, as their remembrance cannot die in your heart, it will only live to torment you. I could not endure to think of my friends when I could no longer think of them with pleasure. Anything may be endured but remorse; it is the dreaded future punishment begun on earth. Sweetly mournful is the recollection of those with whom, and for whom we have lived in tender confidence and unity. Should they depart for ever, when we can look back blameless, in the midst of our sorrow, we are pleased with the consciousness that the

* Ireland.

sacred approbation of virtue consecrates the tender regret. Transient intimacies will never fill the gloomy vacuity which extinguished affections leave in the heart. Vainly, if that were the case, would you endeavour to fill the chasm in your mind with amusements ending in satiety and disgust. Now, in my turn, let me ask pardon for these transgressions on your patience; be assured they are owing to the anxiety of a heart which, though fully convinced of your present regard, dreads few things so much as your future indifference.

You would have gratified me by saying more about your new acquaintances and present employments. What have you been doing? Your worked gown unfinished, all your friends neglected, and all this in a place so remote, and, by your own description, unsocial! What will become of you in the hurry and dissipation of Dublin, if you contrive to be thus mysteriously engrossed on the banks of the notorious Shannon, which one might suppose to be the chosen retreat of dulness? Yet, when I think of it, it is not lead, but brass, that people are said to acquire by plunging into it. Alas, for our poor unhappy brother!* How afflicting is your history, and yet how well we might foresee what has happened:

* Henry Letch, referred to in a previous letter, who delighted to style himself our brother, was, at an early age, with eleven other youths, the children of wealthy parents, placed under the care of the too well-known Dr. Dodd; and, in common with the rest, received very flimsy and superficial notions of morality and religion, and an extravagant taste for elegance and false refinements. He was fond of walking with us, reading to us, &c.; and we hoped, betwixt reasoning and ridicule, to wean him from his absurdities; but to little purpose. Adversity, however, seemed to produce the desired effect. After leaving the army, he took orders, and obtained some chaplaincy about Dublin Castle, and seemed to apply seriously to the

"Curse on his virtues, they've undone himself."

But what is virtue, or can it indeed exist, without self-command and self-denial? What avails to poor Henry that he had no vicious propensities, when he has contrived his own ruin, and, what is much worse, rendered himself contemptible, by indulging inclinations tending to elegance and virtue, beyond all due bounds? This it is to be a mother's darling, and to be Dr. Dodd's pupil, and to skim the smooth surface of knowledge, and, as Voltaire said of Rousseau, "to talk of virtue and philosophy, till nobody shall know what virtue and philosophy is." . . . . . Dearest Nancy, let this sad example teach us to go higher than essays and novels for our divinity and morality. These must be gathered with labour, and are worth the labour of gathering.

Now spirit of Lycurgus, and soul of Leonidas, and shade of King Agis, and all other laconic powers! assist me, to cram, and crowd, and crush together, in a few pithy sentences, the narration of domestic transactions. Know, then, that after the dissolution and scatteration of last year's happy trio, another sprung up in its room, of which triangle I am the base, as you right worthily were of the former. Christina Macpherson made one of the sides, and you easily guess the other. Well, for a time we rejoiced together with perfect harmony, being in such an easy, sauntering, playful humdrum way, that we all insensibly became more and more necessary to each other, because, in fact, we saw no

duties of his function; but was, about the year 1778, cut off by the jail fever, which he had caught by a voluntary attendance on sick prisoners.

great motive to care for any one else. However, this was too good to last. I found the thermometer rising too high in a certain point. I thought it was being too like the world to see what was right in my friend's case only, and not practise it in my own, and so, finally, I did what formerly I advised you to do. And now, being very proud, we think it incumbent to be very sulky; but every nursery-maid knows that the best cure for sulkiness is just—to let it alone. Adieu! my dear friend; tell those that remember me, that I never forget any one I ever cared for. I have a thousand good wishes to send you, which this paper cannot hold. Remember me, and set it in your tablet, or——my ghost will haunt you. I am, with unchanged affection, most sincerely yours,

A. M.

Letter XXVIII.

TO MISS ISABELLA EWING, GLASGOW.

Fort-Augustus, March 15, 1777.

My dear Isabella,

The last hasty lines you had from me were so rapidly scrawled, that you would hardly make out the little meaning they contained. The sage bearer was on the fidget at my elbow the whole time I was writing them. I have been a good deal indisposed, great part of the winter, with colds, and, your old enemy, the toothache. Now that I am better, I have a double enjoyment of everything. You, who have the bustle of a crowded town, and a succession of amusements, to steal away the long dark evenings, must wonder how we manage to get quit of them. Exiles as we are from the gay and fashionable walks of life, we fall upon wondrous contrivances to soften the rigour of the season, and

"Twine a garland round dark winter's brow."

You can form no idea of our multiplied resources, unless you were to pass a month among us. Reading, walking, and all speculative and solitary amusements, you well know, can be enjoyed here as well as in town. But you have no notion how townified folks are in all these little garrisons; and how these small circles, which necessity has driven together, ape the manners of the great world that they have reluctantly left behind. We, too, have our visits, our scandal, brought from thirty miles distance, our tittle-tattle, our jealousies, our audible whispers, and secrets that every body knows. When any one marries within the county bounds, we all sit in judgment, and are sure to find some fault with either party, as if it were our own concern; and when any one dies within twenty miles, we are all very busy in sounding their praises, and contrive to rake a great many virtues from among their ashes, for which we never gave them credit till they were out of the reach of our envy. Then when Mrs. Newmarch,* or Madame la Commandante, receives any new article of dress, we all fly to admire it, and then hurry away to wash gauzes, or in some other imperfect manner to contrive an imitation of it. Not

* Daughter of Governor Trapaud, married to Captain, afterwards Major Newmarch, of the Seventh Regiment. She was a pattern of conjugal affection, and domestic virtue.

to dwell on each minute particular, believe me that our handful of antiquated beaux and rusticated belles just do everything in the country that yours do in town, only with more languor and ill-humour. People habituated to that manner of life, carry its follies and impertinences into the very bosom of tranquillity. When they walk, it is on the hard gravel road, to get an appetite; when they read, it is some periodical matter, to dose away time till the stated card-party begins. These people always give me pain; they appear like fish out of water, gasping and struggling in a strange element. It provokes me, in a place where nature seems to reign paramount, enthroned in the centre of her sublimest retreat, and surrounded by her genuine children, to see these insipid aliens insult her with their ennui. I mean no reflection on a town life, but merely to observe, that people, who have no resources within themselves, and aspire at no improvements, can hide their defects best in a crowd.

I have been talking all the while of we and us, without telling you whom I meant to comprehend under these terms. We have, besides the old immovable set, an Officer of Invalids, and his wife and daughter, from Edinburgh, who are ever pining for want of company they could ill afford to keep, and public places, which it would ruin them to frequent. They strive much to exalt our idea of their former consequence, by regretting that there are no noblemen's seats at a visible distance, and that tumblers and rope-dancers never come this way. Then we have a pair who are a great acquisition; Captain Donaldson, of the 42d, an excellent officer, and accomplished gentleman, who is also beloved for his worth and good-nature. He is married to a daughter of Colonel Gordon Graham, of the same regiment, who, till now, lived always in a gay circle of the first company, but is wonderfully domesticated, and appears to be a good wife and tender mother; so, among all this group of originals, Mr. G.'s satirical wit, and Mr. D.'s dry humour, find abundant food. . . . .

Alas! these Americans, ungrateful favourites of Heaven; not satisfied with throwing away the happiness they possessed supereminently, what public disturbance and private misery have they occasioned to others; and how do the remotest corners of this extensive empire vibrate with the shock of their calamities! My cordial love to our Harriet, and believe me, with unchanging affection, your friend,

A. M.

Letter XXIX.

TO MISS OURRY, KINSALE.

Greenock, August 9, 1777.

What are you doing, my dearest friend, my only sister, and why are you thus forgetful of her to whose imagination you are ever present, and whose heart glows with affection for you, which not even your negligence can extinguish? Alas! how ingenious am I in finding excuses for you, and in vexing myself with anxious conjectures about your health and welfare. No wonder the pleasing idea of our social intercourse, and the lively and tender attachment it gave rise to, should warm my heart amidst the gloomy solitude of Fort-Augustus; but this summer, which I have spent so happily among the dear friends of my earlier years, has not in the least obliterated the remembrance of my beloved Nancy.

How foolishly I ramble. I meant to tell you how I have spent this summer, in the pleasing hope that you are still interested in my little concerns. Soon after I wrote you my last letter, I went, in company with Mrs. Pagan (the American friend I formerly mentioned), and one of the young ladies of the family, to Edinburgh, where we arrived in time of the races, which afforded us a good deal of amusement, being entirely new to all of us. The friends in whose house we staid, with others whom we met there, were assiduously attentive to promote our entertainment, by showing us everything in and about the town that was worth seeing. Crowds, and the gaieties which generally engage the attention of the capital, at that joyous time of year, could give little pleasure to a damsel so totally rusticated as your friend; yet the princely dwelling of Holyrood House, majestic in decay, whose echoing halls and desolated chambers suggested strongly the mournful ideas of fallen grandeur and departed dignity, awaked in my mind a thousand different emotions, all solemn and interesting; not to add the enthusiastic renovation with which I viewed the pictures of our ancient sovereigns, and those heroes to whose memory we owe at least the sigh of retrospective gratitude. But I will not bewilder myself in this diffusive theme; nor yet lead you through the delightful labyrinths of the Botanic Garden, where I wandered with the most exquisite pleasure, amid the united beauties of art and nature, and saw the products of every soil and climate blended in regular confusion and endless variety. Nor shall you accompany me in the delightful excursions I made into the country to see the gentlemen's and noblemen's seats in the neighbourhood; and what need you, for my fancy gratified me with your presence in every pleasing, every interesting scene; and I still pleased myself with imagining myself addressing you, and pouring out my overflowing heart as usual.

But this will not do; I must tell you how I came here. Mrs. Pagan, then, is going out to America to her husband, and she and I have passed the summer together in the most agreeable manner. The family used their united influence to persuade me to accompany her here with two of our young ladies, and see her on board. This is a melancholy task to us all, for she is the darling of her new relations, who feel the utmost regret at parting with her. The wind is contrary since we came down, but we have spent the time (three days) very agreeably. Her father-in-law and two other gentlemen came down with us, and we have not been able to stir out of the house since, being an incessant flood of rain. I should have told you that I staid a fortnight in Edinburgh, and had the pleasure to hear last week of my friends at home being all well. Mrs. Pagan's vessel puts in at Cork, whence this will be conveyed to you. Would to Heaven you did but see each other, you resemble so much in mind and person, that, through mere self-love, you would be charmed with each other at first sight. Adieu, my much-loved sister. Tell your father and mother how kindly they are remembered by your

A. M.

Letter XXX.

TO MISS ISABELLA EWING, GLASGOW.

Perth, May 6, 1778.

My dear soul, I would give anything that you knew the family in which I now am.* Your mind is fitted to taste the pleasures which angels may share with us; that of seeing a happy family living in love and harmony, and enjoying the heartfelt consciousness of living in the faith, and imitation of our blessed Redeemer, with all the hope and comfort such a life inspires. Such is the excellent person whose tender care I now experience; and such are the children of her heart and of her prayers; the heirs of her humble piety and meek benevolence. Her eldest daughter† is certainly one of the worthiest of human beings; and the ease and good-breeding of the whole family would soon convince one that it requires neither constraint nor austerity to live among religious people. How glad I am to have found out these "less than kin, and more than kind," for they do not exactly know our connection, and have the more merit in their attention. I can taste no pleasure without trying to share it with

* The family of the late Rev. Mr. Black, one of the Ministers of Perth.—(1807.)

† Miss Bridget Black, afterwards married to the Rev. Mr. Bonar of Cramond, near Edinburgh.

you. Oh, my true friend! how eagerly do my hopes fly forward to the time when we shall once more share every hope and wish together. Yet, should this be denied, I would fain look forward with trembling hope to our reunion in that state, which excludes cares and wishes, yet excludes not ——. But I will avoid presumption, which must result from endeavouring to mingle, too fondly, the affections of this mortal state with our dimly-discovered views of the world unseen.

Did I tell you of an excursion to Scoon Palace, which we made in company with a large party of the *beau-monde* of Perth? I think I caught cold while contemplating the forsaken mansions of departed greatness. Yet I do not repent going; I love originals dearly, and antiquities vastly; I was pleased, too, with a monument of conjugal affection in the chapel belonging to the palace. Lord Stormont, it seems, was first married to a foreign lady, who had the strongest desire to accompany him to Scotland; but, dying abroad in the prime of life, she earnestly requested that her heart might be brought here, and deposited in his family burial-place, that it might repose near to the object of her former attachment. It is deposited in a white marble urn, with a Latin inscription, expressive of her virtues and her lord's affection. I was pleased to think how good that heart must have been which could retain such warmth, amidst the frozen formalities and frivolous dissipation of a court.

Letter XXXI.

TO MISS ISABELLA EWING.

Blair Athol, Tuesday Evening,
May 28, 1778.

My dearest Isabella,

Having written to Jean this morning about my setting out, I must refer you to that letter for the motives of my journey. I found an honest man, whom I knew very well, from our place, driving an empty carriage north; he is driver in ordinary to the Fort, and as wise and careful as a patriarch. I have passed a most agreeable day of solitary enjoyment. I travelled in silent state, without meeting a creature to interrupt my musings. I did not even read, but amused myself with my knitting, in up-hill roads. I did not speak a sentence till I had some necessary communing with my landladies, except getting the history of the famous battle, as I came through the Pass of Killiecrankie. My driver was very intelligent and distinct about the antiquities of the road. The singular beauty of the morning when I set out, and the satisfaction of getting my mind free from many doubts and fears that had hung upon me, with the hourly change of charming scenes, raised my lately dejected spirits to a sweet serenity. I looked forward with pleasure towards home, the dear centre of all social and rational happiness. The beloved friends I had left behind rose in my mind, not with the pensive parting look they usually wear to my imagination, but all cheerful and benignant; warm with the hopes of that reunion in which I have placed so much of my earthly happiness. The day arose with increased beauty, the scenery was enchanting, and all nature smiled around me; my mind had over-wrought itself before, and was now settled into a calm, and overflowed with pleasing reflections; gratitude to my friends, and gratitude *for* such friends, inspiring a sublimer aspiration towards the great original source of pure affections and intellectual joys.

I shall not go into a minute description of places you have heard so much of, but content myself with saying, that this day's ride afforded more noble and pleasing objects than ever I met with in the same space of time; for you must remember that I went southward through Breadalbane; so all this is quite new to me. The rich and variegated country you pass through on leaving Perth, forms a fine contrast with that gloomy barrenness, and those frowning heights, that mark the entrance to the Highlands, far more savage than the interior, where the green-wooded vales, which open towards Dunkeld, relieve the eye, and the ear is soothed with the deep distant sound of streams "that wander not unseen" through these dark retreats. Dunkeld has a singular air of romantic grandeur,* derived from its wild situation, the remains of antiquity round it, and the soothing gloom of its fine woods, which abound in weeping birch, drooping its pensile branches, and sighing to every wind. These are contrasted by large solemn firs, that stand unmoved, in sullen dignity,

* The Cathedral of Dunkeld, though ruinous, is still a fine object: the chancel and choir remain, and still are used as a place of worship.—(1807.)

amidst the fury of contending elements. You will think me very fanciful, investing plants with sentiment, but you may trust me, when I assure you I do not borrow from Harvey. The reverence I have for his character and intentions has made me often try to like his flowery style, but I never could succeed. I hope your efforts, too, like mine, being, I am sure, equally sincere, may prove more successful.

After leaving Dunkeld, you enter a wild, but not dreary country, in which the sun, looking upon Fascally "with farewell sweets," called my attention to "vales more soft than Arcady of old." The sweet winding stream of Argentine brought poor Strowan * to my recollection, with all his wanderings and hidings. If he were not such a sot, I should not think his life at all so unhappy as other people do. Poets have skill to complain, and, no doubt, feel acutely. But, if their own imprudence, and the cruelty of the world, did not drive them into corners sometimes, they would neither muse nor warble, nor taste the sweets of nature, so peculiarly their own. And, in the bustle of the world, they would run all the risks other people do, without the common defences of caution and suspicion. Now, this furnishes an excellent apology to the rich and powerful, for permitting the ingenious and highly-gifted children of nature to languish in obscurity; and accounts for their letting them starve in corners, while they themselves choose their associates among those whom delicacy and sensibility shrink from; the dull, the callous, and the servile. I am growing ill-

* Robertson of Strowan, the Poet, born 1670, and died 1749.

natured, and should have been better employed in telling you what a fine twilight scene this other princely seat of the Athol family forms, at this moment, opposite my window—

> "But now the fairy valleys fade,
> Dun night has veil'd the solemn view;
> Yet once again, dear parted *maid*,
> Meek Nature's child, again adieu!"

Letter XXXII.

TO MISS ISABELLA EWING, GLASGOW.

Fort-Augustus, June 5, 1778.

Now, my dear Isabella, as you have my letter from Inverness,* containing much weighty matter, it only remains to tell you, that I met my father, in the Governor's carriage, at the Fall of Foyers, vulgarly called the half-way house; and of joy there was abundance, which consoled me for parting in the morning with those dear creatures, Mr. and Mrs. Tod, and various other privations, one of which, though a fanciful, was to me a heavy one; for the delight I should have had in riding through the woods on the side of Loch Ness was so embittered by thoughts of how you would have enjoyed it; and then I was so teased with the affected rural taste of one of the Inverness beaux, who accompanied me, that I was tempted, like Phœbe's lover, in the song, to

> "Cry Sirrah! and give him a blow with my crook,"

* This letter has not been preserved.—Ed.

as he did to his dog Tray, for fawning when his lovership was out of humour.—Well, my father and I proceeded by ourselves, and, after much fair discourse, arrived here by tea-time, where I found Mrs. Newmarch and the Miss Campbells of Duntroon* waiting for me. I leave you to judge my feelings at meeting my dear mother, and finding myself safely and happily arrived among a circle of kind friends.

We have had a visit from the new married couple, who are, doubtless, oddly matched. "Speak ye who best can tell," whether sons of light or not, and inform us how this woman came to take that man, who is a good creature too; but her refinement, and her prospects, and her brother! She is the person whom Johnson mentions in his Tour, whom he met at Rasay, and again at her brother's house, in the Isle of Skye. She looks much up to that surly sage, and receives letters and presents of books from him.†

The eldest of the fair Argathelians‡ is really astonishing for womanly appearance; and I am told her genius, &c. I heard much of her at Perth. By all I hear and see, I have taken it in my head that she is a kind of female Quixote, but a very improvable subject; and when she begins to know the importance of

* Sisters of the late Colonel Sir Neil Campbell, who accompanied Bonaparte to Elba in 1814, as the British Commissioner. One of these ladies was afterwards married to the Rev. Mr. Grant of Duthil, Inverness-shire.—Ed.

† Mrs. Macpherson, the lady here alluded to, was daughter of the Rev. Dr. Macpherson, Minister of Slate, in Skye, well known by his Writings on Celtic Antiquities, and sister of Sir John Macpherson, Baronet, Governor-General of India in 1785. She had married, about this time, Mr. Macpherson, at Culachy, near Fort-Augustus, —Ed.

‡ Argathelians, natives of Argyllshire.

common duties, and the value of native elegance, and modest merit unaccompanied by talent; when she discovers that there is something in the world worth loving, besides virtue mounted on stilts, and genius soaring among the clouds; so benevolent a mind, brought down from these false elevations, may be the delight of her friends, and an ornament to society.

Here follows a list of worthies, to whom, in my name, you must say something tender, grateful, kind, and emphatic, according to the various characters you address, beginning always with Miss Pagan. . . . . . . By discharging these debts of love, you will make me easy. Then shall the soul of your friend rest in this *Limbus Patrum*, purifying, and refining to fit it for the society of those blessed, who inhabit Clydesdale, Cartside, and Kelvinside, and say their prayers in the dear land of my nativity. Adieu, collectively, ye worthies of Clydesdale! Farewell, individually, friend of my forlorn heart.

Letter XXXIII.

TO MISS ISABELLA EWING, GLASGOW.

Fort-Augustus, June 8, 1778.

My dear Isabella,

The joy of Christina's* meeting and mine passes description. Yet she is somehow melancholy, and for this there is some cause. She has too strong and

* Miss Christina Macpherson, who resided at Culachy, near the Fort, and was a very dear friend of the Author. Miss M.'s brother had, as already mentioned, lately married Miss Macpherson, a native of the Isle of Skye, and sister to Sir John Macpherson, Bart.

steady a mind, and is too constantly occupied to sink causeless. Her sister-in-law is, when in health, a well-bred, good-humoured woman; but so nervous, and those complaints recur so often, and are so fatal to the peace and to the temper of those afflicted with them, who are generally uneven and capricious. In her case this only shows itself in sudden attachments, and a great fondness for new favourites, and prejudices against others at first sight. I am at present a great favourite, but no ways desirous of cultivating that favour. I am not in a humour for studying tempers; the days are fast receding that saw me prone to admire, and to deck every one merely tolerable with a thousand fancied charms. Besides, I grow deaf to the lamentations of those who meet no person or thing that is right or upright. The new light that has flashed in on my mind, shows me that the evil lies often in the sweet sufferer's own downy bosom. Now I must not dismiss this "Sunbeam of the Isle of Mist," without telling you that she is formed like a nymph, moves like a grace, sings like a syren, and plays like a muse; in short, if she wore a mask, we should expect an angel; but, alas! where the loves and smiles were wont to live so amicably together, and play at hide and seek in dimples, their arch-foe, the small-pox, has exalted his repulsive trophies; and surely never was victory so complete.

Now here is enough of Culachy gossiping. But there are two new stars risen in our horizon, of whom I must say something. The eldest Miss Campbell, then, is a wonderful girl of her age, scarcely sixteen, has a fine understanding, seems good hearted, and has a turn for reflection, which, properly directed, might be a source of improvement and advantage to her. But her mind seems to have been in a hot-bed; everything is premature beyond the simplicity natural to that age. I cannot develope her; one minute I think I know her, and the next she is out of sight: I am sure she does not wish to deceive me, but so young a philosopher may possibly deceive herself. In the meantime she is much inclined to muse and warble, and would have me tune a responsive lyre; but her muse and mine are of a different family; hers is in waiting from dawn to twilight, and, moreover, "visits her nightly;" while my inspirations come like angel's visits, few and far between, and have for some time ceased entirely. Two or three times short answers have been forced out of me, all deprecating further solicitation. I send you two very comely efforts of hers. One stanza of my last shall serve as a sample:

The leisure hour, alone, the Muse requires,
The still retreat, to peace and virtue dear;
From vulgar eyes conceals her sacred fires,
But calls on heaven, and heaven-taught souls to hear.

But this hint is unavailing; and so are all my attempts at reformation; nothing, indeed, but woeful experience can reclaim wilful wit, though its ways are not ways of pleasantness, nor yet its paths peace. But it is a sad thing to want a mother, and be tost about among artificial characters, of whom I have seen so many, even in this retreat, that I sicken more and more for you and the other children of simplicity, in whom all my delights are placed. Adieu, my daisy, my violet, my all that is native and genuine! Fondly adieu!

LETTER XXXIV

TO MISS JANE EWING, (AFTERWARDS MRS. JAMES BROWN,) GLASGOW.*

Fort-Augustus, July 1, 1778.

My dear Jane,

Now that I am settled, and have leisure to be angry, I am out of all patience at not hearing from any of you this age. I had letters by Perth only once since I arrived. As for my trunk, it has been so well treated by your cousin, that it still remains peaceably, though the carrier be arrived. What to do or say, I know not, and far less, what to put on.

I lost a good conveyance for a letter, and that a letter to Lady Isabella, by going on a grand party of

* This lady, the younger sister of the Author's correspondent, Miss Isabella Ewing, was married in 1788, to James Brown, Esq., of Glasgow, whom she survived for many years. The Author maintained a warm friendship, and frequent correspondence, with this excellent friend, until her death at Glasgow in 1832. In the lately published "Memoirs and Correspondence" of Mrs. Grant, she thus expresses herself in a letter to a friend: "I write to you at present with a heavy heart, the recent death of a much-valued friend, Mrs. Brown, having severed a tie which subsisted above fifty years, without a shade of difference. The deeper and more frequent were my afflictions, the warmer was her sympathy, and the more anxious her endeavours to soothe and alleviate what could not be cured. Her husband, who had been called many years since from her solicitous tenderness, was a man of virtue and talents, with the finest taste and the kindest heart, and of manly sincerity and independence of mind. His warm attachment to me was very gratifying to his excellent wife, to whose sainted spirit I would fain pay a due tribute of applause, were I to indulge my own feelings."—*Memoirs and Correspondence*, vol. iii., p. 219. Mrs. Brown is survived by two sons, Robert Brown, Esq., and William Brown, Esq., both merchants in Glasgow.—(1845.)—ED.

pleasure on Loch Ness. There was the Governor and his new espoused love, who, by the by, is very well, considering, frank, and cheerful, and so forth; and there were the two Miss Campbells of Duntroon, blithe bonny lasses; and there was the noble Admiral of the Lake,* and his fair sister; and the Doctor, and another beau, whom you have not the honour to know. We went on board our galley, which is a fine little vessel, with a commodious and elegant cabin. The day was charming, the scene around was in itself sublime and cheerful, enlivened by sunshine and the music of the birds, that answered each other loudly from the woody mountains on each side of the loch. On leaving the Fort, we fired our swivels, and displayed our colours. On our arrival opposite Glenmoriston we repeated this ceremony, and sent out our boat for as many of the family as chose to come on board. The Laird himself, his beautiful daughter, and her admirer, obeyed the summons: they dined with us, and then we proceeded to the celebrated Fall of Foyers.

I had seen this wonder before, but never to such advantage. Strangers generally come from the high-road, and look down upon it; but the true sublime and beautiful is to be attained by going from the lake by Foyers House, as we did, to look up to it. We landed at the river's mouth, and had to walk up nearly a mile, through picturesque openings, in a grove of weeping birch, so fresh with the spray of the fall, that its odours exhale constantly. We arrived at one of the most singular and romantic scenes the imagination

* Captain Gwynn, of the Government yacht, attached to the Fort.

can conceive. At the foot of the rock over which the river falls is a small circular bottom, in which rises, as it were, a little verdant hillock of a triangular form, which one might imagine an altar erected to the impetuous Naiad of this overwhelming stream; this rustic shrine, and the verdant sanctuary in which it stands, are adorned by the hand of nature with a rich profusion of beautiful flowers and luxuriant herbage. No wonder, overhung as it is with gloomy woods and ăbrupt precipices, that no rude blast visits this sacred solitude; while perpetual mists, from the cataract that thunders above it, keep it for ever fresh with dewy moisture; and the "showery prism" bends its splendid arch continually over the humid flowers that adorn its entrance. Now, do not think me romancing, and I shall account to you in some measure for the formation and fertility of this charming little *Delta*. Know, then, that the nymph of the river Foyers, abundantly clamorous in summer, becomes in winter a most tremendous fury, sweeping everything before her with inconceivable violence. The little eminence which rises so oddly in "nature's softest freshest lap," was most probably, at first, a portion of rock forced down by the violence of the wintry torrent; and as the river covers this spot in floods, successive winters might bring down rich soil, which, arrested by the fragment above said, in process of time formed the altar I speak of. Along with this rich sediment left by the subsiding waters, are conveyed the seeds and roots of plants from all the varieties of soil which the torrent has ravaged; hence "flowers of all hues, and without thorn the rose;" at least I would expect flowers worthy of Paradise in this luxuriant recess. While you stand in this enchanted vale, there is nothing but verdure, music, and tranquillity around you; but if you turn to either side, abrupt rocks, and unsupported trees growing from their clefts, threaten to overwhelm you. Looking up, you see the river foaming through a narrow opening, and thundering and raging over broken crags almost above your head; looking downwards, you see the same river, after having been collected in a deep basin at your feet, rolling rapidly over steep rocks, like steps of stairs, till at last it winds quietly through the sweet peaceful scene at Foyers House, and loses itself in Loch Ness. Now, to what purpose have I taken up my own time and yours with this tedious description, which, after all, gives you no just idea of the place?

When we returned on board, our spirits, being by this time exhausted with walking and wonder, and talking and thunder, and so forth, began to flag. One lady, always delicate and nervous, was seized with a fit, a hysterical one, that frightened us all. I cut her laces, suppressed her struggles, and supported her in my arms during the paroxysm, which lasted nearly two hours. What you must allow to be very generous in the company, not one of them seemed to envy my place, or made the smallest effort to supplant me in it. We drank tea most sociably, however; landed our Glenmoriston friends, and tried to proceed homeward, but adverse fate had determined we should sup there too, and so arrested us with a dead calm four miles from home. Midnight now approached, and with it gloomy discontent and drowsy insipidity. Our chief took a fit of the fidgets, and began to cry Poh, poh; his lady took a fit of yawning; his little grandson took a fit of crying, which made his daughter take a fit of anger; the Doctor took a fit of snoring; even the good-natured Admiral took a fit of fretting, because the sailors had taken a fit of drinking. All of a sudden the Miss C.'s took a fit of singing, to the great annoyance of the unharmonious group; when I went on the deck, fell into a fit of meditation, and began to say, "How sweet the moonlight sleeps upon this bank." Indeed, nothing could be more inspiring; "now silvery calmness slumbered on the deep;" the moonbeams quivered on the surface of the water, and shed a mild radiance on the trees; the sky was unclouded, and the sound of the distant waterfall alone disturbed the universal stillness. But the general ill-humour disturbed my rising rapture, for it was now two o'clock, and nobody cared for poetry or moonlight but myself. Well, we saw the wind would not rise, and so we put out the boat, some growling, others vapid, and the rest half asleep. The gentlemen, however, rowed us home, and left the galley to the drunken sailors. You may judge how gaily we arrived!

I fancy Solomon had just returned from a long party of pleasure on the Sea of Tiberias, where one of his mistresses had the hysterics, when he drew the pensive conclusion that "all is vanity and vexation of spirit." Adieu! Affectionately yours,

A. M.

LETTER XXXV.

TO MISS ISABELLA EWING.

Fort-Augustus, July 26, 1778.

My dear Friend,

Governor Campbell's* family left this place on Monday, and we are all very melancholy, for we never shall see the worthy old veteran more. He has a complication of disorders, one alone of which would be enough to make life miserable. Yet one unused to such scenes cannot avoid surprise to see how those we love best can divert themselves and be very merry while we are in agony. I suppose I was more affected than other people merely because the scene is new to me.

My poetical correspondence, after which you inquire so kindly, has been somehow in a declining state, and is dying, if not already dead. It did not begin with me, and I think it will end with me. I wish I had kept copies for your amusement; but I have not, as yet, set so much value on anything of my own writing, as to preserve a duplicate. This indifference is not affected. I do not give myself airs of despising poetry; on the contrary, I not only love, but revere the Muse, as believing her the priestess of Virtue.

* Governor Campbell of Fort-George, who represented the family of Barcaldine in Argyllshire. He had been on a visit to Governor Trapaud of Fort-Augustus, who had married his sister, Miss Campbell, about a year previously. Governor C. died at Bath soon after his visit to Fort-Augustus.

Her sacred and boundless influence over the heart and the imagination, may, properly used, produce the happiest and noblest effects. Witty and profligate poets have, no doubt, perverted their talents to the worst purposes; but this only affects their contemporaries, for I do not believe they are ever read by the next generation. In the public opinion their productions rot and corrupt with their writers. Who cares now for the wits of Charles the Second's days?—or who would wade through their dunghills? But truth and nature are for ever new and delightful; in all the vicissitudes of time they hallow and preserve the very language in which they are written. Whoever is capable of being delighted by poetry, sees nature and virtue in fairer lights and brighter colours than others. But that reverence for the Muse, which arises from a conviction of her divine origin, and boundless influence, makes me touch the lyre with a trembling hand. Indeed, in my own case, as well as others, I feel a dread and remorse, as if writing without genius were something akin to prophesying without inspiration. But in this playful way of writing, merely for each others amusement, which one may call rhyming conversation, I feel less reluctance, because I know it is to die in the little circle where it was born.—Adieu, my dear friend; send me fireside intelligence, my chief delight.

A. M.

LETTER XXXVI.

TO MISS ISABELLA EWING.

Fort-Augustus, August 10, 1778.

My dear Friend,

I would willingly convey a share of all my pleasures to you; but then I fear you will have a bad bargain, by taking my pains into the account. Now I have a knack of adding other people's to my own stock, which will give you little profit from the transmission (may I call it) of my few wild, simple pleasures. You inquire of Mrs. Campbell?* But for the small-pox, she would have been very handsome, on a large scale. As it is, she is very comely, and possesses uncommon powers of pleasing; there is a masculine strength and dignity visible both in her figure and understanding. But she mingles such perfect ease, pliant attention, and constant good-humour with her dignity, that you respect her without being overawed. Her language is pure and elegant, and gives the idea of a woman of fashion, without the modish phraseology. Then you can easily discern that though she lives in the world and knows it, she thinks her own thoughts, and expresses them in her own words. . . . .
" The world is frantic—fly the race profane!" How often does this quotation occur to me, when I see

* Mrs. Campbell, sister to Sir John Sinclair of Ulbster, married to the Governor of Fort-George, and mother to the Countess of Caithness. She died many years since.—(1807.)

the struggles of vanity and avarice, and mark the end! Yet will these votaries of the world go on crying, "We are the people, and wisdom shall die with us;"—and they look upon us that love peace, and would eschew that world, as poor visionary recluses, without any desirable object of pursuit. I could find in my heart to give them back their pity with interest, and daily relish more your happy project, of being doubly blest in our single blessedness, in that same air-built cottage behind the hill. If we are as happy in it as we were last winter we may think our lot enviable. Indeed the incursions of the husband and bairns, which your sister resolves to have, will now and then disturb our tranquillity; but when they are gone, we shall put on our spectacles, and contemplate our lap-dog and parrot with new delight.

Talking of social ties and endearments, I am sure I get enough, and too much of them, without being bound in ties never to be broken. I wish I could make you sensible how close the ties of neighbourly kindness necessarily draw in these little places. Every one that is sorry solicits your sympathy, and every one that is sick claims your attendance, if it is supposed you have any kindness to spare. Their distrusts and quarrels with each other make every one fly to me with complaints against each other. This new married lady at C., too, has taken a most inconvenient fancy to me; and, like all other indulged invalids, cannot bear to have any of her fancies crossed; and so violent is her kindness while it lasts, that, betwixt her and one drooping soul or other (Mary Gwynn, not the least nor last), my very spirit is worn down with attending sick folks. Miss M'Culloch's sister bears heavier on my mind than any one of them. She is left by herself, her father and mother having gone to some medical wells, where, I fear, the good primitive man will die. I never passed such a confused summer; and my poor Christina Macpherson, that used to cheer my soul "with songs divine to hear," must be away too; and poor Pastor Fido* is also gone. The sweet evenings, and bright silent noons, that we three were wont to spend in tracing up the river Tarffe, and wandering and lounging by turns on Drimen Duie,† with our whimsical broken starts of conversation, as detached from the rest of the world, and as unlike it as the kids that played over our heads, rise to my memory like the music of other times. I would not grudge the absence of this nymph and swain, if they were as happy where they are; but I am sure they are not.

When shall I again dwindle into my dear insignificance?—A thousand things used to charm me when my mind was vacant and easy, which I cannot relish

* Pastor Fido, a playful name given to Mr. Grant, the companion of our walks; he was afterwards Minister of Laggan, and had then just gone to settle there.

† Drimen Duie, often mentioned in these Letters, is a very singularly shaped eminence, nearly three miles to the south of Fort-Augustus, in the deep woody recesses of Glen Tarffe. It projects forward with an angle, formed by opposing precipices on the opposite side of the Tarffe, from which it is divided by the river, which makes a quick turn round the base of this beautiful height, the summit of which is flat, and covered with verdure and flowers; while the steep sides are adorned with the most beautiful shrubs, and the opposite cavern reverberates every sound in such a manner, that music in this spot has a singular and fine effect. A beautifnl rocky basin in the Tarffe receives a small fall of water which descends from the lofty rock that bounds Glen Tarffe, half a mile below Drimen Duie.

now that these restless beings have disturbed me, by making me the depositary of their self-created troubles. This it is to live so plaguy near people, and meet with them continually: though neither estimable nor amiable, they get hold enough of one's affections to make one uneasy. Factions in miniature are like a swarm of musquitoes; they cannot kill you, but they tease you incessantly, buzz about your ears, and hinder your sleep. I wish I could communicate to them some of our "rapture for the Muse," to cure them of slander and captiousness. When I am Czarina of some new discovered region, one of my first edicts shall be, that every one of my subjects who is incapable of being amused in a rational and elegant manner, shall work hard from morning to night. And in this regulation I will consult the happiness of my said subjects,

> "Nor let their everlasting yawn express
> The pains and penalties of idleness."

I have now in my eye a person of plain common sense and much humanity, who, without a grain of literature, a scruple of taste, or an atom of fancy, contrives to be as busy as a bee, and as cheerful as a lark. The whole year round she rises early, regulates her family, and then sits down to work and to sing. When her own work is done, she works for her poor neighbours; does not care a straw whether she is praised or they are thankful, but goes on with the pure motive of doing good; without any gratification in view, but the mere joy of seeing the poor children look well in their new clothes. Thus she goes on. Never inquires what others are doing, unless she can help them; and never goes out of her usual routine, unless there is something unusually good to be done. And all this costs her no effort:

> "Her duties walk their constant round,
> Nor make a pause, nor find a void."

"If I was not Alexander, I would be Diogenes," said the hero of Macedon. If I were not "a muse-rid mop," I would be this serenely happy being, saith your friend.

You see what rural pleasures I am likely to enjoy! Will. Houston, sitting behind the counter between his day-book and his bible, tastes the sweets of summer more than I do.—"Daughter of winding Clutha! walk forth in the light of thy beauty, among the waving willows of Duchnafall. There let the breeze sigh among thy heaving locks, while thy white hand, thrown over thy trembling harp, awakes the memory of joys that are past. Then, in the bright stillness of noon, while the hunter pants wearied in the shade, and no sound is heard along the desert heath; let thy sister, who mourns solitary in a distant land, visit the musings of thy secret soul!" Think of me, who have not, since I came home, walked beyond the garrison or village, except indeed to Culachy,* and that was always in *quick time*. I have not once seen my Penseroso Grot, on the banks of the Lake, nor been in Thicket Island. My rural enjoyments are confined to a twilight or moonlight walk under our own trees; and there, indeed, I resume my wonted pleasure of contemplating the calm bosom of my own lake, the purest of mirrors, exhibiting a prospect awfully solemn and wildly mag-

* Culachy—the place of residence of Christina Macpherson; a beautiful farm, romantically situated at the opening of Glen Tarffe, about a mile from Fort-Augustus.

nificent; while the mountain-tops seem sleeping on its surface.

> "In truth I am a strange and wayward wight,
> Fond of each dreadful, and each gentle scene."

In this favourite scene of my meditations, many a glowing and pensive sigh is devoted to you. There, with other associates of my early days, your image comes full upon me, and I indulge in reveries that end in pain. Farewell, friend of my solitude!

Letter XXXVII.

TO MISS ISABELLA EWING.

Fort-Augustus, September 12, 1778.

My dear Soul!

I have been very agreeably engrossed for some days past. You know how closely Mrs. Sprott and I drew to each other, from similarity of taste and sentiments. She has corresponded with me since she came to Urquhart, and twice attempted to come up here, but was somehow hindered. A week ago I was confounded at receiving a letter from the *wee* advocate; your sister will tell you who that is. I demurred upon the occasion, with modest hesitation, and opened it with consternation, and no little trepidation, which caused a small palpitation; for I dreaded a declaration, too bold to be made by any in the nation, to merit that needs no more elevation, in a maid whose bright graces illume her dark station. But I found my mistake on more near observation; so, being ashamed of my supposed penetration, I saved my vanity by an evasion, and imputed his silence to deep veneration, which often accompanies great admiration. Were I not afraid of the imputation of pedantic affectation, I could make this clear by a learned quotation from M. T. Cicero's fortieth oration. Therefore, upon due deliberation, being moved by your vexation, beyond any other consideration, I must resume the thread of my narration for your further edification, and my thorough vindication, which concerns you as much as any relation; for scandal, you know, spreads like an inundation, and even your prudence and my moderation cannot always silence a false imputation, which would at least raise our indignation, though we bear greater evils with calm resignation. So be sure to exert yourself for my justification whenever you hear me blamed in mixed conversation; mention my virtues with great exaggeration, and my faults, if I have them, with some extenuation; for even vices admit of some palliation, except when they rise, by a fatal gradation, to a climax beyond all alleviation. A friend should never attempt aggravation; for though we live among a perverse generation, each of us may keep peace in our own habitation, and, by lying in bed, to escape observation, become worthy patterns for general imitation, and not sleep in the face of a whole congregation, which would afford Andrew great delectation. So I conclude, in hopes of your full approbation, for I am sure you must be tired of so many long words in rotation, as you always delight in concise abbreviation, as much as I do in fluent and diffuse narration, &c.

Well, but this letter from our *wee* friend meant nothing but to recommend to our attention the two brothers Sprott; one, my acquaintance through his mate, who, by his worth and engaging manners, can always recommend himself; the other, a bachelor brother of his, who is newly come home from India, not at all like his brother, but, I believe, a good kind of man. The brothers and the lady came purposely to spend a few days with us. We enjoyed each other exceedingly, and should have done so much more, had not other company interrupted us. Mrs. Sprott* improved upon me greatly; like Swift's Stella, she has lived in a circle of men and books, and has acquired certain peculiarities from so doing; yet she has a great fund of good-humour, and has a spirited ease in her manner that is very pleasing. She possesses genuine sentiment, and great sincerity; has a warm heart, and an excellent taste, which appears in her dress, furniture, books, &c., but more especially in her friends,—I was going to add, in her husband, but she, more properly, was *his* taste. I forbear to tell you how modest and amiable he is; I content myself with observing, that I never saw a husband whose behaviour to a wife pleased me so well. They would have induced me to go with them to Fort-George, where I had promised to go on a visit to Mrs. Campbell,† but I could not, being the week of our sacrament, which shortened their visit. . . . .

September 21st is come, and I have not gone to Stratherick, having been agreeably prevented by a

* Sister of the late Charles Grant, Esq., long Chairman of the India House, and M. P. for Inverness-shire. She was married to the late William Sprott, Esq., Solicitor in Edinburgh, who, with his brother, the late Mark Sprott, Esq., are referred to in this Letter.—(1845.)—Ed.

† The wife of the then Governor of Fort-George.

visit from a cousin; not P., but a married cousin, a great favourite. He will stay some days, which I rejoice at: I dearly love my relations when they are tolerable, and would fain blind myself when they are not. I have got much information from him with regard to our mutual friend, who continues to roll a stone up a hill with the usual success. He, indeed, seems born to a froward fate, if indeed it is not rather his folly than his fate. His late adventures are as singular as himself; but I will not swell this overgrown epistle with them. You ask if ever he and Pastor Fido met? He was a month here at the very time P. F. was in the gloomy humour I told you of; and their behaviour to each other was so haughtily cold on one side, so saucy and biting on the other! One never unbent from his haughty reserve, so far as to cast a glance at any of the kindred; only, on going away, he would look back to see if I were alive after all this. The other spared no reflections, and would barely allow him the advantage of a tolerable exterior; and was out of patience when I assured him P. F. wanted neither good sense nor good nature, though he did not think proper to spoil them with daily wear. At that time P. F. would think it beneath his dignity to rail at any one, but show his displeasure by a disdainful silence, when the object of it happens to be the subject of conversation.

I rejoice sincerely to hear of our dear Harriet's speedy recovery. The world cannot have too many like her, if her children resemble her.* Adieu, dear friend.

* Referring to Miss Henrietta Reid, to whom some of the Author's earliest Letters, in this collection, are addressed. Speaking of his

Letter XXXVIII.

TO MISS ISABELLA EWING, GLASGOW.

Fort-Augustus, October 3, 1778.

I have now to thank you for two of your kind letters since you returned from the Fairlie: but, before I advert to their contents, will carry on my narrative as usual. The day I sent you my last letter, I received one from Inverness, with an account of poor Mr. MacCulloch's death, which is a loss to society in general; but to this place, as well as to his own family, irreparable. He was a man of primitive simplicity of manners, and undeviating rectitude of principle; and discharged the duties of his useful, though humble station, with peculiar diligence and fidelity, and was, indeed, the principal bulwark of religion in this place since Mr. Grant left us; for our present pastor does not reside here. I was desired to communicate to

different correspondents in a letter to a friend in America, in 1809, who inquired as to their fate, Mrs. Grant says of Miss Reid,—"She being uncomfortably situated among relations very unlike herself, married, with their consent, early, but not happily. Her husband knew her worth, and did not want sense or integrity; but he was unfortunate in his temper, and most unfortunate in his affairs. He was an accurate man of business, but nothing that he touched could prosper. Much was done for him on her account, but a certain fatality rendered it impossible to serve him essentially. She was a perfect model of patient meekness, always suffering, never complaining; frugal, industrious, and preserving not the magnanimity only, but the dignity and delicacy of her mind through all exigencies. I, who could not serve her, found means, however, to make others do it;—every one earnestly desirous to attain an end, can do something. Her family, meanwhile, increased fast, and she was called to peace on the birth of her eleventh child."—*Letter to a Friend in America, 12th August* 1809.

the poor girls the loss they had sustained. I can give you no idea of the terror I felt at being forced to perform this task. Yet the scene was even beyond what I had feared. The widow was at the mineral wells where he died: so the poor souls were in a house by themselves, in a lonely place half-a-mile from the village, where scarce one of our circle had the humanity to go near them. Our family, and that at Culachy, were indeed the only exceptions. The pretty gentle creatures at the G——— have so much sensibility, (how that poor word is hackneyed!) "that they really cannot bear such scenes of distress; it is too much for their feelings, sinks their spirits," &c. So they prudently avoid everything that can wake in their hearts those emotions which certainly result from salutary impressions, and produce the best moral effect. The divine pattern of every excellence, who was a "man of sorrows, and acquainted with grief," set no such example.

"O for the sympathetic glow,
Which forc'd the holy tear to flow,
When, weeping over friendship's grave,
Even He forgot his power to save!"

My dear love, I beg you will join with me in despising this selfish, sordid kind of sensibility, for I am just now particularly angry with it. Dear soul, your too recent experience will teach you to judge, though others cannot, of the anguish and despair that overwhelmed these poor orphans. Poor indeed! for their whole dependence was their father's exertions. But they have a good and generous brother; and, what is better still, they have their father's good works, his prayers, and his example. They will not be left desolate. I never behaved worse; I had, I thought, resolved, and fortified myself in the best way I could, but in vain. Indeed, the scene was new to me; I never witnessed one of the kind, and it was the worse that I liked the poor sufferers so well. I wrought myself up to a forced composure; but when I told, as softly as I could, what every one else knew, the violence of their anguish was overpowering. I went up twice every day since to assist with their mourning, &c.; but got so much cold at last, with walking in wet weather, that I have been feverish and confined since; but I am beginning to mend.

I will not plague you with a detail of petty grievances, but tell you, in general, that I have been teased and plagued beyond sufferance with people of a very different description. . . . . . . To bear our share of the sorrows of our friends is a duty we are born to; we are the better for it. But to be worn out with the follies and absurdities of those who are incapable of friendship, is truly hard. Were I to wish myself anything but what I am, it would be a hedgehog. Happy creature! that can be all collected within itself, and there lie wrapped, indifferent and insensible to all that passes without. I have seen human hedgehogs; but those I do not envy, for they never unroll themselves. Now the genuine hedge-hog only does it occasionally, when it runs the risk of being injured; and so would I.

I suppose you have heard me speak of the brother of the new married lady at Culachy, who, at a very early age, and in the most honourable manner, has made a fortune in India.* He is an uncommon, indeed, I may say, an exalted character; one of those of whom Pope says,

> "Great souls there are, who, touch'd with warmth divine,
> Give gold a price, and teach its beams to shine."

I know you agree with me in taking a strong interest in valuable and singular characters, though not personally known to them. I shall give you a slight sketch of this estimable person's history: He has just left us, and is to return, on his way from his native island (Skye), to visit his sister; and we are daily entertained with anecdotes of him. His history includes his character. In the first place, he was a son of a worthy clergyman of the Isles, distinguished for his learning and abilities, and whose writings have thrown great light on the antiquities of his country.†

* * * * *

Now this is as pretty as fiction, and as true as history. It is inconceivable what good these small pensions, so judiciously distributed, have produced.

* Sir John Macpherson, Bart., the person here mentioned, is a well known and much esteemed character; who succeeded to the interim Government of India in 1785, on the return of Governor Hastings to England.—(1807.) In a letter to Mr. Hatsell of the House of Commons, the Author says, speaking of this gentleman,—"Had I a laurel, or rather civic crown to bestow, I know no head that would better become it than his. The much that I have said, and the more that I have omitted regarding him, is strictly true; and, besides esteem, I have a real affection for him on account of his liberal kindness to his old tutor, Mr. Evan Macpherson, affectionately mentioned in my published Letters as "the Prophet."—*Letter to John Hatsell, Esq., 20th February,* 1807.—Ed.

† The particulars of Sir John Macpherson's history were probably omitted on account of his being still living when these Letters were published in 1806. They would have been inserted in the present Edition, but the Editor could not recover the original letter.—(1845.)

They have cheered dejection, enlivened hope, and supported industry. Here is a man that makes more than a dozen families happy, at less expense than half a contested election would occasion. These small sure streams of bounty, that never dry up, do people more good than a large sum, which would put it in their heads to be proud and idle, and sit down to hatch imaginary wants. Whenever a shower of gold falls upon me, I certainly will go and do likewise. His wealth, the reward of scientific service, as one may call it, to a native prince, was not got in the common manner, and is just as uncommonly spent. Two hundred pounds, which he sent to be distributed among the poor of his father's parish, in the Isle of Skye, I had almost forgot to mention. Advert, that this is not done from the overflowing of an immense fortune; he is not rich in the Eastern acceptation yet. But, as Burnet says of Tillotson,

"He is rich in good works."

Excuse repetition and confusion. I tell you once more, the people hereabouts tease and harass me with their hollow friendship and undesired confidence; civilities that demand a return, and would extort gratitude, where there is neither principle or steadiness; and to devote your time where you cannot give your esteem, and then to have the only estimable person in the whole group injured and neglected by the rest; to see that estimable person sinking under a secret load of heart-breaking sorrow, which I cannot alleviate, and must not seem to know; how vexatious! My dear creature, you know nothing of the strife of human passions. It is here they rage and swell, and are seen in their full magnitude. Confined to a few objects, and within a narrow circle, their agitation is more violent, and their effects more visible. From the dreadful effervescence of idleness and malignity fermenting together, may all I love be preserved! The last is a most profound and mysterious sentence; but if I ever see that blessed sight, your face, I will give you a very full explanation of it, which will make you wonder at least, if not cross yourself.

I turn to a more pleasing subject, the contents of your letters. I am glad you were so well entertained at the Fairlie* by my old acquaintance "Clarissa Harlowe," and your new acquaintance Mr. Monteith. I observe you frequently preferred the company of the former to the latter, and am pleased to find you so partial to my favourite heroine. Never, surely, were characters so well drawn, discriminated, and supported as those in Clarissa;—her own in particular. Never was anything so uniformly consistent, so raised above common characters, and yet so judiciously kept within the bounds of nature and probability. I know very well there are those who, from a very indelicate species of delicacy, object to the conduct of the story in certain instances. Those who can, in the midst of such distress as hers, withdraw their minds from contemplating the trials of a suffering angel, to pollute their imaginations, are very unworthy indeed to be admitted into even the ideal presence of a Clarissa. I know not any criterion by which I should be readier to judge and

* "The Fairlie" is a watering place below Largs, on the coast of Ayrshire, nearly opposite to the Isle of Bute.

try any one's character and taste, than by observing with what degree of interest and feeling they survey this correct drawing from nature. You cannot think with what scorn I listen to little misses, and *very little* masters, who tell us, in parrot phrase, "Nobody reads Clarissa now; people *now* think it languid and tedious." Just as if the effect of good sense, wit, humour, pathos, and, in short, pure Christianity, could vary with the hour, like fleeting modes and manners. Ranting tragedies, written while rant was fashionable; or vile comedies, where wit and talents are lavished in painting manners which happily no longer exist: these, I say, may go out of fashion; but truth is immutable, and nature, if you will bear a quibble, has invariably the self-same variations. Who, then, would affect to despise a clue that leads through all intricacies to her inmost recesses, because the thread of which it is composed is very fine, very long, and artfully twined of many filaments? The means are proportioned to the end. The story, no doubt, unfolds slowly; yet every sentence answers the great end of bringing the actors in the scene so immediately before your eyes, that you seem to have known and lived with them. The approach is long, but it is to a noble object, and the avenue is planted with such endless variety of flowers, both pleasing and useful, that you must be dull and incurious indeed, if you stop or linger by the way. I know nothing, out of the Volume of Inspiration, equal to the death-bed of Clarissa. I feel the effect always new; wrapped in the delusion of this overpowering fiction, I have dreamed, as the Patriarch did at Luz, that I saw angels ascending and descending. Generally in every story, real or fictitious, the interest ceases with the life of the hero or heroine. But, in this instance, we hover over the vault, and trace every circumstance relating to the departed saint, with fond veneration.

Yet, after being so partial to our own sex, as to allow Clarissa to be a natural character, we may be so just to the other, as to suppose Lovelace carried almost beyond possibility. A man could not exist, who, to so fine an understanding, such courage, wit, generosity, and talents, could unite so much cunning and cruelty, folly and villany. The author has, however, so far preserved probability, as to make him act and speak as such a being would do, if any being could unite such contradictions. Modern history, indeed, refutes my wise conclusions, by presenting us with an almost similar character, Lord Bolingbroke, whom Pope distinguishes by the epithet of all-accomplished St. John; he addressed his Essay on Man to him, and speaks of him on all occasions with the most enthusiastic admiration. Swift does almost the same; and Chesterfield, who only saw Bolingbroke in extreme old age, when he might be thought to have outlived his talents and his graces, was yet dazzled with his person and address; and talks of him as the complete model of a finished fine gentleman, as to manners, conversation, and eloquence. Yet this man, after running into the most violent excesses in libertinism, and prostituting his fine talents to serve the meanest and most corrupt ends of a party, without reforming his innate vices, had turned them into a more dangerous channel, by endeavouring to undermine those principles which the tenor of his life had disgraced. Still he had, after all, the art to persuade even the virtuous Pope, and that all-observing cynic Swift, of his sincerity and rectitude; and this merely by the force of eloquence, shining parts, and a kind of constitutional something, that passed for generosity and good nature. Thus, without a heart, without truth or morals, this man was enabled to captivate and do mischief, not only all his life, but even after death. The deistical writings he left behind were not the result of self-conviction, or a desire to convince others, but the mere vanity of exploring the trackless wastes of speculation, of overthrowing established opinions, and thus creating a region in which to rule. It was like Satan's expedition in search of some domain, where he might exercise power, and produce misery. . . . . I do not know what tempted me to wade so far out of my depth after Lord Bolingbroke, but you wish me to say all that comes in my head, and you must take the consequences. Farewell, affectionately!

Letter XXXIX.

TO MISS ISABELLA EWING.

Fort-Augustus, November 14, 1778.

My dear Friend,

Your letter from Stirling is not arrived. I have desired this bearer, who passes through that ancient city, to call for it, and send it by Edinburgh. It is very childish to say that the perusal of your letters makes so much of my happiness; but in this deserted place there is so much mistrust, so much serious trifling, such a dearth of the language of truth, of nature, and the affections, that they are "the sunbeams" of my soul, and I count the intervals between them impatiently.

I must pique you into punctuality by telling you I have a more witty and eloquent correspondent. Though I cherish your "retiring softness" with perverse preference, I am tempted to transcribe some original poetry from her last letter, because it is the prettiest I have seen her write, and not because I am the subject. Read this "Address to Memory."

* * * * * * * *

Our *Drimen Duie* friend is still indisposed: what if he should walk off to the Elysian fields without ceremonious leave-taking? I think it were as well to take the female Quixote's way, and send him word that he may live if he pleases. If raillery could relieve anxiety, it were well; and if diseases in real life would yield to the sympathy of friendship, it were also well. I keep my indignation at all the offenders here within very moderate bounds; for I only preserve my serenity; that is, when they would be jocose and familiar, as formerly, I look grave, and pretend not to understand them. For Mrs. Newmarch's sake, I carry my righteous wrath no farther.—Why do you desire me to burn your letters, while you so religiously preserve mine? You can have no motive for this, which I have not in a higher degree for keeping the pictures of your soul. I have cut all the leaves out of a great old goose of a book, and there I have placed those pretty pictures in regular succession; with Miss Ourry's, and Mrs. Sprott's. Cousin Jean's letters, which I value much for the vein of original humour that runs through them, are there too: so are some of Beattie's poems. You cannot think how diligently I peruse this good book. "Watts on the Passions" is not dearer to you; for, as warm as he is in your work-bag, do you think your paper-bag of epistles can ever lift its head in competition with my great book? No; it has too much respect for its betters, and has learnt from me the doctrine of gradations. To counteract the vile influence of the vile world, I am always sending you some true story of good deeds performed, or good souls acting or suffering, from my Alpine nook. (I do not mean the Fort.)

Did you ever know so good a creature as Sandy the primitive? See now, he insists on his mother and his sisters coming to live with him, and means to support the whole family in ease and abundance. Is it not like Joseph sending for his brethren—and Joseph, too, was a factor. You may suppose the good blind Duke to be Pharaoh, if you please; and, to complete the resemblance, the Highlanders are all herdsmen, and the vulgar in the Low Country hold them in abomination. It just now occurs to me, why, in a country so near as England, and even in one so assimilated as Ireland, Scotch manners are so little understood. They never write a page on these subjects without making some blunder, which to a Scotchman seems very ludicrous. This comes from confounding the peculiarities, dialect, &c., of the Highlanders with those of the Lowlanders, the two most dissimilar classes of beings existing, in every one particular that marks distinction; the former, indeed, are a people never to be known unless you live among them, and learn their language. Smollet, in Humphrey Clinker, is the only writer that has given a genuine sketch of Scotch manners; and in what relates to the lower class of Highlanders, even he appears allowably ignorant, not knowing their language, and having left the country so young, that he was in a great measure a stranger to the Highlands, though born a borderer on it. The Highlanders are Celts, as Pinkerton in the bitterness of his soul calls them. Now I and my ancestors are genuine Britons, who, retiring with surly independence before the red eye of the King of the world, and his imperial eagles, made the strength of rocks ours, snuffed like wild asses at the voice of the pursuer, and still retain "the garb of old Gaul, and the fire of old Rome." As for you, good sober souls of Clydesdale, and all other dales, sung by the Pastoral Muse, your ancestors were good plain Saxons; who, begging to be excused from any particular intimacy with Danish ravens, and Norman leopards, and all foreign birds and beasts, came northward to shelter under the Scottish fir, and wear for their badge the self-righted Scottish thistle. If proofs were wanting, Shakspeare supplies abundance. King John's cooks and footmen, it is evident, spoke much the same language with the caddies* of Edinburgh; and any of us, who have taste to relish Shakspeare, understand readily terms that have puzzled all his southern commentators. In short, you dwellers of the dales, in manners, cookery, &c., are just what the old English were in the days of the rival Roses. I have been

* Street-porters.

greatly amused at hearing an unfledged English Ensign pour contempt upon our good national barley broth, in almost the very terms used by the Constable of France in deriding the heroes of Agincourt:

> "Can sodden water
> (A drench for sur-rein'd jades), their barley broth,
> Decoct their cold blood to such valiant heat!"

Now, pray do not forget to lodge this discussion and quotation in your paper-bag, where much digression and excursion already dwells. To return to Sandy the primitive, the deserving hero of my tale:—he will at length so colonize the banks of the unrivalled Lake, that the prophetic Valkyria may once more say,

> "Those whom late the desert's beach
> Pent within its bleak domain,
> Soon their ample sway shall stretch
> O'er the plenty of the plain."

Adieu, and do not be angry at me for making you "Look into the pit, whence thou wast digged; into the hole of the rock, whence thou wast taken;"* though a more exalted origin is claimed by your high descended and high minded friend,

A. M.

* A scriptural expression by which the Prophet reminds the Israelites of their origin. This the Author applied here to her friend's Saxon descent.

Letter XL.

TO MISS ISABELLA EWING.

Fort-Augustus, April 5, 1779.

My dear Friend,

These promises are very fine, and I suppose generally made on such occasions, but I have no wish for any such homage. I never desire or hope for more confidence, tenderness, or attention, than you and I have shown towards each other. Indeed I expect not even to taste the sweets of a more perfect union of minds. I am neither surprised or chagrined at what you tell me of people's notion, that my supposed attainments will disqualify me for ordinary duties; that is, for discharging them with diligence and propriety. I shall always think myself obliged to you for every information of this kind, without the least desire of knowing from whom it comes. It is very natural, and perfectly allowable, if one is charged with any matter of fact which one knows not to be true, that every means should be immediately used to disprove it. But when we merely hear of those vague and general censures, which we constantly, and often justly, pass on each other, instead of a hot and hasty vindication, we should endeavour to profit by this indirect instruction, and remove the pretexts of blame. These good people only think of me what I have often thought of myself, that I am not well qualified for the constant exertion, self-command, and caution requisite in a married life. There is no passion implanted in the mind but for some good purpose ; vanity for instance. Now I think there is nothing I should be so vain of as the conquest of my own habits, and other people's prejudices. To excel in a sphere that is thought beyond me, would be a proud boast indeed. Whatever one bends one's whole mind to, there is some chance of excelling in. But time must decide ; and, in the meantime, I must hope and endeavour. I may be rash or indolent, but, on the other hand, I am pretty easy, being sensible I am not so obstinate, opinionated, and self-loving, as pretenders to literature among our sex are generally said to be. I give you no directions. Suppose yourself a bride, and apply the money as far as it will go.

As to what has been said of what I have written, I am far, far from assuming the least merit upon it. But this I am very proud of, that, possessing from infancy that glow of imagination, and facility of expression, which the owners are so apt to mistake for genius, I have written so very little. That little, too, was thrown off in such a careless manner, as made it evident that I had not given much time or thought to it. In the meantime, I send two poetical pieces for your amusement, merely to have them out of the way of more serious concerns. One is from my fanciful correspondent, that you wot of; I think it her best; perhaps I am the more partial to it, knowing the subject to be real. I knew the young lady who is the theme of this tale of sorrow. She died last winter, in the twenty-third year of her age, a victim to the struggle betwixt duty and attachment in a delicate and well-principled mind. Her conduct, though imprudent, was perfectly innocent. But she was every way delicate, her feelings nursed by indulgence, and all made of tenderness and music. It is cruel to bring up anybody so very helpless. I will tell you all about her in my next. The Ode to Hygeia was written by your friend, and intended for Mrs. Sprott, who has long been urging me for something of the kind.

How happy it is, since I am destined to forsake a place so dear to me, that the ties are loosened that held me to it :

> " The shades, the streams, the groves remain ;
> But friendship there I seek in vain."

One by one, everybody that I cared for, dropped off, and I saw nothing around me but dreary vacuity. We shall see what kind of a world the odd beings, so peculiar in tastes and opinions, will create amid the central mountains.* No people, however, have their happiness so much in their own power as we may have, if we were not so much in the region of tempests. We may, perhaps, be obliged to go to a cave, like Ajut and Aningait.—With love to your dear sister, believe me ever yours.

Letter XLI.

TO MISS ISABELLA EWING.

Fort-Augustus, April 18, 1779.

My dear Friend,

When I finished my last, I meant to begin another directly, but was prevented by indisposition. I am

* Alluding to her approaching marriage, and removal to the Highlands of Inverness-shire.

now, thank God, much better. My grandmother's death, which happened in the beginning of last week, has occasioned my being in a perpetual hurry ever since, with mournings, &c. She has been thought dying for half a year past. The days of her pilgrimage were neither few nor evil (comparatively speaking); she was above fourscore years upon earth, doing all the good that singular activity and benevolence, directed by very sound sense, could enable her to perform in her contracted sphere: and in consequence of this constant exertion, and the general good will it excited, she was always cheerful, and very resigned in affliction. She departed, in her eighty-first year, full of hope and comfort, with a full confidence in the merits of her Divine Redeemer; and the looking back on a well-spent life, supported her in the hour when all other dependence fails. She retained a singular freshness of complexion, and evident remains of that beauty for which in her youth she had been distinguished.* Few have met with severer trials than this worthy person had to struggle with. The family from which she sprung, and the principal ones with which she was connected, were unhappily involved in the fatal error (I must call it, for they, surely, acted on

* The Author's maternal grandmother, here referred to, was a daughter of Stewart of Invernahyle, an ancient house of the Appin Stewarts, in Argyllshire. The Baron of Bradwardine, in the novel of Waverley, is said by Sir Walter Scott to have had his prototype in Alexander Stewart, Esq. of Invernahyle, who fought in the battles of Prestonpans and Culloden, and was afterwards well known to Sir Walter. This Laird of Invernahyle was granduncle of the Author, that is, the brother of her grandmother, whose death is recorded in the above letter. See farther as to Invernahyle, Note subjoined to Letter IX. of this volume.—(1845.)—Ed.

mistaken principle); well, the error, the blunder, the mischance of 1715 and 1745; and her house was crowded with the orphan children of her sisters and other relations. This tried her feelings, and wasted her little possessions severely; but still she was cheerful, and thought it all well bestowed. It is astonishing what good a superior mind can do, in any situation of life, providing (and be it always provided) that they walk straight on in the path of practicable duty, and do not "waste their strength" in the "strenuous idleness" of spinning systems, and dreaming dreams, and seeing visions of conferring great benefits, when they should, by vigorous exertions, like those of my grandmother, enable themselves to pour forth a series of small yet essential ones. Now peace be with thy liberal spirit, my grandmother! and peaceably mayst thou rest with thy fathers in that green and sea surrounded Isle, where, undisturbed by the sons of little men, or the spades of venal sextons, so many of thy race rest in social slumber.* Oh, to be buried in one of those sanctified islands, where no little boys jump over grave-stones, or no great ones trample over the hallowed dead with callous indifference! It is hard to leave this sacred asylum of the warrior and the hunter, over which the Æolian tones of airy harps

* Referring to the beautiful little island of St Munde, situated in Loch Leven, Argyllshire, near the place where the river Co, after issuing from the celebrated Glen-Co, discharges itself into the Loch. Here, the Appin Stewarts (the Author's maternal ancestors), and the inhabitants of Glen-Co, have long buried their dead, and continue to do so, amid the ruins of a chapel which formerly stood on this island. The proprietors have lately planted the Isle of St Munde, which will soon add to the beautiful and romantic character of the place.—(1845.)—Ed.

sound to the passing blast, while the midnight rowers glide by in solemn silence; but as we must stay in the great island of Magna Britannia a while longer, " and in this harsh world draw our breath in pain," we must refresh our spirits with the best things we meet in it.

Now as I am in the humour of telling stories, and take it for granted that you are in the humour of listening to them, and as female friendship, that stands the test of time and his fellow-traveller adversity, is one of the best things this untuned sphere affords, I shall tell you something I have had often in my mind, and as often forgot to amuse with. You must have heard of Mrs. Buchanan, and the poor contemptible, whom her friends persuaded her to marry, when she was a mere child incapable of choosing; but perhaps you have not heard that this laird had before paid his addresses to her cousin, the beautiful and accomplished Miss Lucy Campbell of Glenure, who refused him in favour of Mr. Cameron of Fassfern, in this country, a man every way worthy of her. It was this disappointment which led the " Lowland laird" to seek an alliance with his present wife, with whom he lived but a few months, his outrageous follies and her inexperienced and rash attempts to restrain them, occasioning an irreconcileable difference. They separated, and " the laird," who was no niggard, allowed her such an annuity as would enable her to live genteelly anywhere. From her youth, and natural love of society and the world, every one thought she would live in the capital; but this, and every scheme of what is called enjoying life, was prevented by her strong attachment to her cousin, Lucy Campbell, above mentioned. Indeed, to use Shakspeare's words on a similar occasion,

> "Their loves
> Were stronger than the natural bond of sisters;"

which their former rivalship in Buchanan's affections had never diminished: and whenever Mrs. Buchanan got in some measure free from the matrimonial yoke, she went to live with her cousin. Mr. Cameron's abode, in a sequestered Highland glen, much retired, and surrounded with a fast increasing family, and with the endless cares of a country life, could have few attractions for a very young lady, to whom all this was new and foreign. Yet, actuated by the spirit of heroic friendship, she forsook the world, and secluded herself from what are usually looked on as the pleasures of it, on her cousin's account, whose tender gratitude you may imagine. In this singular and happy union they lived above seven years. About the time I was in Glasgow with you, Mrs. Cameron died on the birth of her sixth child. Her cousin, though overwhelmed with sorrow at this melancholy event, did not seek for comfort by returning to the world, or to her other friends. She has taken the charge of her cousin's family, and is to her children the most anxious and tender of mothers; and to this painful duty she has devoted the best years of her life, in this remote place, occupied by cares, that nothing less than necessity, or a mother's feelings, could induce any one to undergo. I do not know whether you will view this in the same light, but I think it the most affecting and heroic instance of true friendship I have met with in real life. One cannot help comparing it with the lively and impressive portrait Rousseau draws of Clara and Eloisa. I wonder if there is any such friendship among men. Their way of showing friendship is to venture for each other those lives which they are so apt to squander in duels; but where was friendship, among them, ever so persevering, so graceful, and so tender? Much good may their stern virtues, and their public virtues, and their shining virtues, do them; while ours, that flourish in the shade, are their consolation, and the chief blessing of society after all. I am sure I neither envy their turbulent pleasures, or dear-bought honours. But we must not speak treason of our protectors.—Adieu, friend; can I call you anything dearer or kinder?

Letter XLII.

TO MISS OURRY, IRELAND.

Laggan, Inverness-shire,
August 5, 1779.

My ever dear Nancy,

You have indeed fully made up for your past seeming negligence, and, what I once thought was impossible, you have really got beyond me in attention and kindness. Yet do not too soon overvalue yourself, and distrust me, on the strength of this great effort; I refer you to my past punctuality, and hope to convince you further by future steadiness. Without preamble or circum-round-about, I will satisfy the anxiety you express about the hints in my last. Know, then, that I was at that time engaged in preparations for an event (to me very important) which took place the following day.* It is very odd that our letters, containing intelligence so interesting, should thus have crossed each other. I am no longer my own, and yet I will be always yours. I have not formed a connection that will chill my affections, or contract my heart. I share all your sorrows as you recite them, and still am most uneasy at the effect which your too acute feelings must have on a constitution so delicate as yours. But you have a weighty duty yet demanding your attention. You will find comfort to yourself in administering it to your remaining parent. The sublime and solid consolations which true religion and right reason afford, are all your own; and, though well assured that there is indeed

> "No pang like that of bosom torn
> From bosom bleeding o'er the sacred dead,"

yet I trust those truths, which claimed so much of your attention in your gayest and most prosperous days, will support you in your heaviest hours.

It remains now to tell to whom I have made the greatest of all possible sacrifices. It is to a Reverend acquaintance of yours, whose name you will find at the conclusion of this. The change, so important to me, happened in the end of May last. After staying near two months at the Fort, and wandering many hours every day through our old delightful haunts, to "talk the flowing heart," and compare past conjectures and meditations, we have at length taken up our residence in the Pastor's cottage, which is literally

* The Author was married on 29th May, 1779, to the Rev. James Grant, Minister of Laggan, Inverness-shire, who has been occasionally mentioned or referred to in previous letters.—Ed.

pastoral. Here we have since continued; not enjoying the ideal felicity of romances, but that rational and attainable degree of happiness which is derived from a sincere and tender mutual esteem, health, tranquillity, and an humble and grateful consciousness of being placed in a situation equally remote from the cares of poverty and the snares of wealth, from pinching, want, and languid unenjoyed superfluity. You know, of old, my notions of matrimony, and how meanly I thought of the usual degree of happiness enjoyed by those who enter into willing subjection. This has proved an advantage to me, as I had no sanguine expectations to be disappointed; and, contrary, I suppose, to what happens to most people in similar circumstances, find more of the complacency and attention of the lover in the husband than ever I expected. We were indeed much mistaken in the character of our friend; he has neither the tranquillity nor the indifference we gave him credit for. Wrapt up in his natural reserve, and a restraint arising from some very particular circumstances, he baffled our penetration. Would you think it, he is generous, impetuous, and singularly acute in all his feelings. His delicacy is extreme; and he has as nice and jealous a sense of honour as any Spaniard whatever.

I once more cordially thank you for your last kind letter, which, by the by, does not satisfy me as to what you are about, and whether you think to remain in Ireland. I confess myself surprised at your staying there so long. Mr. Grant begs to be cordially remembered to you. Offer my affectionate respects to your good mother, and believe me most kindly, most truly yours,

ANNE GRANT.

LETTER XLIII.

TO MISS ISABELLA EWING, GLASGOW.

Laggan, August 24, 1779.

My dear Friend,

I observe, with shame and concern, that I am so far fallen behind, that it is necessary for me, in the mercantile way, to acknowledge "your several favours duly received," namely, two from Edinburgh and one from Glasgow; besides one which I find is on the way, and daily, eagerly, I assure you, expected.

You see where I am by the date of this letter. It is a month since I came, accompanied by my father and the awful man who tied the fatal knot. Christina Macpherson, our old associate on Drimen Duie,* was also here. They said they came to see whether "the said knot sat easy on the bound," &c. So these good folks departed after assisting us to receive some ceremonious visitors, and left us to ourselves. Now, it is time you should know who *ourselves* are. Know, then, that Mr. Grant's mother was in the house with him; remember, I have notified this in form, and expect additional congratulations on that account, for I should have been lost and bewildered on my entrance on such a new scene, as the govern-

* A hill near Culachy, above Fort-Augustus.

ment of more than half a dozen country-servants, and the complicated economy of a farm, without such a monitress. You will not wonder that I am already very fond of my mother-in-law, when I tell you she is just what our dear Harriet Reid will be thirty years hence, in mind and manner; and an expression in the faded beauty of her countenance that one might be tempted to call heavenly: such eyes you never saw in a head that one may call a fine antique. It would fatigue you to describe the gauntlet we ran of visitation and re-visitation; though it might give room for a farther display of my picturesque manner of conveying characters to you by comparison and analogy, I cannot as yet enlarge. My neighbours, the wild braes of Badenoch considered, are more than tolerable; some of them rise to agreeable, and some soar up to very agreeable. This accounts for much of my time. The weather, too, has been so very fine, the lord of the cottage is so fond of walking, and I am so fond of accompanying him through the pleasantest of all meadows which surround us, that much time is wasted in that way; then there are the cares of a family, of which family I am hitherto very careless, but care will come too soon; then the early mornings are no longer mine, because, alas! I am no longer my own. Yet you shall always find me most affectionately yours,

A. G.

Letter XLIV.

TO MISS ISABELLA EWING.

Laggan, July 12, 1781.

My dear Friend,

Ever pleasing and acceptable as your kind, kind letters are to me, your last was doubly so, arriving as it did most opportunely, "to cheer the heavy hours obscured by pain," and suggesting the comforting idea of your being not only in health, but in better spirits than I have known you for some time past.

I am tired of quaint devices, and quite of your mind as to that of your ring. It shows the utmost humility, in the first place; and I am so far from thinking with Jane, that it betrays a poverty of invention, that I am charmed with its simplicity. A pretty fanciful motto might apply to anybody, but A. G., that significant cypher, is I myself, I; and the laurel wreath inclosing it, may mean the perpetual verdure of friendship, or my invincible courage, when I used to protect you from those cows whose armed foreheads used to fill you with such tender fears, pretty coward that you are! Were this memorial embellished with such fine sentences as you and I could easily make or steal, vanity and friendship might have equal claims; but now it is an unequivocal offering to the sweet social power that has smiled so long upon us. I am glad the fashion of despising things, common and easily attained, is so prevalent; infidelity and licentiousness will soon lose the charms of novelty and singularity, they will be so despicably common; and religion and common sense will add lustre to their own weight, and be sought after as respectable oddities, at least.

I enjoy, in your description, the entertainment you received on the bank of Carron's sounding stream, where Oscar, King of Spears, rose bright in arms to curb the King of the World, and made the Roman eagles stoop before the race of Morven. Time has been when the "light of my soul arose" at the name of this young hero, so long deplored by Malvina, so mourned by the sweet voice of Cona.

Receive your parcel, all but the poems; these, being copies, and you possessed of the originals, I keep till you reclaim them. I am charmed with the freedom, ease, and gaiety, which reigned in your little society at Arran, and which has not passed uncelebrated, or unsung. The Laureat of Arran seems to wear his bays with becoming carelessness, and rather to laugh at than value himself for having them. He certainly possesses original genius, and a vein of humour not extremely refined, but genuine, easy, and Fergusonial. He has made his dog very eloquent, and, like another talking animal of old renown, he reproves the madness of his master with justice and severity.

How could it enter into that adamantine heart of yours to keep me so long in suspense about a matter that concerns me so much to know? As for lovers, they are a generation born to be teased; but me you shall still tease no longer. Have you no compassion on the fatigues of my imagination, drawing numberless pictures of my friend that is to be? On pain of my displeasure, let his name, age, and complexion, be immediately forthcoming; "let me not burst in ignorance, but tell me:" I will not whisper it to the rushes. In hopes of your speedy compliance, I remain yours as you demean yourself.

Letter XLV.

TO MISS ISABELLA EWING, GLASGOW.

Fort-Augustus, Nov. 6, 1781.

My dear Friend,

From this "region of silence and shade" I thought to have written at length and at leisure: but leisure so often slighted I now vainly solicit. I have been so engrossed by visitors, and engaged with preparing, for the loom, the purple and fine linen which my maids have been spinning in the glens all summer, that I have not so much as wandered on the Loch side, or lounged in the garden since I came here. This last is now withered, but to my fancy it was so a month ago. I look at it as I suppose divorced people do at each other, when a little lurking love remains. I must forsake it, and all I love here, before nature opposes her irremeable bar. You will think I am talking very solemnly about travelling the twenty-five miles between this and Laggan; for I do not know that ever I told you how peculiarly we are situated with regard to each other. This district is divided from ours by an immense mountain, called Corryarrick. That barrier is impassable in the depth of winter, as the top of it is above the region of clouds; and the sudden descent on the other side peculiarly dangerous, not only from deep snows concealing the unbeaten track of the road, but from whirlwinds and eddies that drive the snow into heaps; besides an evil spirit which the country people devoutly believe to have dwelt there time out of mind.

I was rather urgent in requesting permission to make this visit, because my little daughter is here, who loves me and smiles on me irresistibly, and whom I must needs leave as a substitute for myself;* and then I resolved to enjoy the last fading gleams of Autumn here, and embrace my dear parents before I should be separated from them all winter by this dreadful barrier. The society is varied by some new characters; not military ones, but just such harmless, good-humoured people as one takes pleasure in pleasing, and leaves without a pang. My mate has chosen this time to visit his Strathspey friends. I am beginning to be on the spur homeward; snow is now beginning to fall; but though I should "ride on clouds and skies," I must get home immediately.

Now, I will give you a sketch of our situation at Laggan, and you will say it is time. After ascending this awful mountain, we travel eastward through twelve miles of bleak inhospitable country, inhabited only by moor-fowl, and adorned with here and there a booth, erected for a temporary shelter to shepherds, who pass the summer with their flocks in these lonely regions. On leaving this waste, you enter a vale six miles in length, and half a mile broad, which wants nothing but wood to be beautiful; it has indeed some

* The Author's eldest daughter, Mary, is here alluded to. She was born at Laggan, 8th May, 1780.—Ed.

copses, or what the Scottish bards call *shaws*. This vale consists entirely of rich meadow and arable land, and has the clear and rapid Spey running through the middle of it. About the centre of this vale, at the foot of a mountain which screens it from the north wind, stands our humble dwelling; just such a cottage as that at Greenlaw, only higher, admitting of attic chambers for you to repose in. You will wonder we have not the good house to which the Pastor's office entitles him. That should be built on the glebe, and can be nowhere else, and this glebe is a nook which none but a hermit would inhabit. Then we are so far from market, that, unless the ravens were commissioned to feed us, we could not do without a farm; which, affording us every necessary of life, we send to Inverness (only fifty miles off) for elegancies and superfluities; elegant sugar, and superfluous tea, for instance. The last incumbent preferred getting this farm at an easy rate, and living in a cottage of his own building, to a more elegant mansion without that advantage; and we have made the same sacrifice of vanity to convenience. We have a great extent of moor and hill grazing, where they say we may feed some hundreds of sheep; a very suitable flock for a person who ought to be much detached from secular cares, having a shepherd kept purposely to attend them. They require even in winter no food or shelter, but what the hills afford. Our neighbours abound in courtesy and civility, and many of them, having been abroad in the army, are sufficiently intelligent. I remember, before I knew anything about these countries, being much delighted to hear of the Swiss; who, they say, after serving in the French army, and sharing in all the gaieties of Paris, retire, towards the decline of life, to their own country, and there immediately, and with alacrity, resume their pristine, simple, and hardy manners and habits. But there is no *amor patriæ* like that of mountaineers, everywhere. The people here so entirely resume their early modes of living and thinking, that they give probability to all we hear of those children of the rocks in other countries.

Now I feel I have tired you; for when I flag I have always a happy consciousness of my own stupidity, and shall therefore bid you farewell, to write to one who will think all my nothings very interesting; so indeed do you:—forgive, then, this implied preference, and believe that I am to you unchangeable. Adieu.

Letter XLVI.

TO MRS. SMITH, GLASGOW, (FORMERLY MISS ISABELLA EWING.)*

Laggan, March 8, 1782.

My dear Friend,

I have now to thank you for your long, kind letter, and for introducing me to that most desirable place, your fireside. Long, long may the genius of domestic happiness smile in your chimney-corner! and, if in process of time, some other friendly genius should set me down smiling in the opposite corner, with you and

* Miss Isabella Ewing had been married some months previously, to James Smith, Esq., afterwards of Jordanhill, near Glasgow.

your Caro laughing in the middle, and sister Jane and my Caro simpering together behind, we should form a charming group, and I should be as happy as is permitted to us in this probatory noviciate of being. This, perhaps, as we are all circumstanced, is a romantic wish; but I have no notion of throwing cold water upon those glimmerings of hope which occasionally cheer and enliven one's gloomiest moments. From the more extended circle of your connexions, and your happiness in being the centering point of that circle, it is altogether impossible that you can feel my absence as I do yours. But I know you will have influence enough to bring your beloved here, and that will be a second spring of the affections, and we shall then all know and love each other. This I feel certain of. With you it rests to realize this cordial presentiment. Surely, people that can go through this cold world, unloving and unloved, do not feel its sorrows as I do, or they would sink under them.

You inquire if I left Mary at Fort-Augustus; I durst not do otherwise, she is so firmly established in the affections of the good old people, that it would be a breach of the peace to deprive them of her. This does not please her father, who is afraid of his dear daughter being spoiled, but, in fact, very unwilling to part with her, though he affects to be too manly to be fond of an infant; but he wants a pretence to lament her absence without descending from his dignity. For my own part, I honestly confess, that my heart ached at parting with her. I would not wish these human flowers to breathe their first fragrance on any breast but my own.

I am sorry to hear that the Naiads of my native Clyde have paid you such an abrupt visit. The more substantial water nymphs who inhabit the square temple of purity in the green could not be ruder. You dwellers in the Stockwell and Bridgegate must be an iniquitous generation to be so inundated. We have, notwithstanding our primitive innocence and rural simplicity, met with a still severer shock, having had, for two months past, a winter as rigorous and terrible as those of the honest Laplanders, who, as the sweet singer of Tiviotdale tells us, "love their mountains, and enjoy their storms." I could have done so too, while they only afforded us a tremendous amusement, but now that our poor sheep are perishing in scores under the wreaths, I see it in a very different light. You will be very sorry to hear that our loss in this article has been considerable.

Now be correct, diligent, lively, and communicative; in short, be a peerless correspondent, for you are the link that holds me to Clydesdale; and if you break— but you never can, because you are the faithful friend of your ever affectionate

A. G.

Letter XLVII.

TO MRS. SMITH, GLASGOW.

Laggan, February 2, 1783.

My dear Friend,

When I sit down to write to you, after this too long interval, and begin to taste the pleasure of reviving in this manner the delightful ease and tenderness of our past intercourse, my heart glows at the recollection, and I am surprised at myself for allowing so long a time to elapse, without indulging myself in so pure a satisfaction. But, when my crowd of worldly cares rush in to interrupt this delightful reverie, the fervours of friendship, like those of a sublimer kind, are drowned in the clamours of the world. I never experienced so much of this tiresome turmoil, as since I wrote to you last. But, before I proceed to my wonted egotism, let me acknowledge your kind letter, which, after lying in state two months at Perth, reached me when I, too, was lying in state; of which more hereafter.

I rejoice to hear that you are become "the joyful mother of a hopeful son." How thankful should you be to Providence, which has enabled you to fulfil the first duty of that fond relation! I am sure you will pity me, who, though earnestly desirous, and in some respects well qualified, am not permitted to nurse; the wise people about me being of opinion that it would endanger my small stock of health at this season.

"He that's convinc'd against his will,
Is of the same opinion still."

I shall have endless remorse, if any thing happens. My mother was kind enough to risk a winter journey over Corryarrick, and it is by her advice that Miss is sent to grass. I am anxious to hear more particular accounts of young master. Whom do the wise people say he resembles? I am sure they have discovered him to be either his father's picture, or his mother's image, for these are the invariable phrases.—I am truly obliged to Jane for her letter. It is great charity in you and her to write on, without minding my suspensions.—You know I long ago remarked to you, that people get no extraordinary gifts, without having some extraordinary occasion for the exertion of them; so it is with the spirit and fortitude of your left-handed hero, who, it seems, has had these heroic qualities not a little exercised. He seems to be a perfect Ulysses in his woes, his wanderings, and his perils. I hope the conclusion of them will be equally successful; that he will escape the fury of the American Læstrygones, and enticements of the West Indian Lotophagi; and that some fond and faithful Penelope will soothe and reward him after all these scenes of danger and distress are over.

You would see the death of Mrs. Sprott* in the newspapers. That warm and liberal heart is now cold indeed; that friendly and expanded breast, which heaved so long under the pressure of sickness and sorrow, is now at rest. She was indeed "the friend and lover of the tuneful train," and possessed that "rapture for the muse, that heart of friendship, and that soul of joy," which Thomson ascribes to his loved, lamented Hammond. I think of her very often, and alway with fresh sorrow. There are some circumstances which embitter the recollection of that amiable woman to me with a poignant regret which I cannot describe; but, alas, what do they now avail!

Take your own time for the expedition of the trusty and well-beloved party; but it would suit me best in

* See Letter XXXVII. above.

the beginning of July, for then the sheep-shearing would be over, and I could afford time to go to Fort-Augustus with you; and you could return by Fort-William, a short and easy road, though not so picturesque as the Athol braes, which you will take on your way here. This interview, however transient, will afford me an opportunity of saying unwriteable things, and returning in person the sacred flame of friendship, to burn to perpetuity. I cannot touch this subject but it elevates me, rekindles the glow of youthful enthusiasm, and carries me, in an instant, "beyond the visible diurnal sphere."

I send you a great, comprehensive benediction, including your brother and my dear Harriet. May every return of this season of good wishes bring health and felicity to you and your beloved! so prays, so wishes, yours, with true and tender regard,

A. G.

Letter XLVIII.

TO MRS. SMITH.

Laggan, August 7, 1784.

My dear Friend,

I hope this will find you safely arrived in town with your mate, and relieved from all apprehensions about the *son of your love.* I have no doubt but your dear little sufferer has gone through much distress; but your timidity of temper makes me hope you have, in fancy, aggravated the danger.—I rejoice to think you are so partial to all my dear retreats, to Spey, Corryarrick, and, above all, to the lord of the cottage. I should not have died in peace unless you had seen and liked us all.* I am quite gratified to think how much *you* please *him*. Nature, delicacy, and gentleness, is all in all to him; he revolts at every shadow of affectation, and detects pretensions with a glance. I dare say, in his whole lifetime, he never said a word, the intention of which was to bias any one in his favour. You must like him as he is, or not like him at all; but I was sure you would and must like him. Never were two unpretending beings more congenial in their manner of thinking; he was extremely partial to your letters, before he saw you. You and he, too, have this in common, that you both appear to most advantage on paper, where your diffidence does not stand in your way. He admires my application of Collins's Address to Simplicity to you, and says you really are,

> "By nature taught,
> To breathe her genuine thought
> In language warmly pure, and sweetly strong."

Now the least thing you can do in return for all this, is to tell me how your beloved likes me, and the cottage, and so forth. What an ingrate he must be, if not partial to the wife of one who loves his wife so well, especially when the lady in question is so well disposed towards him. My dear, we ought, as Caius says of Dr. Evans in the play, "to pray our pibles well," that matters happened as they did. Nursing our delicacy and our affection as we did, in tender friend-

* Alluding to the recent visit of Mr. and Mrs. Smith, and her sister, Miss Ewing, to Laggan.

ship and voluntary retirement; and cultivating our taste to a degree which circumstances might have rendered very inconvenient, we should have been wretched caitiffs, had men fallen to our lot, such as the generality of our friends are very well satisfied with. For my own part, I could never have endured grossness, or indifference, or twenty things I see better people put up with, who do not seem to think there is the smallest occasion for common tastes and inclinations. In such a case, I think, "I would never tell my *hate;*" but, I dare say, concealment would, like an envious worm, "feed on my meagre cheek." Alas, how I play with a subject that should touch us both very nearly, when we think of her who has full as much feeling and delicacy as any of us, who always suffers, and never complains! With her disposition she would have been too happy, had she met, like us, with gentleness, attention, and indulgence.

"Turn, hopeless thought, turn from her."

Your other letter is come, and I am so pleased! I began to fret and wonder, and my very Caro, who hates impatience, began to look solemn and significant, and wonder if you were well. These post-horses are brutes void of all finer feelings; and, so far from improving by the literary commerce they are the means of carrying on, they seem insensible of the loads of information, consolation, and ratiocination they carry on their backs, and will not budge a foot faster to relieve even the impatience of lovers. For instance, your letter was full sixteen days on the way. I am sure you will be glad to hear that we have a delightful prospect of a fine harvest; flax in abundance, potatoes, your favourites, in superabundance, and "the breezes wave the ripening corn" in profuse luxuriance; but then you will be sorry again to hear, that for a few days past, all this fair promise of plenty was like to be drenched in floods of rain, and overwhelmed with the swelling of Spey. However, you must be glad, again, to hear that this is only the equinoctial storm, and that we still hope for good weather to enable us to rejoice in the blessings of Providence. Mr. G. joins in affectionate good wishes to your lord; I have no room or time for other remembrances; but, while I can think, I shall be faithfully yours.

Letter XLIX.

TO MRS. SMITH.

Laggan, August 18, 1785.

My dear Friend,

Your kind letter, and the little volunteer that came with your sister's, gave me more pleasure than you can imagine, considering what a variety of pains and pleasures engross, agitate, and divide me by turns. Before I enter on the subject of yours, I must tell you how we went to Fort-George,* in the little machine, and took Catherine with us, who was not alarmed, as on a former occasion when you were with us, but, on the contrary, seemed highly delighted with the journey, and all its accompaniments. The journey, by the by,

* The Author's father had removed in 1783 from Fort-Augustus to Fort-George, near Inverness, where he held the office of Barrack-master of the Fort until 1791, when he removed to Glasgow.

was a very pleasant one, being a continued series of visits, as the road passed the houses of our connexions and friends all the way. The scene of the meeting between the two sisters was more pathetic, and less ludicrous, than the one you witnessed formerly. Their mutual joy and affection was really edifying. The eldest has made great improvement; so great that it would be no wonder if, like other little prodigies, she should disappoint all expectation. There is a lady, whom I heard lately speaking on the subject, who is so impressed with the idea of premature children's disappointing hope, that she told me, with great tartness, she never liked *progidies*, and was very glad there were no *progidies* in their family.

Fort-George is a gay and polite place; the society well bred and agreeable, and the neighbourhood populous and pleasant. I made a short excursion to Ross-shire, saw the pretty little town of Fortrose, and the coast of that fine country, thickly planted with gentlemen's seats, being the residence of the powerful clans of Ross and Mackenzie. . . . . . . After spending three weeks very agreeably at the Fort, we set out very early, before the *bairns* rose, to avoid the struggle of parting; because both their hearts were set on coming home with us, and we had settled to leave Catherine there, for her improvement in the elegancies of the English tongue. I do not speak of conquering our Scotch, alias Doric, dialect, the sweet simplicity of which I think pleasing in a child; but you are to know, that I make a point of making my mountain nymphs speak the language of the mountains in the first place. I am all anti-Pinkerton, and delight in the Celtic. You cannot think what a source of pleasure my little acquaintance with that emphatic and original language has afforded me. I am determined my children shall all drink "from the pure wells of Celtic undefiled." They shall taste the animated and energetic conversation of the natives; and an early acquaintance with the poetry of nature shall guard them against false taste and affectation. I never desire to hear an English word out of their mouths till they are four or five years old. How I should delight in grafting elegant sentiments and just notions on simple manners and primitive ideas! This is just the forte-piano character that we always wish for, and seldom meet. How, indeed, should we? People, whose circumstances confine them to breed their children at home, are so apt to have them spoiled for want of culture, and by vulgar association. Then, if they send them to the common seminaries, there are so many of them together, spoiling each other with trifling conversation; and the love of vanity and dress rages like a contagion; their manners, nay, their very ideas, are so artificial, that their minds and manners wear a tiresome uniform. Now, I am going to make an experiment on my mountain nymphs. If it fails, your laughing at me will be only the smallest part of my mortification. Know, then, that I propose, in the first place, to attend, above all things, to the culture of the heart; and at leisure, and in due time, to that of the understanding; and, having secured these main points, to let the manners, in a great measure, shift for themselves. I pre-suppose a tolerable good disposition, and some degree of sensibility; and, taking these for granted, I cannot easily believe that an unpolluted mind, unaccustomed to fear from without, or reproach from within, bred in the centre of kindness and confidence, and having all its best affections constantly exercised,—I cannot, I say, suppose any other than soft and artless manners to flow spontaneously from such a mind, so formed, and so circumstanced; especially, when unaccustomed to vulgar language, and, what is far more degrading, vulgar sentiments, which I have heard conveyed in very good language from very pretty mouths.

Forgive this digression from our homeward journey; even the strong temptation of wandering in my favourite path can scarce excuse this long scamper. So we set out, as I told you, from Fort-George, and, after proceeding five or six miles, spent the rest of the morning in surveying the antiquities of Calder Castle, a venerable and gloomy edifice of grey renown; for this is the Cawdor of Macbeth, and it was a few miles to the north of it, that the witches anticipated his titles. I fancy their hagships resided hereabouts; at any rate, I am sure the demon of black-despairing melancholy dwells in some of those caverns that echo the roar of Calder Water. The Castle has no other inhabitant at present than an old sybil, who lives in the cellar, and some legions of rooks and daws in the lofty towers, that add strength and horror to this antique dwelling. You enter over a very narrow drawbridge, laid across a deep chasm. We saw some good paintings, and tapestry frightfully fine; for Pharaoh was there driving so furiously after the Israelites, and the Red Sea rushing so fiercely upon Pharaoh, that you started back instinctively, not knowing which to fear most. Small gothic "windows that admit no light, and passages that lead to nothing," or, at most, to a small dark room with a thick, heavy door, strengthened with iron; these, and resounding, dusky halls, and narrow, winding staircases, give no very high idea of the enjoyments of the virtuous and stately dames, who wrought tapestry here in the days of feudal grandeur, and perpetual hostility. You are shown, in a very high tower, the self-same bed in which Duncan, of pious memory, was murdered by Macbeth. It was brought from Inverness, on the demolition of the castle there. The fact of Duncan's being killed in it is hard to establish; but the bed is certainly unique in itself, and very unlike the beds of these degenerate days. It is, in the first place, very large, and exactly square; it is magnificent in its own way, yet it is evident that curtains were an unknown luxury when it was framed; the wooden canopy which forms the roof is surrounded by a moulding or cornice two feet deep at least, of wood exquisitely carved in flowers, with many imitations of palm and pine branches, and good store of thistles. Round the frame of the bed, or bedstead, which is very low, though the canopy be lofty, is another moulding, seemingly formed to prevent the possibility of his Majesty's tumbling out. This, too, is richly carved; so are the posts, and certain raised ornaments, not inelegantly representing branches, at the corners. In short, the expense of carving this bed, if the artist's recompense was adequate to his labour and ingenuity, might purchase the most costly curtains.* From the battlements of the Castle you see, in the back-ground, a thick forest, old beyond history or memory, and solemn beyond imagination. Tremendous rugged rocks appear emerging from the wood; on one side you see the chasm and drawbridge aforesaid; on the other, the river Calder, dark in its colour, and devious in its course, howling, groaning, and boiling through a rocky channel, worn into many dismal pits and caldrons: at the foot of that rock on which the Castle stands, it is so deep and dark, that it dizzies one to look down from the tower. In short, the gloomy pools below, and pendant branches above, might almost tempt a love-sick maiden, or fog-sick Englishman, to hanging or drowning. There is a wide view towards the sea, including the heath where the weird sisters announced the fatal career of successful ambition to Macbeth, whom I always figure to myself saying, "Is thy servant a dog that he should do this thing?"

After looking down with complacency on the numerous families of ravens, whom we used to look up to at a great distance, in the vast old elms that were planted, before the Union at latest, round this venerable pile, we quitted Calder, with an emotion of gratitude for being born in happier times; when high-born dames and barons bold are no longer forced to seek security from rugged manners, and feudal outrage, in those terrific mansions. Now, after this hopeful outset, consider what a fair field of description lies before you, for this is only the morning scene; and,

* This interesting relic was accidentally burnt by a fire in the Castle a few years ago.—(1845.)

after performing an *act of recollection* on the moor, the whole country of Strathspey opened upon us—Castle Grant,* and the surrounding pleasure-grounds and gardens, which are very fine, though surmounted by rude environs. There are numerous paintings there, to my great delectation. Some of these are very characteristic of the amiable propensity of this family, to cherish the inferior gentry and their humble relations, who "dwelt under their shadow." There is a pleasant summer parlour, opening, with a glass-door, to the garden, the walls of which are entirely covered with the portraits of those lesser gentry around, who were attached, many of them, by the double tie of kindred and feudal subjection. This last was rather patriarchal sway, as they managed it. Never, surely, was power so gently used, or protection so gratefully acknowledged. Those endearing, though invisible and undefinable ties, that have for generations held these people so strongly to each other, and to their chief, produce united effects, which afford one of the most pleasing views of human nature that can be met with. The family, luckily for you, were from home, but had left their effigies behind. Caro was quite charmed to see with what reverence I beheld his kindred shades. He is to-night extremely anxious about saving my poor eyes. So it shall suffice, that the Castle is a spacious, convenient, and elegant mansion, where many heroes of the family, "on animated canvass seem to frown;" and where everything evinces an

* The fine, old baronial seat in Strathspey of the late Sir James Grant of Grant, Bart., and now (1845) of his son, the Earl of Seafield, Chief of the Clan Grant.

abode where baronial pomp and hospitality still continue to linger, softened by the milder graces of modern elegance. These eyes I must save, and therefore I bid you heartily good-night, and will begin a new letter to-morrow; for if once I resume the reins of government, I shall not lay them down for landscape painting. Adieu! my true friend.

LETTER L.

TO MRS. SMITH, GLASGOW.

Laggan, August 19, 1785.

My dear Friend,

Again I resume, and I insist on being allowed some merit in resuming, when the meadows, glittering with dew, the ascending larks, the fresh flowers, and the curling mists that climb the opposite mountain, all invite me out to enjoy the sweetest hour of day, the soft shadowy twilight excepted. You know not how sweet and sacred the hour is that I devote to you.

To return to Strathspey. We spent two days with a relation of Mr Grant's, and on Sunday went to hear my old friend's lord preach. After sermon we went into the manse, and with difficulty escaped their kind compulsion, for we were engaged. She* becomes the holy state very well; seemed composed and cheerful, domesticated, and in a fair way of being rusticated. Strathspey is quite a civilized country compared to

* Mrs. Grant of Duthil, formerly Miss Beatrice Campbell, who is married to a clergyman in Strathspey.—(1807.) Mrs. Grant died in 1845.

this, and has a good neat village in it, where the father of the district* has been cherishing some exotic manufactures, which do not seem to find the soil congenial. In fact, a Highlander never sits at ease at a loom; it is like putting a deer in the plough. We made a circuit of two days more, and then came home, and found all well and happy. I am glad to hear such good accounts of John Beverly, who, I trust, will do credit to my recommendation. He appears a well-disposed boy, strongly marked with the true English character of sincerity, integrity, and plain sound sense.

Rochefoucalt says, very ill naturedly, that people always find consolation very easily for the misfortunes of their friends. Painful experience assures me of the contrary. My very spirit is wounded by my dear Harriet's accumulated sorrows; and reflection, instead of soothing, aggravates my affliction; when I think over all our early friendship, animated by the ardour natural to that innocent age, on her side so pure and genuine; when I think on all her truth, her gentleness, and meekness, and the dignity and delicacy that were intuitive, (for of *whom* could she learn them?) My dear soul, you never knew her so well as I did. The powers of her understanding, and the graces of her mind, never met with the sunshine of encouragement. At the very time when they were expanding, we know how she was secluded from improvement, and crushed by arbitrary harshness. What a moderate degree of prosperity would have been hap-

* The late Sir James Grant of Grant, Bart.

piness to a spirit so regulated and so tranquil! But, alas, to sink under the cold hand of poverty, and have so many innocent sufferers looking up to her! I greatly fear, too, that he who should support and comfort her is by no means what we should wish him to be. We know not even what to say to her; sympathy, so sweet, so soothing, in other cases, avails not here. For, to a person who has so much delicate pride, when one cannot alleviate pecuniary distress, it is insulting to mention it. What shall we, what *can* we do for our friend?

Remember us with much esteem to your beloved. What a tide of information you must pour in upon me in return for this descriptive effort in folio. Be conscientious, and then you will not be concise. Adieu!

A. G.

Letter LI.

TO MISS JANE EWING, AT GLASGOW.

Laggan, March 1, 1786.

My dear Jane,

I hope this will find you safely returned from England, much improved by your travels, and so replenished with candour and good nature, that you will excuse my sending this by the post; which, I protest, proceeds from no hostile design against your purse, nor from any vain conceit that you will have here the value of your sixpence, but to relieve me from a weight of perplexity and concern that I can support no longer. But in case there should have been mistakes or misapprehensions, I shall give you a clear retrospective view of the whole state of our correspondence since Mr. Grant brought me your May letter. . . . . Now, my dear, I think no scruple can remain; and I beg of you, by all that is dear and friendly, to send me, by the very next post, sixpennyworth of your own characteristic truth and intelligence.

New objects, new pleasures, and new attachments obtrude themselves so frequently, from the very nature of the gay shifting scene around you, that it is no wonder they should insensibly exclude the old ones, whose distance, both in regard to time and place, make them appear remote even to your imagination. But how different is my situation! Placed on a serene and distant eminence, whence I view the toils and pleasures of the gay and busy world with tranquil unconcern, I am absorbed in the delightful contemplation of those virtues and graces, either budding into hope or arriving at maturity, which my partial fondness fancies in those who are united to me by those tender ties which nature forms, and sentiment rivets. Thus, free from the tyranny of caprice and custom, thus, disencumbered of those hollow friendships, the offspring of interest or vanity, which divide the attention without sharing the heart, I have balanced and closed up my books of attachment; am scarce so sanguine as to expect I shall find truth and sensibility enough to induce me to open them for the reception of a new object; and am proud and pleased to think that I have bartered away my affections for such advantageous bargains of merit and real friendship. I have now, like an opulent trader, retired to my country house, placed my fortune (of friends) in the stocks (that is, my heart); and it is become my great speculation, like theirs, to watch the rise and fall of the funds; and, to tell you the truth, I begin to fear having fallen much below par with you.

Pray allow me here, however foreign the subject may seem to you, to claim your sympathy in the deep concern I feel for the death of my friend Christina Macpherson.* Her departure was very sudden; she was nursing her second son,—was attacked by a kind of fever incident to nurses (though rarely fatal), and died the second day. You cannot think how I was affected by her loss, though already lost to me in an unequal marriage. Her sense was strong and masculine; her sentiments just and liberal, though neither soft nor polished; and her affection for me, such as now wrings my heart to remember. What a deep and dismal chasm is left in the imagination, when the mind wanders in search of what is torn for ever from its grasp, and, for the open heart and melting eye of friendship, meets only the solitary mansions of the dead! Now that I am in the figurative mood, you must indulge one more allusion to the sybil's books, which increased in value as they decreased in number. Even thus it is with my dear remaining friends; so you may contemplate your own importance as a volume of increasing value.

Catherine goes on improving amazingly; she has

* Who had sometime before married Mr. Kennedy. She has been frequently referred to, in these Letters, as residing at Culachy, near Fort-Augustus, and as the constant companion of the Author's walks in the beautiful scenes of that neighbourhood.—Ed.

an uncommon memory, lively and delicate feelings, and a strong desire to please and excel.* Her junior, Isabella, has much pastoral expression of countenance, which, in the Arcadian language, means gentleness and innocence. She is prudent, regular, and exact in all her little transactions. John Lachlan is a great lump of generosity and good-nature, and shrewd withal: whose mind, I take it, will be as open as his countenance. Peter has a more marked countenance than any of them; his features are regular, and, for a boy, delicate: he has much fire and alertness about him. He was very healthy, and so quiet that it was a pleasure to nurse him; which pleasure, however, was interrupted by a severe attack of the rheumatism. He now walks, and speaks many words. Apologies for egotism between you and me are affected and unnecessary. Of whom, or of what can I write here so interesting to you as myself? and the same holds from you to me. Caro sends many, very many, and kind compliments to you all. This letter is levelled partly at you, and partly at your sister; the very idea of her neglect is wounding. Remember me with esteem to all your brothers, and to your mother; and let me know by next post, whether you think it of importance that I am yours unalterably,

A. G.

* These passages refer to the Author's children.

LETTER LII.

TO MISS JANE EWING.

Laggan, July 5, 1786.

My dear Jane,

With all due gratitude, I acknowledge your three letters, which, from a travelled lady, just arrived from England, to a rusticated Highland matron, are no small marks of condescension. But you will never assume a character, and have not been long enough from home to acquire a new one. The merit of your kindness is augmented by considering what small returns of entertainment you have to expect.

We, here, have been all in a hurry with public amusements for this fortnight past. You will be quite at a loss to conjecture of what kind they could be. Roups,* then, are a source of great amusement here, and a very expensive one to the roup-makers. At the dissolution of any family, by the death or removal of its head, it is customary to send out letters of invitation to all the connexions which inter-marriages have created to the defunct, for a century past, in the neighbouring counties, inviting them to countenance the ceremony by their presence. This invitation tacitly includes an expectation, warranted by old custom, that these allies, as they call them, will purchase things rather beyond their value. The wealth of the family consisting in the number of their cattle, and their pride in the number

* Sales by auction.

of their connexions, the one come to purchase the other, and both are displayed in their full extent. Whether it can be well afforded or not, there is always a plentiful dinner, and very plentiful drink on these occasions, which the friendly greetings of so many people, bound by a common tie, frank, lively, and not deficient in that good breeding which habitual kindness and courtesy forms, render no unpleasing scene to those who witness the conclusion of it. It is indeed a very joyous one. Besides the entertainment for the superior class, there is always a plentiful distribution of bread, and cheese, and whisky, to the peasantry, whose cheerfulness never exceeds the bounds of respect and decorum. The general good humour diffused by this meeting of numbers, who know and like each other, though they do not often mingle, and the emulation of good-will to the entertainers, generally raise things to a great price. Though you want nothing, you must appear to countenance the business; a refusal on such an occasion, would be thought as odd in the Highland world, as it would be in the *beau monde* to refuse an invitation to stand and be shot at.

You always hear Highlanders talk of "countries;" but did I ever tell you what our countries are? not by any means parishes, counties, or any such divisions as you are used to: a country, here, means a habitable track, divided by rocks, mountains, and narrow passes from the adjacent countries, and inhabited by a particular clan. These, in places where only two or three miles of rocky eminence separate them, differ in looks, language, and manners, more than you can imagine possible. Nay, they affect to differ; for bordering clans often live in bitter and jealous rivalship; and though individuals love, and sometimes marry each other, the general dislike continues. Different clans, in their collective capacity, form strict alliances with each other, and are cordial in their attachment; but they are those who live at a distance from each other, and cannot interfere about hunting, hill-pasture, &c. The Grants and Macleans, for instance.

But to return to our roups. We were not, on this occasion, presented with the usual spectacle of festivity mingling with the grief of the widow and orphans. The first was that of a Nabob, as we used to call him, who had been in the army, and made money in the East Indies. He died childless, and, from the caprice of his nature, never could enjoy the gifts of fortune; though he was, at the sametime, a man of such upright intentions, that we all acquiesced most patiently in his removal, hoping he would find that peace in happier regions which eluded his grasp in this discordant world. His heirs-at-law, after giving the widow her annuity, seized and rouped everything; and the whole parish feasted three days on his remains. After picking the bones of our departed neighbour, we all set out to eat the Chieftain* up alive; for you must know he is a Colonel of the Guards, and took a fancy to live on his estate two years ago—built a new house, and brought fashionable furniture from London. For half a year, he lived hospitably in the halls of his fathers; but wishing to have his domain improved and planted, and aspiring, as every Colonel does, to die a General, he

* The late Colonel Macpherson of Cluny, Chief of the Clan of Macpherson.—Ed.

has let it for ten years to a judicious and noted improver, on condition of having it restored with hundreds of dikes, thousands of drains, and ten thousands of trees upon it. Judge, then, how you will find the scenery tamed and improved when you return. To make way for this arrangement, every article of cattle and furniture was sold. The *roup* lasted a week. There were several of our connexions from Strathspey there. We had a cold collation there every day, and as many strangers every night at our own house as it would accommodate. When all this was over, we paid a round of visits with the Grants, before their departure.

Curtis, our surgeon at Fort-Augustus, whom you inquired after, was nearly blown up, in India, in the Cæsar man-of-war, and is come home from that scene of wealth and corruption, with his mind unspoiled and his pockets empty. I am told he is doing well enough in his original profession. He will be happier, but the world will not think so. My cousin, whom you have seen, is returned from India, perfectly qualified to talk of

"Antres vast, and deserts wild,"

for he returned overland. He passed through Syria, and was half a year in Cyprus, and returned by Marseilles. He, too, has failed of enriching himself in the modern Ophir; but I question whether he will bear the privations that obscurity is heir to, as well as the philosophic Curtis, who is too wise for ambition, and too calm to be disturbed by the fervours of imagination. I will write to your sister from the leisure of

Fort-George; and, in the meantime, give you joy of the conclusion of this long, tiresome letter, and bid you heartily, Adieu.

Letter LIII.

TO MRS SMITH.

Fort-George, July 30, 1786.

My dear Friend,

I have been long meditating a stroke at your sixpence, but still deferred it till I should leave home, and reach this haven of tranquillity. Here, amidst the sound of fifes and drums, and small arms, I seek that quiet and leisure which I look for in vain amidst the more discordant tumults of the nursery; where the thorough bass of the bull and the old sow, from without, and the shrill treble accompaniment of the pigs and poultry, form a complete anti-concert. Not that I mean to complain of the country, for, jesting apart, I never enjoyed it more than I did this past summer, notwithstanding the constant fatiguing exertion which my situation demands. You, who are the repository of all my complaints, know very well what a wretched invalid I was all last winter; but the spring, the sun, and health, returning all together, and that so mild and sweet a spring as I never saw in this northern climate, you cannot think how suddenly I benefited from its reviving and gladdening influence. Then my little boy, Peter, the finest creature you ever saw, began to run about earlier than any I ever had, and, from being a trouble, became a pleasure and amusement to the whole family. My eldest came down here in May, where he is to remain, being the darling of his grandfather's affections; so that we have none to disturb us but the two girls and little *Pickle*. We had the warmest, brightest summer imaginable; and when the busy cares of day were done, we used to saunter every evening by the Spey, till eleven o'clock, through meadows literally flowery, for you never saw such a luxury of sweets. There, too,

> "Quiet waters, soft and slow,
> Along the verdant landscape flow."

It was then and there that we tasted, with the highest relish, the true enjoyment of minds detached from the world,—may I add, somewhat raised above it.

> "In that kind school, where no proud master reigns,
> The full free converse of the mutual heart,
> Improving and improved."

But need I describe this kindly intercourse to you, who understand it so well, and who love, as much as I do, to cherish the remembrance of scenes and conversations never to be recalled, but always to be regretted; where that love of sincerity, of nature, and of virtue, which charmed and united us, expanded our hearts, and excluded the scandal, tittle-tattle about fashions and coxcombs, and jealous malignity, which so frequently engross the *tête-á-têtes* of misses in and out of their teens?

You know me made of digressions, and will therefore excuse this long one. After being so long rusticated, and used to quite a different manner of life and style of conversation, you cannot imagine how I was struck with the difference, in manners, dress, and language, between the people I found here, and those whom I left behind at Laggan. I speak singularly, for Mr. Grant is not with me. We are building a new church, and an addition to our cottage, for the reception of these new comers who visit us so frequently—I mean the *bairns*. When my mate left me, he parted with such reluctance, and so many charges of quick return, that he reminded me of Milton's Adam on the fatal morning of the transgression.—To return to the Garrisonians. You can imagine no set of people more polished, powdered, *tonified* and *Englified*, than they are. That rage for elegance, that passion for show, that frenzy for false refinement and artificial luxury, which marks the age, burns here in full ardour. No wonder, when it has banished decorum, regularity, and decent frugality from the sober haunts of commerce, and even obtruded itself, with all its disquiets and dangers, into the more sacred asylums of rural tranquillity, that this passion triumphs here, where it has nothing to obstruct its progress; for the permanent parts of the community are so very idle, and so much accustomed to the company of a successive variety of military beaux, who arrive with fresh cargoes of vanity and fashionable impertinence, that the ladies here are as great adepts in the fashionable chit-chat, the modish games, &c., as any of their sisters in Grosvenor Square. Add to this, an assumed vivacity, and continual pretension to wit, supported by a mechanical giggle, which every one has equally at command.

This, no doubt, is a caricature, which the splenetic turn of reflection, produccd by retirement, with a sickly habit, has aggravated. But now for the reverse of the medal. These people are certainly pleasant, easy, and elegant, though not totally free from affectation. Then, considering they are so entirely unoccupied, and living so much together, it is wonderful to observe the harmony that prevails, and the decorum they observe towards each other. Even in absence, they have, upon the whole, less malignity and slander than any small society I ever knew or heard of. Though they have not warmth for real and tender friendship, yet their manners are so far smoothed and softened by that politeness which is the ape and substitute of benevolence, that they keep all rancour within decent bounds. Indeed, they float down the tide of dissipation so quickly, from one wave of amusement to another, that they cannot be much in earnest in their love or their anger. You will wonder who these residents are. They consist of the Governor and his Staff, four invalid companies, and a company of artillery. Dear peaceful home! where all is native and unsophisticated; this will make me more sensible of the value of my dominion there.

I have at last written to Harriet* since my arrival here. I only deferred in hopes of sending some trifles, which might be serviceable. You know she is in one sense very proud, and so are all people of great delicacy. . . . . . . I never repined at my lot for want of any luxury, but the divine one of bestowing where I love. Tell her, what she will scarce believe, so jealous are the unfortunate, that she is as dear to me as ever,

* Henrietta Reid, the Author's early correspondent.

though I have not the means to convince her of it. Let me know what sort of being Willy has chosen to divide his heart and loaf with.—I have a line from my sovereign lord, just now, upbraiding my delay; and charging me to meet him in his own Strathspey. I will stay there some days, having a grand visit to make. Adieu.

Letter LIV.

TO MRS. SMITH, LINT HOUSE, NEAR GLASGOW.

Fort-George, August 27, 1787.

My dear Friend,

The long letter you promised me from Lint House is not yet arrived. I have been for a month at *my* Lint-house, alias Fort-George; where, being in some measure disengaged from the perpetual hurry which always surrounds me at home, I find leisure to gratify the strong inclination I always feel to write to you. Taking it for granted, that, in the present case, you not only excuse, but require egotism, I will endeavour to explain to you the nature of that bustle, and perplexity of affairs, which I complain of so often, and so justly. Having a great deal to do is not altogether the thing; that, too, abridges my time for amusements of this nature; but it is having a great deal to think of, to contrive and to plan out, that plagues me. It is acting in a variety of characters and capacities, scarcely compatible with each other. I must, after seven years' experience, confess, with deep mortification, and due reverence for that exalted character, that the person who would be a notable housewife, must be that individual thing only, and not mar the main affair by an attempt to introduce separate and subordinate excellencies. She must not even, in any sense, be a tender wife, or attentive mother. She must not walk about with her husband, or be his evening companion in conversation or other amusements; she must not spend her time in instructing her children, nor attend to the forming of their minds. Their food, clothing, and health, is all she must attend to.

You Lowlanders have no idea of the complicated nature of Highland farming, and of the odd customs which prevail there. Formerly, from the wild and warlike nature of the men, and their haughty indolence, they thought no rural employment compatible with their dignity, unless, indeed, the plough. Fighting, hunting, lounging in the sun, music, and poetry, were their occupations: for the latter, though you would not think it, their language is admirably adapted. This naturally extended the women's province both of labour and management. The care of the cattle was peculiarly theirs. Changing their residence so often as they did in summer, from one bothy* or glen to another, gave a romantic peculiarity to their turn of thought and language. Their manner of life, in fact, wanted nothing but the shades of palm, the olives, the vines, and the fervid sun of the East, to resemble the patriarchal one. Yet, as they must carry their beds, food, and utensils, the housewife, who furnishes and

* *Bothy*, a slight, temporary dwelling resorted to in summer only, when the cattle are driven to the mountain pastures.

divides these matters, has enough to do when her shepherd is in one glen, and her dairy-maid in another with her milk cattle. Not to mention some of the children, who are marched off to the glen as a discipline, to inure them early to hardiness and simplicity of life. Meanwhile, his Reverence, with my kitchen damsel and the ploughman, constitute another family at home, from which all the rest are flying detachments, occasionally sent out and recalled, and regularly furnished with provisions and forage. The effect, you know, often continues when the cause has ceased; the men are now civilized in comparison to what they were, yet the custom of leaving the weight of everything on the more helpless sex continues, and has produced this one good effect, that they are from this habit less helpless and dependent. The men think they preserve dignity by this mode of management; the women find a degree of power or consequence in having such an extensive department, which they would not willingly exchange for inglorious ease.

What those occupations are, you cannot comprehend from a general description; but, as it is an hour to breakfast-time, and I find myself in the humour of journalizing and particularizing, I shall, between fancy and memory, sketch out the diary of one July Monday. I mention Monday, being the day that all dwellers in glens come down for the supplies. First of all, at four o'clock, Donald arrives with a horse loaded with butter, cheese, and milk. The former I must weigh instantly. He only asks an additional blanket for the children, a covering for himself; two milk tubs, a cog, and another spoon, because little Peter threw one of the set in the burn; two stone of meal, a quart of salt, and two pounds of flax for the spinners; for the grass continues so good that they will stay a week longer. He brings the intelligence of the old sow's being the joyful mother of a dozen pigs, and requests something to feed her with. All this must be ready in an hour; before the conclusion of which comes Ronald, from the high hills, where our sheep and young horses are all summer, and only desires meal, salt, and women with shears, to clip the lambs, and tar to smear them. He informs me that the black mare has a foal, a very fine one; but she is very low, and I must instantly send some one to bring her down to the meadows, before he departs. The tenants who do us services come next; they are going to stay two days in the oak-wood, cutting timber for our new byre, and must have a competent provision of bread, cheese, and ale for the time they stay. Then I have Caro's breakfast to get, Janet's hank to reel, and a basket of clews to despatch to the weaver; Catherine's lesson to hear, and her sampler to rectify; and all must be over before eleven. Meantime, his Reverence, calm and regardless of all this bustle, wonders what detains me, urging me out to walk, while the soaring larks, the smiling meadows, and opening flowers, second the invitation; and my imagination, if it gets a moment loose from care, kindles at these objects with all the eagerness of youthful enthusiasm. My tottering constitution, my faded form and multiplying cares, are all forgotten, and I enjoy the pause from keen exertion, as others do gaiety and mirth. How happy, in my circumstances, is that versatile and sanguine temper which is hoping for a rainbow in every cloud; nay, so prevalent is this disposition, that were a fire to break out in the offices, and burn them all down, I dare say the first thing that would occur to me, would be to console myself by considering how much ground would be manured by all these fine ashes.

Now I will not plague you with a detail of the whole day, of which the above is a competent specimen. Yet spare your pity; for this day is succeeded by an evening so sweetly serene, our walk by the river is so calmly pleasing, our lounge by the burnside, so indolently easy, and our conversation in the long-wished for hour of leisure so interesting, sliding so imperceptibly from grave to gay. And then our children! Say you wish me more ease and leisure, but do not pity me. Pity with me is like advice with some; I am readier to give than to take it. Adieu! dear and true friend.

Letter LV.

TO MRS. SMITH, GLASGOW.

Laggan, September 5, 1788.

My dear Friend,

I have just had the pleasure of your short, and Mrs. Brown's longer letter. You have not been good *bairns* this summer. Have you not the grace to consider that this is my hurried season? Could I command time, you would be teased with my redundancies. Indeed I have nothing to send you from hence very interesting to town belles. Yet what maketh us to differ, to use Mrs. Hervey's apposite phrase, if we, with our long-established friendship, find no more to interest us in each other, than people incapable of that generous sentiment? Why is spleen, or, to use a more fashionable word, *ennui*, the peculiar disease of fine ladies and fine gentlemen, but because they, of all mortals, cannot have their minds stirred up, and kept in motion, by anything but what relates to their darling selves? Avarice and vanity are the passions which, by turns, sway and agitate them. The card-table exercises the one, and a rotation of public places, filled, as they think, with their admirers, the other. Languor, apathy, and the horrors, fill up, by turns, the dismal interval.

How different is the case with those whom the polite world regards with pity, as beings lost in oblivion, because their cares and pleasures are confined to their own family and particular friends! Yet how animated, how endearing is that circle, to those capable of tasting its attractions with unvitiated relish, with genuine truth and warmth of feeling! The eye cannot turn, without meeting with the expression of reverence, sympathy, or tenderness, in some countenance we love; the most ordinary occurrence excites hopes and fears, pleasure or disquiet, because it must, in some degree, affect those who engross and animate our wishes. Haymaking is not merely drying grass; it is preparing a scene of joyous employment and innocent amusement for those whose sports recall to us our gayest, happiest days. Planting is not merely raising shrubs or trees, so familiar that they excite no new pleasurable idea; it is preparing shelter, and unfolding beauties, for those human blossoms, whose dawning sweetness, whether real or imaginary, we contemplate with blameless rapture. Excuse this rhapsody. It is an attempt at contrasting a life of what is thought harmless dissipation, with that peaceful privacy where the voice of the heart is heard, and attended to.

Why do you not tell me what kind of a wife Jane* makes, and whether she takes matronal consequence to herself? Who that was ill is grown better, and who that was wicked has repented? Who has begun to go to sermons on week-days, and who has left off attending them on Sundays? We have been, by turns, so moral and playful, that, now our name is up, if we should deal a little in censure and tittle-tattle, we can go on, and keep our credit, on the strength of past good behaviour. Where is Dunlop Street, and what sort of a house have you in it? and do you still keep Watts on the Passions beside you, by way of precaution? and do you continue your laudable attention to the *wee* prophets—or do you not rather tell them, in these busy days, that "at a more convenient season you will hear them?" You see how present, all past mirth and sorrow, sports and seriousness, are to me; yet you will gravely talk of my neglecting you, ungrateful being that you are! . . . . I give you this commission, to me important, because I think, if a suitable place could be found for my charge,† she might improve in many

* Miss Jane Ewing, the sister of Mrs. Smith of Jordanhill, who had been married in February preceding, to James Brown, Esq. of Glasgow.

† Miss Charlotte Grant, the young lady here alluded to, and who is frequently mentioned afterwards by the name of "Charlotte,"

respects; and I should flatter myself that going now and then to public places, and associating with other young people, will cheer her dejected spirits, and prevent her taking a turn too thoughtful for her age. I would wish her to pass four or five months in town, and return to me in summer. Adieu, in haste, my dear friend. Mr. Grant has learned to think of you as I do, and sends his love. Dispose of mine where you know it due.—Farewell again.

Letter LVI.

TO MRS. BROWN, GLASGOW, (FORMERLY MISS JANE EWING.)

Laggan, October 10, 1788.

My dear Mrs. Brown,

I will lose no time in thanking you for the very friendly and interested part you take in all that concerns me, of which I have a recent proof in your attention to poor Charlotte's* concerns. If I live till the time of her return next year, I hope to have the pleasure of telling you in person, somewhere or other, how affectionate a sense I retain of all your kindness. You seem so engrossed with this same *Caro* of yours, that you appear quite unconcerned in what passes round you, and never give a word of news to one who lan-

was a relation of the Minister of Laggan, in whose family she for many years found a home. She was much admired for beauty of countenance, and singular elegance, both of person and manners, in which dignity and softness were happily blended; while in her mind the soundest sense and firmest rectitude supported and directed each other.—(1807.) Miss Grant was daughter of the late Captain Grant of Ballintomb in Strathspey.—(1845.)—Ed.

* See the last Note appended to the preceding Letter.

guishes in obscurity, and, moreover, in total ignorance of what the Clydesdale world is doing; which is all the world to me. If you did but know how it renews my youth, and awakens "the light of my soul," to recollect "those happy days, beyond recovery fled!" Not that the present are unhappy, or at all so inanimate as you may imagine. If you would tell what you are all about, I would, for instance, tell you how the Bard of bards, who reached the mouldy harp of Ossian from the withered oak of Selma, and awakened the song of other times, is now moving, like a bright meteor, over his native hills;* and, while the music of departed bards awakes the joy of grief, the spirits of departed warriors lean from their bright clouds to hear, and a thousand lovely maids descend from the hill of roes, and pour forth the tears of beauty to the woes of Malvina; while the fair mourner of Lutha rejoices, in the presence of her love, to hear his fame resound once more from Albion's cliffs to the green vales of Erin. This Bard, as I was about to tell you, is as great a favourite of fortune as of fame, and has got more by the old harp of Ossian, than most of his predecessors could draw out of the silver strings of Apollo. He has bought three small estates in this country within these two years, given a ball to the ladies, and made other exhibitions of wealth and liberality. He now keeps a Hall at Belleville, his new-purchased seat, where there are as many shells as were in Selma, filled, I doubt not, with much better liquor. . . . . . .

* Alluding to James Macpherson, Esq. of Belleville, near Laggan, the compiler of Ossian's Poems, who had realized a large fortune in India, and recently purchased estates in the Highlands of Scotland.

I make no apology for haste and inaccuracy. It is a fine harvest day, and I write with my son in my lap. Adieu, my dear friend. Accept our best wishes for your chosen, and assure him I consider him as a new and near connexion. I am always much yours,

A. G.

Letter LVII.

TO MRS. SMITH, GLASGOW.

Laggan, Christmas-day, 1788.
(Ink frozen by the fire.)

My dear Friend,

Festivals I always choose for writing to you, for then I am at leisure. Doubly so to-day, for my lord and sovereign is out, at a meeting of country gentlemen, and has left me here starving in such intense weather, as none but ultra-Grampians have any conception of. I hope Charlotte has given you my epistle from Dalwhinnie; a very meritorious one, too, considering what a cold vigil I kept to write it. I long much to hear how far she answers to the sketch I gave you of her; if I were less happy in my family, I should be inconsolable for want of her. Even the inexhaustible fund of *entertainment* I possess in them, can scarce alleviate my chagrin for her departure. She, to whose mind early sorrow has given early ripeness, is unusually domestic and companionable. Her having no great compass of acquired knowledge, or powers of imagination, is rather an advantage in our retirement, because she could attend to common things, and be interested in such occurrences, as a person soaring in the balloon of romantic elevation could not descend to. Then she has a very pleasing vein of humour, which I would call peculiar, but that it in some degree resembles Caro's. She has not his singular vein of delicate irony, but rallies very like him; and, like him, too, is very much awake to the ludicrous, and very quick-sighted in detecting all pretensions. She is also, like him, invariably true; neither deceived nor deceiving: sound judgment, indeed, is the *forte* of these relations. Therefore, when I take a flight into the ideal world, it must be a solitary one. People at her age are generally too much engrossed with views and schemes for that new scene which seems to open wide and boundless before them in the world, to settle their giddy minds to that calm and rational enjoyment which time and experience teach us to value. But *she* is always present and at home, careless of admiration. I was not bewildered in the usual way; but, though loving as I did an occasional excursion beyond this cloudy region, I think I, too, could always claim the merit of sitting very quiet in the chimney corner. Indeed I find, that tranquillity of temper is very useful in the lot which Providence has appointed for me.

This is not the region of select society, yet by no means lonely. One meets with people willing to please, not deficient in point of understanding, and having manners superior to expectation, when you consider everything. I should, perhaps, enjoy their society more, if what I have at home were less pleasing. No one can be more sensible than I am of what I possess in this respect. Yet there is no perfection; affection, delicacy, and discernment, may have their excesses.

As there is no pure happiness in this region of shadows, mine is not without alloys and interruptions; not merely such as are common to every one, but some peculiarly my own. . . . . . . And yet my advantages are such, that I should be wretched without them; and my drawbacks such as I can bear without repining, and trust, in time, to conquer without any mighty effort.

Alas, how sadly does my reluctant heart assent to your too just observation! This is, indeed, the time our children will afford us most pleasure. Should wealth and honour be scattered in their paths, should their merit attain applause and distinction from surrounding multitudes, still they will be weaned from our arms, never more to dwell in them with pleasure, and depend on us for happiness; never more will they read their hopes and fears, their rewards and punishments, in our eyes. Oh happy obscurity, that hides the future from us! Happy they, who are not appointed to drain the dregs of life, to outlive those they love, or what is ten times worse, to see them become unworthy of their love!

"Spare my eyes, my heart *the last.*"

Adieu, dear friend, affectionately yours,

A. G.

Letter LVIII.

TO MISS CHARLOTTE GRANT, GLASGOW.*

Laggan, March 8, 1789.

My dear Charlotte,

I have got your letter and your long journalizing packet, which has been just six weeks " suspended in mid air," that is, lying at Dalnacardoch. No person could possibly enter into its details with more interest than we did. I was sure you must needs esteem Miss R.; her mind is very pure, and she is a person whose truth and uprightness may always be depended on. Now this is one of my tautologies. People of very pure minds are sometimes so hurried away by imagination and credulity, or so fickle and uncertain, that you are not safe with them. In her you will find a rational companion and a steady friend. Principle built on piety is a pedestal on which one may safely lean. The piety of a young woman should be, like all her other virtues and graces, quiet and void of ostentation; yet, depend upon it, besides the horror which a mind rightly turned must always feel at an impious character, a young girl without pious impressions must needs be very unamiable. She must either have resisted such impressions, or have been so unhappily circumstanced, as to have no creature among her early connections solicitous about her present safety and eternal felicity. How one's blood chills on reading Savage's tender complaint:—

" No mother's care,
Shielded my infant innocence with prayer."

* See Note as to Miss Charlotte Grant, subjoined to Letter LV.

A helpless, feeble creature, born to obey and to be protected, who is only amiable while she is gentle, only endured while she is spotless; such a creature as this rejecting or slighting the protection of Omnipotence, bold in presumption, and fearing nothing but the breath of her fellow-mortals, is a being that imagination revolts at. There is a melancholy truth too little thought of during the triumph of youth and beauty. It is the consideration of young women being the sole material of which old women are made. Now, an infirm old woman,—a female who has made her way through all the peculiar sorrows that sex is heir to, and passed through a long life without seeking peace and consolation in the bosom of Infinite Mercy, is so much the object of a peculiar, undefined kind of horror, that our ancestors, more pious, though less wise than their children, were very apt to consider such as very bewitching creatures, and feared to meet or look at them.

Lest I should lose your attention by over-solemnity, I shall return to your Christmas letter. One of the first things that seems to have struck you was the great scarcity of beauty among my townswomen; and the next, the frequency of those burials that met you whenever you went out. Now, in my time, there were as many beauties and as few burials there as in most other places; and though I cannot account rationally for all this, I can do it poetically, by supposing all the fine women in town died of grief on your arrival, seeing themselves outshone, and that it was their burials that so frequently disturbed your feelings in your walks. Seriously, you feel strange and cold;

you are not partial to the people, and therefore see nothing in a flattering light: their manners do not generally please strangers. Yet remember, I predict that you will yet grow very fond of these very people, and then you will find wit, beauty, and politeness wherever you go.

I am glad to find you sensible of the merits of those most estimable sisters,* to whose protection I recommended you; but I do not wish you to think that there is nobody like them. You never in your life formed a more mistaken opinion than in supposing certain friends of mine to resemble C. I will not refute such an idea, but trust your own good sense and discernment with discovering and rectifying this and other errors of opinion. Having once been very young myself, I can easily understand the triumphant satisfaction young people feel in finding out the mistakes and deceptions to which their seniors are liable, and how ready they are to cry out with David, "I wiser than my teachers am." But you, like other people, will find every year "a critic on the past;" and I do not wish you to adopt my opinions merely because they are mine—"Time and I against any two."

Your last letter, which is just arrived, will supersede its elder sister's in my notice and attention; but I will yet return to my comments on them. In the meantime, I congratulate you on the well-timed and considerate attention of your relations, on Mrs. Douglas's goodness, which I hope you will never forget, and even on Miss Douglas's beauty, with

* Mrs. Smith of Jordanhill, and Mrs. Brown.

which you yourself are dazzled, and which, at any rate, can do no harm to herself or others, while she is so good-natured and unaffected as you describe her. I have enjoyed all your enjoyments, worn your white plumes, or rather delighted to see you wear them, danced along with you at your assembly, and enjoyed, with my friend, Mrs. Smith, the pleasure of seeing you dressed for it, and of hearing you and your lovely (not fair) cousin contrasted like Bessy Bell and Mary Gray. May you both, like those charming cousins, be as long celebrated for fidelity in friendship towards each other, as for grace and beauty.

It is odd enough that you should light on your namesake C. G. for a partner. They say he is generous and good-natured, yet I think such a sudden tide of good fortune rushing on one bred to no expectations, at so early an age, must be very dangerous. I consider the Will as mere caprice. Had his father really loved him, he would have taken some care to fit him for the enjoyment of all this wealth; as it is, his very good qualities may be fatal to him, and it is most likely "that dogs and men will drink him till he burst."* I am glad you formed no other acquaintance. I am told you and Miss R. are visited by a swain of a very different description, just the kind of person I should like, were I as free to choose at will; but probably he is a mere acquaintance, or possibly knows that Miss R. has "that within which passeth show," and looks on you merely as a *fine child*, as indeed you would be little more, if lessons in the school of calamity

* This prediction has been literally fulfilled.

had not prematured your reasoning faculties. Your little cousin is quite charmed with the acquaintance you have made in the * * * *; he desires you to remember his last lesson about your morning studies, and I appeal to your own feelings for testimony of the comfort resulting from beginning the day as every rational creature, conscious of being liable to error, and requiring protection, ought to do.

We have very great pleasure when we talk you over (as indeed you are our frequent theme), in observing to each other your noble veracity. I call it noble, because your never stooping to warp in the least, even when truth is disadvantageous to you, denotes an innate dignity of mind. This is very well indeed, yet I would have it on a solid basis: "On piety morality is built," built like the pyramids we used to talk of, liable to no change or diminution.

I always begin with the intention of amusing you with anecdotes, domestic and parochial, but you engross me so, that all centres in yourself. The New Year and Christmas were passed in the accustomed way; the young folks very happy, the old folks enjoying their reflected happiness, and the wonted interludes of fiddling and dancing, shared at times by a pastoral dialogue between the pastors and their mates. The Christmas was this year spent at Dell; our friend's ancle would not allow him to come out. We went up, found him *grumpy*, and his mate willing to soothe him and be agreeable. I rallied her, and Caro was in the humour of being very facetious. We projected some matches among the little folks, and finally became quite joyous. Our friend shone out in his native colours, all cheerfulness, candour, and benevolence. What a pity he should ever have mingled with the dirty world! and how honestly he tells us of the embarrassments it involved him in. He made us laugh by the hour with his London adventures, particularly his reading Greek to the Bishop, to promote a project of General Johnstone's, which proved abortive after all. You cannot think how much interest he takes in you; so does his mate, which is, in one respect, more valuable, for he, as Caro says, scatters his good will among the whole human race. They spent the New Year with us, which was succeeded by a less welcome visit, more convenient and amusing to the visitors than the visited. But I leave an account of this to a young lady of the party who has promised to detail it, and much other petty history.

I am glad you find so much entertainment in my "Clarissa." What you say of wigs, formality, and change of manners, is all true, but will hold more forcibly with regard to all other writings of the former age than this; particularly the abominable comedies of King Charles's time, from the heroes of which two modern heroes, whom you and I know, have taken their model of a fine gentleman. Modes are adventitious, but nature is always the same; and where was ever nature so truly and distinctly painted? The little touches often repeated, not only unfold character, but imprint it on the mind, with all its shades and variations. The tediousness you complain of is necessary in so long a work to prevent your tiring. This is odd, yet true; when once you are intimately acquainted with a person who has any marked features of character, you are interested in all he does and says, and how shall you be intimate with one whom you only see, as Job's friends saw the vision, in an indistinct and transient manner? I will make you understand me at once: I sincerely believe you when you say that the remembrance of our cottage is very dear to you, and that you often dream pictures of it in your solitary musings. Say that you saw a fine landscape of the surrounding hills, the green valleys, and serpentine windings of the river below, and our cottage, with its sheltering hills, and rushing brook, in a corner,—you would be pleased, no doubt. Say, again, that some laborious Dutch painter had drawn our cottage as the nearest object of a piece, in which all its appendages should be faithfully delineated; where you would see the honeysuckle on the porch, the pigeons sunning themselves on the thatch, Peter in manful contest with the gander, Ann Mann milking the cows in the outer yard, and the children listening in the court to a sermon preached by John out of the wheel-barrow, while Caro, in serene dignity, overlooked the whole from his wonted stand. Say the picture were so very minute as to include my favourite ash-tree, and the house, which the literal Jack did literally build, to shelter the hatching goose. Now here are the shadows of two shades, or pictures of imaginary drawings. Which would you prefer? The last, by all means. Well, Richardson is the Dutch painter, who has produced a drawing of superior interest and equally minute detail. The shoe strings of a person familiar to my imagination, and dear to my heart, are more to me, even in description, than the imperial purple which invests a form too great and too remote to come near my affections. It is no proof of "Clarissa's" being a less valuable work that it is less fashionable. All I have told you formerly is true. "Clarissa" is the shore; fixed and unchangeable as truth and nature must ever be; the fashionable world is the ship, sailing away from it, but steering without chart or direction.

I tell you, Charlotte, I am sometimes tempted to say with Wat Tyler's mob, "It was never a merry world since gentlemen came up;" that is to say, since all manner of people must needs be ladies and gentlemen. There is no fixed standard for rank and opinion, more than for rank or place. Change, endless mutation is the thing, and while people are chasing a Proteus with vain diligence, the pursuit leaves no leisure for friendship, or for any serious and tranquil enjoyment. People must wear everything that is new,—must read everything that is new; and for that only reason must be everywhere, see everything, and know everybody. The consequence is, that they are like rich people's children, who know no pleasure but getting new toys, breaking them, and throwing them away; while ours build a house of turf and pebbles, spend a whole day in gathering materials,—call, and almost think it a palace when they have done, and then rejoice over it for a week, from the triumph of their conscious efforts in producing it.

Dear Charlotte, whatever you learn, do not learn to despise peace, friendship, and needlework. That unquenchable thirst for amusement that urges some people without a rural idea, without materials for thought, to fly through these recesses in summer, merely to change, and say they have been in odd wild places, is a fatal symptom of a deranged system. What can one expect of young people intoxicated with conceit, idleness, and boundless liberty, but what happens to other drunken people,—transitions from the feverish joys of an irregular imagination, to irksome languor and intolerable self-reproach.

How I have run on! Young said,

"The grandeur of my subject is my muse."

By the same rule, talking of Richardson, one may allowably be minute and tedious. Paper, fire, eyes, and candle fail me, or I could give you such curious anecdotes of the learned Hamlet, and of David and Jonathan, who are in a temporary state of exile from our dominions; and of Moome, whose hitherto uncontested power as queen of the hamlet has, lately, been in some danger. But Caro has great merit in her eyes just now for vindicating her rights. I wish you had seen her in all her vindictive majesty; you never heard one so eloquent. All the aggressors were forced to hide their diminished heads before her. I beg you will lay in a good stock of patience against your return; for she declares, as a mark of peculiar grace, that she will tell the dear creature, Miss Charlotte, every word of the dispute. Be very proud, for Caro's very self is going to write to you; parish news you will get from other quarters. I have long messages from all the children, the general purport of which is, to bid you return soon; the epoch fixed for this event is when the daisies come out My sister, Pastorina, sends you her kindest wishes, valuable for their sincerity, though unvarnished. I send you a thousand benedictions, on the express condition that you will no longer haunt my dreams. Is it not enough that you keep possession of my thoughts all day? Adieu, dear Charlotte; believe I pray for you as well as dream of you. Yours tenderly, faithfully, maternally,

A. G.

Letter LIX.

TO MRS. BROWN.

Laggan, March 9, 1789.

My dear Mrs. Brown,

As low as you rate your critical abilities, they have altogether captivated and dazzled my goodman. He desires me to keep the letter for my girls, to moderate the poignant affliction they will feel, some time hence, in weeping over Werter.* He considers this pathetic hero as a weak though amiable enthusiast, and looks upon Charlotte as first cousin to a coquette. Albert is his hero; with him he sympathizes, and for him he feels more than for the lover of nature and of Charlotte. I execrate the plan, detest the example, reprobate the reasoning, shudder at the catastrophe, and am most perniciously charmed with that vivid colouring, that fervid glow of sentiment, that energy of thought, and that simple, unadorned pathos, which,

* "The Sorrows of Werter;" a novel translated from the German language.

without the pomp of sounds, penetrates and melts the very soul. In all his afflictions, I was afflicted. Yes, with all his agonizing horror, I saw the dreadful brink, saw the last pang of dissolution, " like a flash of lightning, illumine the dark gulf of futurity;" but it was lost in a moment in impenetrable obscurity; nothing remained but the lime-trees, beneath whose shade he wished to rest, and the silent grave, where " Pity trembles while she weeps."

Do not laugh at me for catching a spark of Werter's enthusiasm, amidst so many cares and children. Judge from thence its fatal effects, at an earlier period of life, on " a heart oppressed with love and grief;" its destructive tendency, in representing people worthy, amiable, and enlightened, cherishing destructive errors, shutting their eyes to visible consequences, and inflicting misery on others as well as themselves, by the indulgence of feelings, ambiguous even in their dawn. Without one exertion of fortitude to conquer them, without any generous regard for the peace of others, without, indeed, that disinterested attention to the future peace of the person beloved, which true affection should produce in a pure and elevated mind, these selfish lovers go on to the precipice of destruction with the gross and vulgar subterfuge, that while the person is inviolate, no rights are invaded. I have some compassion for Werter, but very little indeed for Charlotte. In all points of delicacy, a woman of a mind at once cultivated and untainted is a natural judge. Such a mind repels the idea of a divided affection, of giving to the fond and faithful lover, possessed of her earliest affections (what fond and faithful love will spurn at with disdain), chill esteem, and half-hidden sentiments. Yet, this is the person we are taught to admire, and to consider as having a slight blemish lost in a blaze of excellence, and atoned for by unavailing remorse.

After treating these hazardous Platonics with due severity, I will tell you, however, in a whisper, what I think the better tendencies of this novel. It depicts nature truly, very truly indeed; for, when I read the short letter, expressing his rapture at the discovery of his favourite fountain, where, he says, "Fairies and genii seem to hover over it," &c., I felt my early days renewed; having on such occasions, in the morning of life, felt the very same sensations, and gone about restless with the desire of meeting some one who could derive as much joy from as simple causes. I am sure I have loved particular spots as well as some people are capable of loving those dearest to them. There is no wonderful adventure, no splendid scenes shown to dazzle and mislead the imagination; no sudden accession of wealth to make those happy, to whom heaven has allotted happiness, with which wealth has no connexion. Sentiment may have slain its thousands; but has not vanity slain its ten thousands? The great danger of novel reading, is a restless desire to be seen and admired, kindled by the surprising adventures of the heroines, the wonderful events which the admiration excited by their beauty produces, and the splendid destiny which generally awaits them. It is this that makes young people so impatient of peace and retirement, so sick of the plain realities of common life. In Werter, there is no exaggerated description, no unnatural or inflated language, no gilding or glitter. You feel always at home, and find yourself among such people as you daily meet; and it is this truth of painting that communicates the strong interest we feel in the persons, while our judgment is in arms against their conduct. It is the manchineel tree, whose apples attract us as much by their resemblance to the fruits of the same form, as by their superior beauty. We go with the ease of familiarity to repose under it, though its shadow is danger, and its fruit destruction.

I have said so much of Werter, that I shall refer all I would say of myself to another letter. Judge how our imaginations have been impressed, when I tell you Werter has enlarged our phraseology. Last October, the Spey very often inundated the valley we inhabit; the various weather that caused this overflow, occasioned many of those nights in which the moon bursts out, and vanishes by turns in total gloom. This partial light makes our mountain scenery appear very awful, and the tremulous effulgence on the wide expanse of troubled waters heightens the effect. These we familiarly called *Werter* nights. You cannot but remember the horrors of his nocturnal rambles, while meditating the perpetration of "a deed without a name."—Rejoice that my critical quiver is emptied, and believe me your unchanged and unchangeable friend,

A. G.

Letter LX.

TO MRS. SMITH, GLASGOW.

Laggan, May 16, 1789.

"Pity me, O my friend! for the hand of God hath touched me;" touched me to the very quick, and that in a manner so utterly unexpected, I feel still like a person stunned by a thunder-bolt, beginning to pant for breath, and look about to see what I have left, and to feel for what I have lost. I know I need not have recourse to declamation to interest your tender sympathy. You know that the dear creature it has pleased the Almighty to deprive me of, was my pride and my delight.* The spirit and animation of that fine countenance no one ever beheld without being struck with its marked expression; and that fair promise of every human excellence which dawned through every word and action, his fond parents viewed with secret exultation! Ask Charlotte if I exaggerate, or if ever she saw such manliness, generosity, and tenderness, appear in a child. There was nothing he dreaded like giving me a moment's pain. O! what have we lost; but what has he escaped by this early removal! Ripening, as he was, for immortality, he lived more in these four short years than most children do in ten. He walked, spoke, thought, and felt sooner than any child I ever saw or heard of.

* Her son Peter, born 9th March 1785, died 12th May 1789.

> "Why wanders wretched thought about his tomb,
> In infidel distress?"—

I know the vanity of these fond, foolish recollections. I know how well it becomes a Christian to render his own gifts meekly to the Divine Giver, when demanded. This, and a great deal more, is often and easily said; nay, I could say it all myself, but nature will have her way. When Mary the Second of England was on her death-bed, early finishing a pious and exemplary life with a suitable conclusion, having been asked if any of the various remedies she took did her good, she answered, that nothing did her good but prayer. I may say something like this; but, alas, my efforts to seek this relief are, like my dear child, cold, dead, inanimate!—the heart speaks not, moves not, under the oppressive weight. Here is great room for censure. Be it so: it is not your approbation, but your sympathy, that I solicit. When I wrote last I dreaded the measles; John took them, but very favourably; we had not the least apprehension for this darling. . .

Excuse my dwelling on minutiæ so dear to my remembrance. Yet how shall I speak of the three following days? or how procure some oblivious draught, to wash them for ever from my remembrance? The unspeakable pains he then endured still press upon my heart. Yet he was sensible to the last minute, expressed pity and tenderness for us by words, and then by signs, when his speech grew languid and imperfect. As he became weaker he grew calm, and, at length, expired, "as soft as balm, as mild as air." At six in the morning, May 12th, this human wonder forsook its earthly prison, and mingled with its kindred angels. We saw him depart without a tear. *Now* we can weep, and that is some relief. O pray for us !—Adieu !—I pity poor Charlotte, to whom our beloved child was very dear, and she thinks and feels deeper than most people. I have announced to her, in a separate letter, *her* loss, for such I know she considers it.

A. G.

LETTER LXI.

TO MRS. SMITH, GLASGOW.

Laggan, May 26, 1789.

My dear Friend,

Were you as happy as your great worldly prosperity, and the esteem of all that know you truly, can make you, you would be very unfit to enter into the present feelings of my heart, these acute returns of pain, these agonizing recollections, that darken the summer's sun, and throw a veil of universal sadness over the fair face of nature ;—the recital of such sensations would form poor entertainment for a person engrossed or elated by the pleasures and gaieties of this world.

28th June.

Since writing the above, I went to Fort-George, by particular desire of my worthy parents ; but, alas, I found, to my sorrow, that "change of place is only change of pain." The regiment* in which my father served during the years of my childhood, and to which

* The 55th Regiment of Foot, in which the Author's father served in America.—ED.

he is still much attached, he imagined would interest me; but whether it be that the habit of a retired life has made me think differently from what I used to do, or that my mind is entirely engrossed with one sad and tender idea, I see them not as old friends, but merely as worldlings fluttering after trifles. I am now at home, after spending a dreary month at the Fort, without being awake to anything but poor Catherine. We thought she would be the better for change of air and salt water. Her rapid growth enervates her. We have brought your relation home with us. . . . . . .

Charlotte will be home this week. I am relieved at the thought of it. To her I dare talk fully of what is ever in my thoughts. With her I can venture to feed my insatiable sorrow with every little anecdote and recollection that will serve to keep his dear memory alive. His father, though he cannot get over it himself, blames me very justly for repining at my darling's happiness. I will not be surprised or angry, though you should reprove me for this extravagance: but I am not well; and returning here, I find my beloved child's image in every place, in some of those lively and striking attitudes which were almost peculiar to himself. I cannot go to the door without seeing the spot where the cold earth covers that lovely countenance, which I never could behold without an emotion of pleasure, only exceeded by my present anguish. Happily I have preserved his dear profile, taken when he was out of humour. His sensible frown adds strength to the expression of the most animated countenance I ever beheld. I do not acknowledge your kindness to Charlotte; nor have I answered a sentence of your most affectionate letter, which I thankfully received a month ago. I can speak of nothing but the only thing I think of. Do not think I neglect the only method of procuring true consolation. I earnestly implore strength to bear my sorrows; but I am not able to pray or wish, in any degree, to be enabled to forget the object of them—his remembrance is so sweet to my soul, and my aspirations after a reunion with him, where we shall part no more, are so consequently strong.

Pray read Dr. Gregory's Comparative View,* and observe particularly the last section on the Influence of Religion; that on Taste; and the Strictures on False Refinement. I long to have you share the entertainment they afforded to my happier hours. A letter from you is almost the only thing I could read now. Write amply; give me good accounts of Mrs. Brown; and believe you are one of the few that still interest me. Farewell.

LETTER LXII.

TO MRS. SMITH.

Laggan, August 3, 1789.

My dear Friend,

Week after week has elapsed without my gratifying myself by writing to you, or being able to assign a good reason. I shall assign the true one; which, at the same time, I own I cannot justify. When I re-

* Comparative View of the State and Faculties of Man with those of the Animal World.

ceived your letter, in which you animadvert, very justly, on the folly, not to say guilt, of wasting that time and thought in fruitless mourning for the dead, which ought to have been employed in useful attention to those who are left, I was ashamed to discover the state of my mind even to you; and from you how could I conceal it? Truth is, my mind has been either wound up to a pitch at which it could not long remain, or sunk in the deepest dejection. . . . .
But in vain do I weary and exhaust my worn-out spirits in pursuit of a vision that eludes my grasp. Alas! I must turn my eyes to objects more attainable, and more suited to my situation, and the ties that still hold me to this world. I must again run the round of earthly cares and low pursuits, and wait patiently till my appointed day come. "For I shall go to him, but he shall not come to me." A late alarm, from another part of my family, convinced me forcibly of my own weakness and inconsistency. The grief which I could neither soothe or reason down, grew more tolerable on being divided. A bright atmosphere, a busy scene, and the affectionate attention of a pleasing and easy companion, did more to relieve my mind than all that reason or reflection could suggest. I always think of him, but with more composure. I view him as having passed the fiery trial of suffering, and as regarding us with tender compassion. The first thing that alleviated my distress was Charlotte's return, in itself pleasing, but still more gratifying, as her minute details about you all, made you in a manner visible and present to us. This suspended the sense of pain, by renewing the pleasing remembrance of the

innocent happy hours we formerly passed together. My youngest boy, Duncan, had got a hurt, the consequences of which alarmed us, but he is now better. Our busy season coming on, and finding myself incapable of any steady application within doors, I sent his maid to the hay-making, and wandered out a good deal with him in my arms. In consequence of this exertion, I have found that exercise in the open air operates beyond anything towards the relief of depression of spirits. Long may it be before you require any such remedy for that heaviest of evils! I have been indeed very little within, till of late, that the bad weather has confined me.

I have thought much of what you say of a certain friend of mine being in danger of running into the extreme of enthusiasm; but, after all, cannot think the hazard very serious, though I have paused and pondered sufficiently on the subject. The fact is, that it is in vain for us to flatter ourselves that the great work of our salvation is a bye concern, for which we may occasionally set aside a few minutes, which, by chance, are left vacant from business or pleasures. This does not agree with the opinion which the wise and good in all ages, and of all persuasions, seem to have entertained (however different their degrees of light and intelligence); namely, that our manner of existing here is not the final end of our being; that this is merely a state of probation, in which there is a glimmering of light afforded us, barely sufficient to distinguish good and evil; and a degree of choice and judgment, just enough to enable us to make a selection, and hold by the best. Were our intellect strong enough to discern the lucid order and according harmony of the divine scheme of Providence in its full extent,—could the horrors of guilt, and its consequent punishment, be made visible through the thick veil of humanity,—or could weak mortal eyes bear the refulgence of celestial beauty,—there could then be no room for choice or hesitation, no exercise of fortitude, discernment, faith, or hope; no struggles betwixt the erring will and the love of rectitude. Creatures left without choice, and impelled by the clear and glaring certainty before them, not struggling up the hill to virtue and felicity, but swimming with the stream in torpid ease, could not exercise those virtues which our imperfect state so loudly calls for. All the nobler exertions, all the softer emotions of the mind, lose their meaning and their use, where there is no vice to combat, no distress to relieve, no weakness to protect.

All this is so like common-place, that you must consider me as digressing very widely. Yet the perpetual struggle and warfare with guilt and sorrow, which is evidently our appointed task and duty here, leaves little room to suppose that anybody can be righteous over-much. We see our duty imperfectly in this land of shades and apparitions. Thus much, however, we are certain of, that we walk continually on the brink of danger in the open paths of life. If not happier, those are certainly safer, who, in some measure, fly from the conflict. What do people pursue in the world but business or pleasure? The regulation of the mind, and the exertion of that active beneficence which true piety produces, form such an occupation to a mind so turned, as to exercise all its faculties in the most agreeable manner. With those who have made great advances in piety, I should suppose "perfect love casteth out fear;" and that these exercises become a source of pure and lasting pleasure, as incomprehensible to the children of this world, as colours to the blind. Enthusiasm is the wine of life; it cheers and supports the mind; though excess, in either case, produces intoxication and madness. I am not sure that the religion of the heart can exist without a certain degree of enthusiasm. What noble or tender emotion of the mind is excited in any great degree without producing it? Very few affix a precise or determinate idea to the word, used in a religious sense. You will hear many people, who have never thought about the matter, parrotizing about enthusiasm, when they mean bigotry or fanaticism; if, indeed, they mean anything. Religion has not so great an enemy upon earth as vanity; and no wonder, since true piety must needs be founded in deep humility. Wealth, power, and distinction, cannot be attained by all the vain and ambitious; but the prize of wit and wisdom seems always within reach of those who are determined to be wise or witty. Those who wish to purchase these distinctions as cheap as possible, exchange the principles they only seemed to possess, for the character of wit and talents they only seemed to acquire. They hear impious wit oftenest quoted by the thoughtless and dissipated; and, therefore, they think impiety necessarily implies wit, and are indeed very often incapable of distinguishing the one from the other. These are the people who so frequently talk with contempt and ridicule of enthusiasm, in the religious sense of that expression, as they misunderstand it.

I have been very serious, and, as generally turns out in that case, very tedious; but some late instances that I have met with, of absurd pretensions to wit, founded on still more absurd pretensions to infidelity, have really provoked me; especially, as I very well know this pretender believes and trembles in the dark. For his impiety he must account to his Maker; but his impertinent ostentation is an offence against society. I suppose you are very glad that I am going to bid you good night. I fancy you will think, after giving you this lecture on impiety, the next thing I shall set about will be to caution bees and ants against idleness, or our friend W. D. against too much gravity and austerity. I do not know whether you will be the better for reading this, but I am much the better for writing it, and that you will think a sufficient apology. Adieu! my dear; I have taken the declamation, and left action to you. Be ever what you have been, and I shall be at no loss for an example to illustrate some of my sage precepts.

Letter LXIII.

TO MRS. BROWN, GLASGOW.

Laggan, August 13, 1789.

My dear Mrs. Brown,

I am such an economist of your pence, that I have deferred my sincere and cordial congratulations* all

* On the birth of Mrs. Brown's eldest son.

this time, in hopes of getting them sent by one who has cheated me at last. Yet this is the only testimony in my power to give of the unabated friendship I shall always retain for you, and this is simply all; for, with me, despondency and ill health have been so constantly producing and reproducing each other, for some time past, that I have neither the power nor inclination to furnish you with the least degree of entertainment.

Charlotte and I were all last week on a tour of visits on Loch Laggan side, where the romantic singularity of the place, and peculiar turn of its sequestered inhabitants, might, in happier hours, have afforded a subject for amusing description. As it is, I can only say, that the rocks and woods which border this fine piece of water, are equally gloomy and magnificent; while the spot where we spent most of our allotted days, can be equalled by few in a singular assemblage of rural beauties.* The deep silence which surrounds you, in a place secluded even from the Highland world, and distant from every other human dwelling, affords leisure to contemplate the placid features of the scene around the house. This, from a small eminence, surveys a meadowy plain, bordering on the lake, in which large trees have been left here and there, producing a very fine effect to the eye. Through this extended meadow, a stream, delightfully pure, wanders over fine gravel, while you trace its progress by the

* The beautiful residence of Aberarder, on the northern bank of the lake, is the spot alluded to. On the opposite side of the lake the Marquis of Abercorn has lately (1845) erected a fine hunting-seat in the middle of the extensive deer forest, which he holds from Macpherson of Cluny.

copses of hazel and alder, vocal with the sweetest strain of woodland melody, and rich in all the smaller wild fruits that abound in this district. In the immediate scene you are soothed with everything that is beautiful, and in the surrounding ones, awed by all that is majestic. The lofty Corryarder, the haunt of eagles and of clouds, towers behind; before, the lake spreads its still expanse; opposite, the dark remains of the most ancient forest in Scotland borders the whole south side of the lake;* above it rises a mountain wooded almost to the top; and beyond these awful solitudes appear rocks, at whose barren desolation the mind revolts. Of the inhabitants of this recess, I can only say, that they are peaceful and industrious, and seem as mild and harmless as the sheep, who are the sole subjects of this realm of solitude. I should tell you, that the lake contains two small wooded islands, on which are some fragments of buildings of the most remote antiquity. One is called the Isle of Kings; the other that of Dogs; for there, it would appear, their Caledonian majesties, who had here a hunting-seat, used to confine Bran and Luath, and all their other followers of the chase. It was hay-making time; we worked at our needles, or wandered at will, all the long sun-shine day, in the haunt of roes. In the evening, we had regularly a party on the water, and music. You start, but I am correct. When our landlord's sons had worked till tea-time, they came in

* Now enlivened by the erection of the hunting-seat of Lord Abercorn, built close to the water, and, in summer, surrounded by pleasure boats, hunters, and all the usual accompaniments of sportsmen —(1845.)—Ed.

to rest; and whenever tea was over, they launched out their boat, which two of them rowed to the opposite side of the lake, while the third played, on the violin, some of our favourite old tunes, that brought you and your music full on my recollection. But we were not merely regaled with airy sounds; the central gloom of the ancient forest abounds in bilberries, strawberries, and other wild fruits; and having others with us to hasten the task of gathering, we left the youths fishing, returned by twilight, and supped on the trout they caught, the fruit we gathered, and richer cream than ever your Lowland eyes beheld. This literally pastoral excursion has set my pen in motion beyond my own expectations; for I have so far lost the knack of writing upon nothing, which you once ascribed to me, that I seem now no longer able to write on anything.

Were I possessed of descriptive talents, Charlotte's extravagant joy, on the birth of your son, would give full room for their display. As for me, the moral and melancholy turn which my thoughts have lately taken, leaves me to associate even the cradle with the grave, its sure, however distant successor.

"Birth's feeble cry, and death's deep, dismal groan,"

are very properly connected by our favourite plaintive bard; whom, by the by, I am told it is not now the fashion to admire. Dear Jane, continue to love me, till I learn "the last new fashion of the heart," till I cease to have a taste and feelings of my own, and to be in some measure guided by them. I wonder when it will be the fashion to regret that the grass is not blue, or the skies green.—Pray bestow the charity of a letter upon me very soon. A little time from you will now be valued like the widow's mite, because you can ill spare it.—I heartily condole with Mrs. Swanston on the loss of her son, which will wound her pride, as well as her more tender feelings; for I suppose she was vain of having him. I, too, was vain once, but my vanity, I hope, is buried with the cause of it. Charlotte, whose love of infancy is most inordinate, regrets that she is not with you, to assist in nursing your heir. Mr. G. joins me in warm and sincere wishes, that he may be a long continued blessing to you both; and, with best respects to his father, let me add a caution which painful experience dictates—Love him with moderation, as we ought to do every earthly thing. Make my best wishes to your brothers and their mates, and thank the latter for me, on Charlotte's account.

I am, my dear Mrs. Brown, with much affection, yours.

Letter LXIV.

TO MRS. MACINTOSH, OF DUNCHATTAN, GLASGOW.*

Laggan, Dec. 23, 1789.

Madam,

Though I feel a desire of expressing to you, in some

* Mrs. Macintosh, well known both as the wife of Mr. George Macintosh, of Dunchattan, and the sister of the late Dr. Moore (father of General Sir John Moore), was a late acquisition to the Author. Their first acquaintance, which soon ripened into friendship, began from the gratitude expressed in the letter here inserted,

degree, the deep sense we all have of the generous part you have acted towards Miss Grant, I own I am at a loss how to do justice to my own sentiments on that subject, without running the risk of wounding your delicacy, or falling into the beaten track of unmeaning compliment. This I know has, by frequent misapplication, lost its value and significance. Yet I am sure no person, capable of acting as you have done on this occasion, can be at a loss to judge how people must be touched with a kindness of the most essential importance, done them in that instance where they feel it most tenderly; and this by a person whose character (the only thing we know of you), is such, as makes protection and advice doubly valuable, and thoroughly to be depended on. The partial light in which we view this object of our greatest earthly solicitude, endeared to us by innocence, misfortune, and a thorough knowledge of her disposition, led us to hope for the kind offices and good wishes of every well-disposed person. But it required a very liberal and superior mind, indeed, to take so clear and just a view of objects so remote and detached. We will not take all the credit of doing, as you seem to think, what no one else would have done. Your present conduct convinces me that, in our place, you would have acted just as we did; but I am not, by any means, so clear that we, in your place, should have done as you did. Uncommon and disinterested exertions in the cause of

for Mrs. Macintosh's particular attention to Miss Charlotte Grant, the young lady already referred to, who was long an inmate of the Author's family.—(1807.) Mr. Macintosh died in July 1807, and his widow survived him until 27th June 1808.—Ed.

virtue, by people who live in the world, are efforts like swimming against the current. Recluses, like us, walk in the light which emanates from the unbiassed mind, and seek or hope no other approbation than the whispered plaudit of the gratified heart. In this case we have more; we are doubly rewarded, by the distinguished merit of the object of our cares, and the daily improvement that marks her progress in knowledge and in virtue.

Her reception in the family of her worthy relation, Mr. Douglas,* is a circumstance every way favourable to her. Every motive of prudence and gratitude conspire to make it highly proper for her to sacrifice her own views and inclinations to the slightest indication of their will. The circle of acquaintance she made, when she went to Glasgow, though not wide, nor perhaps highly fashionable, was among people of real worth and estimation, to whom she owes much for civility and most useful attention. These it would be most indelicate and ungrateful in her to drop. Yet it will not be proper in her to go anywhere without the full approbation of Mr. Douglas and his family. How to act or apologize in this, or any delicate case, I am sure she will be directed by your candid advice.

Mr. Grant and Charlotte join in offering our most grateful respects to you and good Mr. Macintosh; and believe me, &c.,

A. G.

* The late John Douglas, Esq. of Glasgow, was nearly related to this justly admired young person; and there a most affectionate intimacy began betwixt her and his daughter, now Mrs. Douglas, of Douglas Park.—(1807.)

Letter LXV.

TO MRS. BROWN, GLASGOW.

Laggan, Feb. 13, 1790.

My dear Mrs. Brown,

I have deferred writing to you this long time, waiting the return of as much strength and spirits as should enable me to do it with some degree of fulness and precision. Though somewhat better, I am far from well, and have been this week past crowded with people coming to take leave of the young travellers, who go to-morrow. In the first place, my mind is perfectly at ease with regard to the deposit I am about to place in your own hands;* so much so, that I shall never think of giving you directions about her, convinced that, at this time of life, and in this stage of education, your judgment is far more to be depended on than my own. The arduous task of forming her heart, and instilling into her mind principles of moral rectitude and devout submission to the source of all goodness, is, I hope, in some degree performed. She is docile, and willing to please, without the least tincture of levity on the one hand, or self-conceit and stubbornness on the other. You will find her disposed to pay you implicit obedience, on the best of principles, that of an interior conviction, that you will only order what is right. It only remains for me to hint at the

* The Author's eldest daughter, Mary, was to reside for some time in Glasgow, for the benefit of her education. She had hitherto been brought up chiefly with her grandfather at Fort-George.

defects I observed, yet durst not blame, in her past education, in which I have had little share. . . . . . .

Experience has taught me the evil of this. Kept constantly to my needle (of which application many trophies remain), I was childishly ignorant of everything else when I got the charge of a family. I found Mary, when she returned to me from Fort-George, much in the same situation. But I have employed her in domestic matters and occupation all winter, and find her so ashamed of deficiency, and willing to please and be useful, that I hope she will conquer all indolent habits. While absent from us, she was shut up with old people, without a companion, or any relaxation but what books afforded; in those she took refuge, and in those found consolation; but they were taken without choice or selection. She has, from a kind of necessity, read more, and, perhaps, reflected and digested more than any Miss of her age you know. There is a certain thoughtful indolence, a degree of over-refinement, and an indifference towards ordinary characters, and common though very useful things, to be feared as the result of much knowledge early acquired. This is more especially to be feared in a mind that unites a degree of masculine solidity and habits of reflection with the quickness and sensibility common to the sex; and such are generally those female minds that range beyond the useful limits in search of knowledge and entertainment. However, we need not much fear; when our pupil enters her teens, and acquires the love of dress, and thirst for amusement natural to that period, all this may scatter like morning mists. I do not, however, wish her to read much at this time; and what she does read, I wish to be of a moral and serious cast; sketches of history, biography, poetry, or essays of a graver cast. Richardson's are the only novels in the circle of my own knowledge I would wish to indulge her in. In short, whatever a young creature's mind has a strong bent for, should be checked and counter-balanced, to prevent its running into a blameable excess. Let her write, dance, and attend a geographical class with Mrs. Smith's children. Drawing and music are both out of the question; she has neither ear for the one, nor that turn of fancy which leads to excellence in the other. Tinkling and daubing are tolerable amusements for the superabundant leisure of the wealthy, who have the means, as far as possible, to make art supply the defects of nature; but I would not waste time and money in swimming against the stream, were it but to prevent the painful hypocrisy of those who are forced, from mere compassion, to "d— with faint praise" miserable music, and wretched drawing. I despise the fashionable frippery of fillagree, which neither displays taste, nor forms habits of attention and diligence. Needlework, good old court needlework, is the thing. It exercises fancy, fixes attention, and, by perseverance and excellence in it, habituates the mind to patient application, and to those peaceful and still-life pleasures which form the chief enjoyment of every truly amiable woman. Fashion is an epidemical frenzy, that follows and overtakes us everywhere, though we, in following it, can overtake it nowhere. Would you believe it is partly to shun this that I was impatient to send Mary from her former abode at

Fort-George, which is become gay and fashionable in as great excess as this is retired and rusticated.

There is a daughter of the Duke of Gordon (Lady Madelaine Sinclair), married to the present Governor, who is very young, very good-natured, and extremely affable and unassuming. She began to take much notice of Mary, which, no doubt, would be very flattering to the good people she was with. Considering her as belonging to one of her father's clergy, Lady M. would regard it as a kind of *Highland connexion*, and would, with her usual good-nature, think it meritorious to patronise and bring forward a child shut up in a kind of monastic confinement with two recluse old people. To mend the matter, the abundance of gentlemen and scarcity of ladies there, have introduced an absurd custom of bringing children to the assemblies. It is obvious that to decline such kindness would be both ungrateful and disrespectful; and to remove her by such a quick transition from absolute retirement to the *beau monde*, would be destructive to all my views, whose object it is to bring up my children in the utmost frugality, simplicity, and industry; and, at the same time, to give them that culture of mind, and inspire them with that propriety and elegance of sentiment, which will dignify a blameless and virtuous obscurity, if that should be their lot, and form their manners to such softness and decorum as would not disgrace a more easy situation, if Providence were pleased to bestow it upon them. You ask, how people secluded from the world are to acquire manners? I answer, that where there is mind, there is always manner; and when they are accustomed to treat each other with gentleness and courtesy, they will feel that quick disgust at what is rude and inelegant, which contributes more than any instruction to the refinement of manners. I am sure this homily has worn out your patience.

I regret exceedingly that your sister is out of town, because I could wish Mary to be with her every moment she should be absent from you, except a few formal visits, which she may make to some of my old acquaintances. Children at her age can hardly be considered as making any part of the company, being rather an encumbrance. They, however, amuse themselves and enlarge their circle of ideas by being present in mixed companies; but in general I think they are more improved by being with those they know best, and can be easy with, because they are more interested, and attend more to their conversation.

I am but too sensible of the task I impose, and the trouble I occasion you, but you know not how desirous I am to have Mary in a private family. More I will not say, for it avails not to tease you with apologies. . . . . With true esteem and unbounded confidence, I am, my dear friend, yours most sincerely,

A. G.

Letter LXVI.

TO MRS. SMITH, GLASGOW.

Laggan, March 20, 1790.

My dear Friend,

Your letter, for which I truly and literally longed, came at last, two days after the twins were born. Before I say more of it, I must acknowledge a *lang-syne* letter of yours, which, though singularly acceptable to the state of my feelings at that time, has, through hurry, confusion, and stupidity, remained still unacknowledged. It was that in which you inform me of Isabella Reid's death, whom I well remember when a lovely lassie, and who then gave promise of the sweetest and most amiable disposition. How desirable in the eye of reflection is that early fate for those who are so early ripened for futurity, and whom we absurdly lament the more, on account of that very goodness which insures and perhaps hastens their reward.

Your letter arrived on the very evening of the day when we were preparing the last obsequies of a person for whom I had the highest affection and veneration. It was my honoured mother-in-law, whose modest worth, whose tender sensibility, and every gentle and amiable quality, will never be effaced from my mind. Fourscore years of most useful and irreproachable life, she spent in a constant struggle with various and complicated afflictions. Born to a degree of affluence and distinction; blest with an uncommon share of beauty, merit, and understanding; living among numerous and powerful friends, her outset in life was attended with very flattering promises of prosperity and happiness. From the early loss of both parents, who left behind twelve orphans, she became too soon acquainted with sorrow. She married soon after, in early youth, a man every way worthy of her, by whom she was tenderly beloved, but whose warm and liberal heart admitted not of so much worldly prudence as served to make any considerable provision for his family. She, though in the bloom of youth, and still admired and sought after for her beauty, renounced every earthly wish and enjoyment but what related to her family, and by the most strenuous efforts of diligence and humble industry, contrived to educate her three sons in a genteel and indeed expensive manner, and send them abroad each in a very creditable line of life. They were indeed such sons as a mother might be justly proud of; but they dropt off, one after another, just when they had the prospect not only of doing well themselves, but being in a way to assist her, and left her without earthly hope or comfort but what she derived from her youngest and only remaining son, then a boy at College, who had been left by his father a sickly infant in the cradle. Supported by a confirmed habit of religion through these and many other distresses, though she felt them with exquisite poignancy, she bore them with placid meekness, without having her temper soured or her heart contracted, but continued to the last serene, tranquil, and in full possession of all her faculties. Her death was every way suitable to such a life. We have all our inevitable portion of sorrow to endure, but how few can bear it as she did. I reproach myself, when

I think of the unutterable, inexcusable, and sinful anguish which I have suffered since May last, and consider what greater and more justifiable causes of sorrow other people have; but I charge some of it on bodily weakness, which certainly produces a degree of mental infirmity. And, indeed, you never saw any human creature more feeble and helpless than I was for sometime past. I look back with a kind of tremor on that gloomy period, by far the most painful of my life, and cannot be thankful enough for the returning serenity which I flatter myself with perceiving in my own mind, since it has pleased God to support me through this last great trial.

Yet, when I think on the melancholy alterations which have happened in your family, a family whose remembrance will be ever dear and valuable to me, and to whom you are so tenderly attached, not only by the ties of blood, but by the dearer sympathy of mutual worth and long habits of reciprocal affection,— when I think how deeply you feel these changes, and not the less deeply for stifling and commanding these feelings, I must own that your ground of affliction, though not so visible and apparent, is more rational and justifiable than mine; and to a mind like yours your being yourself in a state of comparative prosperity is no alleviation. I know no circumstance attending the increase of years so painful as the observation of those mournful vicissitudes. I am heartsick of them.

> O ye blest scenes of permanent delight,
> Full beyond measure, lasting beyond bounds;
> Could you, so rich in rapture, fear an end,
> That ghastly thought would drink up all your joy,
> And quite unparadise the realms of light!

Yet from the very frequency of these reverses, I would hope a change for the better, especially as your relatives have youth, merit, and industry on their side. Your mother has most uncommon strength of mind, has been exercised in sorrow, and is, I dare say, much abstracted from this world; and, if it were not for this, I would think her more to be pitied than any body concerned.

I can easily understand the reluctance you had to part with your beloved nephew; but I hope you will have a rich return in the pleasure which his growing merit and success in the world will afford you. When we delight so much in seeing a plant—a mere vegetable—flourish under our culture and protection, how superior, how refined is the pleasure of cultivating an intelligent being, capable of love, merit, and gratitude, and how strong and tender a tie does it form in a recent and obvious instance. I have found it a high gratification, insomuch that it did

> "Almost impress
> On my dark cloud an Iris."

I must now, however, break off. Alas, what sheet of paper can hold the redundancies of my full heart, when it overflows to you! Adieu, my ever dear Isabella; forget not

A. G.

Letter LXVII.

TO MRS. SMITH, GLASGOW.

Laggan, July 27, 1790.

My dear Friend,

By a letter from Charlotte while at Edinburgh, I find there is one from you on the way, so that I can write again without descending from my dignity; and I can do this with the more ease of mind, as my little twins* are now recovered from the small-pox. They are the best children I ever had, and very healthy and pleasant looking.

My eldest daughter is now staying here, and Isabella, your name-daughter, is with Duncan at Fort-George. Mary, with much sedateness and composure of manner, shows every indication of genius and superior capacity, with great modesty and diffidence, and a tranquil, even temper. Catherine is a hasty, heedless romp; yet possessed of great activity and strong sensibility, with a warm heart and most generous disposition, and some lively sparkles of wit and humour. Isabella, again, is the very essence of meekness, complacency, and active good-nature; she not only wishes to please and oblige, but endeavours to do so in every shape. I never, indeed, knew a child of so amiable a disposition.

These are the outlines, as far as I can draw them, of this triad. You will smile, and call it a panegyric. Though very unlike each other in many respects, one

* Charlotte and Petrina, born 3d March, 1790.

characteristic feature of similitude runs through them all. They are all artless and disinterested: no traces of mean cunning or selfish grasping. This is an indication of an enlarged mind; and, besides the future promise, has a present good effect. Whatever they have, they share with each other with readiness and pleasure; so there is one source of wrangling and debate stopped. They all give pretty strong proofs of feeling as well as understanding; and it is by the management of these feelings that I propose, in a great measure, to sway them, till their minds open and strengthen: so that one may reason with them without teaching them *parrotism.* This, perhaps, might not be a safe way in the world; but, if ever children can be brought up with uncorrupted hearts, ours have a chance of being so. Their number, and being altogether strangers to those indulgences which wealth and ease admit of, will entirely prevent their being softened into a sickly sensibility, by those feelings being exercised. For the art lies in directing them to those ends for which, it is presumed, they were bestowed. In the first place, I am at the utmost pains to fix their affections: we should be unhappy if we thought they loved any one nearly so well as their parents. Indulgence will not produce this effect solely, for to that there must at last be limits; and a child, who is very seldom refused anything, considers refusal as injury. When this happens oftener, the fear of being mortified makes him reflect before he makes any request, whether it be a proper one. One or two indulged children might be endured; but a large family of them would be Tophet and Gehenna. The thing is, to endeavour early, so to manage their feelings and affections, that they shall shrink from the idea of giving pain to those they love. Having made sure of their affection, the next point is to secure their esteem, that it may stamp authority on my decisions, and preserve that respect so necessary for maintaining my influence. Shall I confess to you, that the most finished coquette was never at greater pains to appear to advantage before her lovers, than I am to conceal every defect and weakness from my children! Thus I endeavour, by exciting their veneration, to preserve my ascendancy over their flexible and unformed minds. My great object is to form their hearts .to an ardent love of virtue, to a generous admiration of superior excellence, and to compassion, not only for the weaknesses, but even the vices of their fellow-creatures. I would have them cherish those pure and delicate sentiments which make the vices of others appear to them, not as objects of acrimonious censure and self-applauding comparison, but of such a contemptuous aversion, that they shall as habitually turn from the view of human nature thus degraded and deformed, as we do from any object that is peculiarly disgusting to our senses. In that case, they will turn their eyes with pleasure on every view of the human character which still retains any traces of that divine image in which we were created,—

"Though sullied and dishonoured, still divine."

It is not by formal maxims, or frigid precepts, that we teach them the great doctrines of morality; yet we are continually in a powerful, though indirect manner, impressing them on their minds. I never formally forbid them to steal or covet, to envy or traduce, because "they have the commandments," and are taught to reverence them as the dictates of Inspiration; and because I never observed in them the least symptom of a sordid or malignant inclination. But in my general discourse, in the conversation I have with their father or others in their presence, I always set the contrary virtues in the strongest, fairest light; avoid as much as possible talking of other people's follies or crimes; and, should they be casually mentioned, pass them lightly over with an air of indifference or disgust, not calculated to excite their attention or curiosity. It is a sad thing that children should be taught, by the example of their seniors, to pursue vice into all its dirty recesses, and to triumph in their superiority and discernment in making discoveries, which, when they are made, afford neither profit nor pleasure. I prefer the more pleasing task of insinuating instruction, and awaking the generous thrill of emulative desire, by pointing out to their enamoured view all that is great, lovely, or excellent, in the characters of the living or the dead; nay, even of those that never lived or died, except in the creative imagination of poets and philosophers. Not but that I greatly prefer examples drawn from reality. What is necessary to be known of evil, by way of guard or prevention, may be very soon acquired; for the whole world are in a combination to impress that kind of instruction. When I have warmed the hearts, and enriched the minds of my children with abstracts of all that wisdom and devotion, truth, honour, magnanimity, and tenderness have done to adorn and exalt our nature, I descend a step lower in the scale of existence, and make them observe and admire the fidelity, affection, maternal tenderness, attachment, and gentleness, which are seen in little birds and domestic animals. All this helps to impress still stronger on their minds the sense I would have them entertain of these qualities, whenever they meet with them. After thus endeavouring to give a right direction to that generosity and tenderness with which it has pleased God to endow them, I would (though I knew them myself) be at no great pains to teach them those refinements in manners which it is become fashionable to talk so much about. The kind and degree of good breeding I should most approve and wish for, will naturally result from a well principled mind, a feeling heart, and a just and cultivated taste,—especially when the manners of those they look up to for examples are not devoid of that softness which delicacy of sentiment always produces. Forms and punctilio are the mere apparatus of good breeding, easily acquired, and of little value. The ease of fashionable manners,—the determined self-confident ease,—nothing but mixing much with fashionable people can give: at least I should suspect a little *native bronze*, where it grew wild. A person, who, to a good, and in some measure cultivated, understanding, adds modesty, gentleness, and some refinement of taste, may not be elegant, but can scarcely be vulgar. And such manners may, by a slight culture, be improved into elegant simplicity, of all elegant things the most desirable. Though elegance should prove unattainable, I would still have that simplicity, both in their taste and manners, which would be most suitable to the humble station in which Providence has placed them; and, at the same time, have their minds impressed with that true dignity which is compatible with any station which one may suppose the daughter of a gentleman, in the ordinary course of life, either to rise or sink into.

You know what my religious opinions are, and what unspeakable importance I attach to them; so you may believe we are at all times anxious to leave this invaluable legacy unimpaired to those who have so little beside to inherit from us. On these subjects you and I have but one opinion; and I am so unfashionable as to think one never can begin too soon to direct a child's hopes and fears to their proper and ultimate object; though reason must not be addressed till it unfolds, for fear of teaching children to use words without annexing ideas to them, which is just the parrotism that I dislike. You will wonder to see me dwell so much on cultivating the taste, when I am such an admirer of undisguised nature. But I respect taste as an outguard of virtue. A just and regulated taste would make the levity, the absurdity, the cunning and meanness, which often accompany depraved inclinations, more obvious and disgusting. Besides, it places every charm of all-beauteous nature, every grace and ornament of ingenious art, in the fairest point of view; which has the happiest effect upon the heart and temper.

Time and paper so confine me, that I must reserve all that crowds on me to answer the objections you will naturally make to this mode of education. My children, you will say, after being brought up to my wish, will be, after all, but amiable ignoramuses, unacquainted with human life, and unable, from their extreme simplicity, to ward off the blows of malice, or avoid the snares of deceit. Some acquaintance with human depravity, you will say, is necessary for enabling us to act with due caution in a corrupt world. I answer, that they will find too many instructors in this crooked science, and know but too soon what every one is too willing and able to teach. Delicacy and high principle are better guards than cunning and suspicion. A person possessed of the former qualities, feels not at home or easy with artificial characters, and shrinks, unconsciously, from the approach of the callous and designing. A large family is a little community within itself. The variety of dispositions, the necessity of making occasional sacrifices of humour and inclination, and, at other times, resisting aggression or encroachment, when properly directed by an overruling mind, teach both firmness and flexibility, as the occasion may call forth the exercise of those qualities. Respect and submission to the elder branches of a family, tenderness and forbearance to the younger, all tend more to moral improvement, if properly managed, than volumes of maxims and rules of conduct. With regard to modesty and deference, too, people in our situation must needs enforce those in self-defence. In a cottage, where children are continually under the eye of their parents, and confined within narrow bounds, petulance would be purgatory.

This detail of mine wants nothing but a little method and arrangement to be the ape of a lecture.

Regard, however, with indulgence, the hasty sketch which conveys to you some idea of the manner in which we endeavour to discharge the most important of all social obligations, though a most confused and imperfect abstract of our own very imperfect scheme. You will be partial to it, merely because it is ours; if you are disappointed, my best apology must be, reminding you how often you have solicited this brief chronicle. Now, reward my tedious blear-eyed vigil, by giving me as minute an account of your family as I have given you of mine. Mr. Grant begs to be warmly remembered to Mr. Smith, who, I trust, has not forgotten that I cannot endure to be forgotten. I am charmed with the accounts I hear of Mrs. Brown's little family. Make my love acceptable to her; and, believe me, in spite of matrimony, distance, and Drimochter,* most truly, most tenderly, yours,

A. G.

Letter LXVIII.

TO MRS. SMITH OF JORDANHILL, GLASGOW.

Laggan, October 10, 1790.

My dear Friend,

I had the great pleasure to receive your letter some weeks ago. I then was flattered with a prospect of getting franks from Fingal;† and, though I had not, time was never so scarce with me, the children and the

* A bleak extensive mountain between the counties of Inverness and Perth.

† A familiar name given to James Macpherson, Esq. of Belleville, the Translator of Ossian's Poems.

harvest together scarcely leaving me a spare half hour. I am happy to hear you still continue so much interested in me as to make me acquainted, as far as possible, with your family. I have heard of your Isabella's mild shyness, which so peculiarly marks her for yours. Would you believe it, my Isabella * is strongly distinguished by the same characteristic, and I think will resemble you greatly in temper.

I have an ardent desire to see you once more before "I go hence and am no more seen." The distance makes me think it will be vain to flatter myself with hopes of your coming here: my going to Glasgow is equally hopeless. But, could you bring it about to take a jaunt next summer to Kenmore, and bring Isabella and James with you, it would be a fine affair for them, and I should assuredly meet you there, which I could do the more easily, as Charlotte could matronise for the family in my absence. Mr. Grant would be of the party, as would Mr. Smith, I presume. He will be occupied with building his new house at Jordanhill; but what then? You will have your fine new house always, but me you will never see probably, if you miss that opportunity. I am sure it will be more difficult for me to go than for you to come: you see I am for keeping a little merit on my own side. Believe me I am perfectly serious, and shall be very anxious until I hear your sentiments on the matter.

Mr. Grant was at Belleville visiting Fingal, in the beginning of this week. That tender and sublime Bard has, contrary to the usual fate of authors, en-

* Named after Mrs. Smith.

riched himself by his talents of one kind or another. He has purchased an estate in a beautiful spot on the Spey, twelve miles below this, where he keeps a Hall of Shells, and indeed lives with the state and hospitality of a Chieftain, not like

> "A meagre muse-rid mope, adust and thin,
> In a loose night-gown of his own dun skin."

Apropos: he is a full, handsome man, and distinguished among his countrymen by the epithet of "Fair James." He is now engaged in building a house which is to cost L.4000. Only think how this must dazzle people accustomed to look on glass windows as luxury, and on floors as convenient but by no means necessary appendages to a building. I am the only lady in the country that have not tasted of his shells, or been warmed by the flame of his oaks. Judge how domestic I am with my twins.

This night we concluded shearing our wet dismal crop; but, as our children are from home on a visit, we have deferred the kitchen feast and dance we usually give on that occasion; which gives me time to write. Let me hear from you soon, and pray do not mind postage, for I place your letters under the head of luxuries; and being frugal in other luxuries, can afford to indulge in these. Mr. Grant bids me crowd in compliments to you both. Adieu, my dear.

A. G.

END OF THE FIRST VOLUME.

EDINBURGH:
Printed by THOMAS ALLAN & CO.,
265 High Street.

For EU product safety concerns, contact us at Calle de José Abascal, 56–1°, 28003 Madrid, Spain or eugpsr@cambridge.org.

www.ingramcontent.com/pod-product-compliance
Ingram Content Group UK Ltd.
Pitfield, Milton Keynes, MK11 3LW, UK
UKHW040617240426
470322UK00010B/171